D1327333

In the Guise of Democracy

Governance in Contemporary Egypt

In the Guise of Democracy

Governance in Contemporary Egypt

May Kassem

With a foreword by Raymond Hinnebusch

ITHACA

PRESS

IN THE GUISE OF DEMOCRACY
Governance in Contemporary Egypt

Ithaca Press is an imprint of Garnet Publishing Limited

Published by
Garnet Publishing Limited
8 Southern Court
South Street
Reading
RG1 4QS
UK

First Edition

ISBN 0 86372 254 7

British Library Cataloguing-in-Publication Data
A catalogue record for this book is available from the British Library

Jacket design by Neil Collier
Typeset by Samantha Abley

Printed in Lebanon

To My Parents
JAS

Contents

Acknowledgements

This work could not have been completed without the assistance received from many people. Most of the material in this book was accumulated as a result of the kindness, generosity and cooperation of the political activists, academic specialists and voters whom I encountered during my stays in Egypt. They allowed me to exploit their in-depth knowledge, experience and views with regard to the often perplexing topic of Egyptian politics and elections. For this I am deeply grateful. Any misunderstanding or misinterpretation of the information they provided is my responsibility alone.

I would also like to express my deepest gratitude to Dr Charles Tripp, Professor Donal Cruise-O'Brien and Professor Malcom Yapp. The knowledge, experience and scholarly brilliance of each one of these distinguished academics have left an indelible mark on my outlook on politics. I must also thank both Professor Sami Zubayda and Professor Raymond Hinnebusch for having confidence in my work. Professor Hinnebusch's subsequent encouragement and friendship is something I will always cherish.

Although they are not directly linked to this particular project, the kindness and generosity shown to me by Professor Enid Hill and Professor Earl (Tim) Sullivan makes me forever grateful to them both.

On a personal level, I would like to extend my sincere gratitude to L. Gilbert for her friendship and to S. O'Brien for her immense effort exerted during the last couple of years of writing up this project. Last, but certainly not least, I would like to thank my best friend Ms Dzidra Stipnieks, whose support I shall not forget.

Note on Transliteration

For transliteration purposes I have used a simplified version of the
International Phonetic Alphabet (IPA). Given the distinctive inflections
of Egyptian Arabic speech, it has been decided to transliterate Egyptian
names in a way that approximates the forms of those names as they
would be recognised by the subjects themselves, modifying somewhat the
classical Arabic orthography. This method has also been applied to certain
transliterated distinctive Egyptian expressions, institutions or places.

Foreword

This book makes a major contribution to our understanding of Egyptian politics and of the motives and consequences of the political liberalisation experiments on which Middle East authoritarian regimes have embarked in recent decades. May Kassem systematically researches three major issues: (1) the reasons the Egyptian government holds non-competitive multi-party elections; (2) why activists participate; and (3) the role of the wider public in the electoral system. She finds that the function of Egypt's elections is to systematise and expand clientalism in a way that both engages and marginalises activists, co-opts much of the opposition and inhibits the formation of broader political groupings in the mass public.

Most striking is the effect on opposition parties that believed political liberalisation would lead to genuine democracy but that, the author shows, have come, through their co-optation via the electoral system, to accept far less. The book also provides valuable information, based on firsthand field research, on the actual conduct of election campaigns by the parties and on the mechanisms by which the regime controls them. Dr Kassem's research demonstrates the extent to which the Muslim Brotherhood was the only party sufficiently institutionalised electorally to mobilise the public: this probably explains why the regime has excluded it from the political arena.

In getting under surface appearances and national level rhetoric through a painstaking empirical investigation of the actual and complex operations of politics on the ground, this study provides a fascinating glimpse of how Egypt's political system actually works. It shows that the multi-party system is more than a mere façade because notables and activists play the game, but that, paradoxically, because it advances their co-optation, it has, at least in the short term, reinforced rather than undermined authoritarian rule.

Raymond Hinnebusch
Professor, International Relations and Middle East Politics
University of St Andrews, Fife, Scotland
July 1999

1

Patronage in Controlled Democracies

The personalised authoritarian system of rule that was established in Egypt after Gamal 'Abd al-Nasser and the other Free Officers took power in 1952 appears to have been preserved to date, not simply as a result of the immense formal powers that Nasser vested in the presidency, but also as a result of the clientist strategies adopted by him and his successors, Sadat and Mubarak. Such strategies further contributed towards inhibiting the development of formal political groupings and hence the possibility of successful challenges to the system.

In such a context, Egypt's democratisation efforts as reflected in its contemporary electoral framework functions predominantly as a mechanism for reaffirming and, more importantly perhaps, expanding, the regime's informal grip on political participation so as to include political opponents and their supporters. This strategy is based on the logic that, within a specific setting, a multi-party electoral arena could be utilised by the regime as a means of providing, at various levels of the political and social structure, the opportunity to participate in the existing political system and, in most cases, to gain access to a share of the resources it commands. In this way, disparate political activists and their potential supporters would be recruited into the regime's informal system of containment and control.

Elections, after all, constitute the foundation of any democratic system of rule. It is for this reason that the difference between democracy and other systems of rule is gauged by whether elections are held and, if they are, by their characteristics. The term "democracy" itself can mean many things depending on ideological, orientation and historical context, but in general democracy denotes a system of government whereby "the principal office holders of the political system are chosen by competitive elections in which the largest part of the population can participate."[1] In other words, democracy is a method of rule that should meet the following three conditions.

(1) Meaningful and extensive competition among individuals and organised groups (especially political parties) for all effective positions of government power, at regular intervals and excluding the use of force.

(2) A highly inclusive level of political participation in the selection of leaders and policies, at least through regular and fair elections such that no major (adult) social group is excluded.

(3) A level of civil and political liberties – freedom of expression, freedom of the press, freedom to form and join organisations – sufficient to ensure the integrity of political competition and participation.[2]

Definitions by other authors refer to similar conditions or principles.[3] However, while such formal definitions are relatively straightforward, "democracy is not a quality of a social system which either does or does not exist, but a complex of characteristics which may be ranked in many different ways."[4] In this respect, formal definitions can represent a major problem in that, although many political systems may satisfy defined criteria, certain constraints "may often in practice make a system less democratic than it appears on paper".[5] As one author notes:

> The technical regularities of the vote (access to the ballot box, counting the votes and so on) evidently do not guarantee [an election's] competitive character. Nor does a plurality of candidates or alternatives . . . Pluralist regimes are known in which coercion plays hardly any role in the conduct of electoral consultations but none the less have elections that are to all appearances non-competitive.[6]

Multi-party elections of this nature are sometimes classified as "exclusionary elections" and are characterised by the fact that the governments that hold them do not depend upon them for their continuance in office.[7] Thus, if one were to study the nature of such elections, it would be necessary to concentrate attention on their functions for the ruler of a state, rather than on their significance to the individual voter.

Authoritarian rule and the ballot box

Non-competitive, democratic-style elections are mostly established by authoritarian conservative regimes, monarchical dictatorships or well established post-military regimes which have "taken power, creating from above a government or privileged party rather than coming to power with the support of a movement-type party".[8] These political systems are predominantly characterised by a personalised method of rule, and in such cases, the state can best be understood as a government of men rather than laws. Thus, while formal political institutions exist, these institutions are usually devices manipulated to maximise the personal power of the rulers rather than to define and impose universally accepted rules of political conduct and constraint.[9] The adoption of a formal democratic framework can subsequently be understood in such terms. Accordingly, should authoritarian rulers adopt democratic institutions, they will do their utmost to ensure that such measures include "the simultaneous exclusion of the four principles which give such institutions their true democratic content: consensus concerning the rules of the game, political accountability of the rulers, the right to ample political representation, and alternation in power".[10]

The concept of multi-party legislative elections cannot therefore be considered as open competition between various political parties attempting to gain control of government on the basis of rival public policies or opinion. Nor can the implementation of controlled multi-party elections be regarded as planned first steps towards withdrawal from power in the foreseeable future. In fact, since the rulers do not particularly "consider the possibility of losing power",[11] they tend to maintain a considerable distance from the electoral contest and leave such forms of participation to those on the periphery of power.[12]

Electoral competition between political parties in such systems may sometimes produce what appears to be "freely" elected representatives, but in reality these public figures remain subservient to the real power-holders, whether such power-holders are found in the form of a king, president or military leader. The National Assembly in Morocco, for example, comprises elected deputies representing various political parties. However, it is difficult for members to implement public policies since these deputies remain in a deferential position to King Hassan. As one author put it, the king's pre-eminent position dissipates the zeal and rhetoric of multi-party electoral campaigns.[13] In defence of such personalised rule, King Hassan claims:

I am obliged to personify power as strongly as possible, for people do not obey a programme or plan. They obey men, a team of men, and it is all for the best if that team is embodied in a chief and symbolised by one face, one voice, one personality.[14]

Similar situations in which the power of authoritarian rulers overwhelms the power of a multi-party parliament can be found in other Arab states, including Jordan, Tunisia and Egypt, as well as in many Latin American states, such as Colombia, whose former foreign minister once noted: "We have a constitutional façade, but behind that façade we have a military which is very powerful."[15] More recently, several African states, such as Kenya, Botswana, The Gambia, Côte d'Ivoire and Senegal, have also appeared to be developing similar patterns of rule following their respective transitions from single-party rule.

Controlled elections

The rulers who adopt these systems tend to impose a number of constraining conditions in order to ensure that the arena of political contest remains under their stringent control. The laws regulating the licensing of opposition parties, for example, always demand a public commitment to the existing political order and the substantive acts of the regime.[16] As the case of Jordan illustrates, the primary concern of the late King Hussein with regard to legalising political parties in 1991 was to ensure that "such parties agreed in advance to support the constitution and the monarchy".[17] The same occurred in Morocco: when King Hassan attempted to re-create a system based on multi-party elections in 1977, potential parties were forced to demonstrate their allegiance to the king and his policies if they were to be allowed to compete.

In addition, authoritarian rulers can, and very often do, exercise a veto over the participation of certain groups or individual personalities. In most cases, such exclusionary measures are confined to those whom the rulers believe may have the potential to attract wide-scale appeal and who may subsequently use such appeal to mobilise large sectors of the public against the regime. This can largely explain why political parties in certain North African states are granted legal permission to function only if they do not possess a broad social base within society.[18] Linz's observation of government caution towards electoral activities in East European states such as Estonia and Latvia during the first half of the century is also evident in contemporary systems of this nature. He writes that "elections with licensed or controlled parties are unlikely to have [a] festive and revivalist character" and adds: "The rulers are less likely to encourage this, because they are uncertain about the turn-out and the outcome."[19]

Waterbury observed this phenomenon in contemporary Morocco. According to the author, King Hassan did not only place himself as arbiter of all political issues and groups, he also intentionally prevented efforts at large-scale mobilisation of any sectors of society during elections, even favourable ones, for fear that they might eventually turn against him.[20] Such ambiguous electoral tactics can also be noted in Brazil's post-1964 authoritarian regime. One observer comments that there was "a succession of arbitrary modifications to the rules of the electoral game in order to diminish political competition, guarantee predictable outcomes, and to keep party alternation in government under strict control".[21] Again, the same patterns are evident in Egypt, as most patently illustrated before the 1984 elections. President Mubarak, arguably apprehensive of an unexpected electoral turnout during the first legislative elections under his rule, went as far as to completely change the electoral laws in an attempt to curb potential successes by the opposition and to ensure that his National Democratic Party (NDP) maintained its dominant position in the legislature.[22]

Non-competitive multi-party elections

The reluctance of authoritarian rulers to allow large-scale mobilisation of any sectors of society during elections means that, in contrast with elections by plebiscite in ideologically based single-party systems, controlled multi-party elections are not attended by wide-scale political indoctrination and propaganda on behalf of the regime. Instead, political participation is rather indirect and is embedded in a complex network of informal clientelist relations linking the periphery to the centre.[23] In this context the government-supported party is primarily made up of "a conglomerate of personalities, factions and interests without common ideological or programmatic positions",[24] and elections turn out relatively simple and uncontroversial slogans such as "order", "economic progress" and "social justice". In most cases, contestants representing the government party are reduced to commending and advocating the achievements of public officials who do not actually take part in the electoral contest,[25] such as the ruler and certain ministers. Opposition contestants are even more limited by the formal and informal boundaries set by the rulers on their activities. Whatever their opinion of the political system, it is highly unlikely that they would publicly question its legitimacy.[26]

Elections for external consumption

Since non-competitive multi-party elections do not have any profound visible effect within the political arena, if the ruler derives some form of legitimacy from holding them, it is in a limited context. On the international level, the holding of such elections may, for example, help to enhance a regime's standing. Senegal's President Leopold Senghor, for example, initiated limited electoral reforms which subsequently meant that some opposition parties were allowed to compete in the 1978 legislative elections. While he ensured that his own party obtained the majority of seats (82 per cent of the votes cast), this move "probably enhanced his international standing in the West as a leader of a regime that respects civil and political rights".[27] As a result, "his party was the first in Africa to be admitted into the ranks of the moderate Socialist International."[28]

International considerations were also among the main reasons why the late President Sadat of Egypt decided to authorise a multi-party system. His government was, in the words of one author, "seeking political forms that would help its appeals to Western sources of support and cared little about making itself attractive to Communist countries".[29] The fact that legislative elections in which opposition parties participate continue, even under Sadat's successor, to have no effect on the replace-ment or succession of government, they nevertheless continue to help President Mubarak gain Western, especially American, support. Egypt's non-competitive multi-party elections make it "easier for the president and the US congress to provide aid, while very much reducing the possibility that Egypt will be criticised for human rights abuses".[30]

It is worth remembering that a regime's international position, especially with regard to Western democratic nations, is determined on the basis of other, more important, factors than the nature of its electoral system. In some instances, the electoral practice of a regime can count for very little. If, for example, the US wishes to enlist support for a foreign policy item, "no precise criteria of what counts as 'democracy' are needed; but foreign governments that do not share the official American world view, will find it hard to secure recognition in Washington as truly democratic, however liberal their electoral practices or their political philosophies."[31]

Elections in domestic politics

At the national level, it is noted that the whole concept of proclaiming democracy as a central political goal may help to provide some form of legitimacy for the rulers who hold democratic-style elections.[32] But this is likely to be because the ruler is attempting to illustrate his "commitment" to the general principles of democracy rather than to the possibility of government alternation.[33] The underlying fact, however, is that the legitimacy of a regime that did not come to power as a result of competitive elections is unlikely to be judged by the public solely on the basis of electoral dynamics. This is explained in the comments of one author, R.S. Milne, concerning the political system in Mexico. These comments can also be applied to similar non-competitive systems elsewhere.

> Because the regime had originated in a revolutionary transformation rather than through an inclusive and widely accepted electoral process, public perceptions of regime legitimacy depended more on overall evaluations of government performance and the fulfilment of a comprehensive revolutionary programme than on government adherence to particular procedural requirements.[34]

A similar point is also made by the prominent Egyptian writer, Mohamed Hassanein Heikal, who notes (with reference to Sadat) that while in the West, "A new President or Prime Minister . . . will no doubt be expected to implement at least some of the programme he offered before his election . . . in the Third World the leader's legitimacy, and so his survival, depends on his achievements."[35] Defining these achievements depends, invariably, upon the social, economic and political circumstances that each ruler individually confronts. The legitimacy derived by President Nasser following his ascent to power in post-1952 Egypt may have been due partly to his government's role in "evicting the British from Egyptian bases, nationaliz[ing] the Suez Canal, and emerg[ing] victorious from the 1956 invasion of Egypt by England, France and Israel".[36] Socio-economic reforms in terms of land redistribution, and developmental projects such as the Aswan High Dam, may also be regarded as factors that further contributed to his political legitimacy. As Hudson notes: "The Aswan High Dam scheme was not just an economic development project but an important legitimacy-building device, which explains in part Nasir's violent reaction to America's decision not to finance it."[37] Elections therefore played a minimal role in the legitimacy stakes and thus functioned within the limited framework of a one-party system.

Furthermore, the legitimacy of Nasser's successors, Sadat and Mubarak could hardly be attributed to the non-competitive multi-party arena that followed. In fact, opposition parties were not even granted formal authorisation to function until 1978, just over three years before Sadat's assassination. That Egypt's multi-party elections do not constitute the basis of regime legitimacy in the Mubarak era is reflected in the words of one potential voter, who said:

> The government is not all bad. Some are bad because they are corrupt and some because they are stupid and useless. But President Mubarak is good because he is trying very hard to solve the country's economic problems. Hasan al-Alfi [the then Minister of Interior] and 'Amr Musa [the Minister of Foreign Affairs] are also good . . . Al-Alfi tries to control the police and make sure they do not hassle people for no reason at all and Musa seems to know what he is talking about . . . Really, it does not matter how these people get into government. What is important is that they do a good job.[38]

Clearly, the rulers themselves are largely responsible for the fact that non-competitive multi-party elections do not have much legitimising significance on the political stage. In the absence of a dominant party based on a strong ideological or programmatic position, and given their reluctance to endorse wide-scale mobilisation, the rulers' utilisation of such multi-party elections, cannot be as a major legitimisation tool as is the case when single-party elections are mobilised. As one author explains:

> Without being assured of a turn-out that would give symbolic expression to the willingness of the people to participate within the regime, and fearful . . . of the number of votes the opposition might gain, [the rulers] are unlikely to attach much symbolic and legitimising significance to the elections.[39]

The establishment and subsequent regulation of a multi-party system through measures to ensure electoral results with foregone conclusions appear unnecessary for authoritarian rulers. They already control the major levers of coercion and maintain centralised command over the political apparatus without being bound by any rules other than those that fit their own political or personal convenience. However, as Schmitter points out, for such elections to be held in the first place, "they must have some reason or motive; they must contribute in some way to sustaining . . . the mode of political domination. They must have some functions . . . or they would not exist."[40] On this basis, it is perhaps best to turn attention to another aspect: the role of these elections within the framework of clientelist co-option and control.

Co-option and control

In the absence of effective constitutional-legal rules of restraint, authoritarian rulers need to resort to alternative and more informal strategies to maintain control over political activity. These strategies may rest upon attempts to cultivate the support and loyalty of subordinates on the basis of co-option and patronage. Of course they can, and at times do, resort to coercion, but as Jackson notes:

> . . . the method of intimidation and coercion has built-in costs: to the extent that opposition is suppressed, it is possible only to secure acquiescence, not active cooperation. But to survive, most personal rulers . . . rely on the willing cooperation of other political actors, and generally, they attempt to secure it by the stratagems of co-option, consultation, agreement, and patronage – especially the last.[41]

Authoritarian rulers can also attempt to deal with opponents on similar principles: either by actively contriving to eliminate them or by attempting to win their cooperation and adherence.[42] In the long term, broadening the power base of the regime to co-opt potentially subversive new elements appears a more viable option. Extended use of repression can have profound consequences for political stability should opponents turn radical in efforts to counteract government actions.[43] Anderson explains:

> All governments face dissent, but it is usually the government itself that selects the arena and chooses the weapons with which the battle is fought. Regimes that do not recognise [such] mechanisms . . . appear to run a much greater risk of wholesale opposition to the entire system than do governments that permit some form of the expression of dissent . . .[44]

In this setting, the establishment of a multi-party arena can perhaps best be examined as an instrument of control that permits authoritarian regimes to "make sure dissent would be institutionalised and channelled, not spontaneous".[45] Accordingly, by providing a forum for political contest in which disparate political actors can participate, the power-holders are most likely to monitor their activities from a better vantage point than if these opponents were forced to resort to illegal and clandestine methods of participation. It is therefore no surprise that non-competitive elections in Portugal prior to 1974 have been regarded as events that extended the surveillance capacity of the regime and brought "police records up to date".[46] While this may seem exaggerated, the general principles are apparent in some form or other within most authoritarian systems of this nature, including Egypt's, where the electoral register is also maintained by the police and where legal electoral activities are also constantly infiltrated by state security personnel.

As an instrument of control, however, a non-competitive multi-party system may be better understood in terms of clientelist relations. Patronage is extended to the arena of political contest to reinvigorate and expand political clientelism, thereby reaffirming government domination over political activity. Electoral practice, after all, is not embedded simply in a political tradition but also in a specific socio-economic and cultural context. Thus, elections may not necessarily have the same meaning in a complex industrialised society, where political participation centres around organised groups based on socio-economic interests and conceptions, as they do in societies where "the modes of relationship favour primary groups, while secondary groups are weakly developed".[47]

In the former, relatively full employment, social security, diverse opportunities and other characteristics which constitute the basis of modern liberal society lessen the possibilities of personal domination[48] and permit individuals the opportunity to affiliate with groups that are "voluntary, self-generating, (largely) self-supporting [and] autonomous from the state".[49] In this respect, state–society relations are based primarily on generalised reciprocity rather than on particularistic and hierarchical bonds of clientship.[50] In developing countries, however, the scarcity of resources and the general insecurities that emerge when there are no reliable avenues for dealing with problems of economic survival, tend to produce vertical patterns of dependency. This in turn means that the particularistic and hierarchical ties of clientelism are more likely to constitute the basis of state–society relations.

Understanding political clientelism

In general, clientelism can be defined as a "personalised, affective, and reciprocal relationship between actors, or sets of actors, commanding unequal resources and involving mutually beneficial transactions that have political ramifications beyond the immediate sphere of dyadic relationships".[51]

The difficulty of defining political clientelism in more specific terms derives largely from the fact that it varies in form not only according to the political system in which it prevails, but also according to the level of the political system in which it is operating. Lemarchand and Legg also emphasise a similar point: "'Clientelism' cannot be meaningfully considered apart from the setting in which it exists. The forms which it takes depend to a considerable degree on the structure of society and on the political system in which it operates."[52] Basically, however, a clientelist structure is characterised by the patron–client relationship, which J.C. Scott defines as

> an exchange relationship between roles [or] . . . as a special case of dyadic (two-person) ties involving a largely instrumental friendship in which an individual of higher socio-economic status (patron) uses his own influence and resources to provide protection or benefits, or both, for a person of lower status (client) who, for his part, reciprocates by offering general support and assistance, including personal services to the patron.[53]

It is the process of reciprocity that distinguishes patron–client ties from other relationships – such as those that are based upon formal authority or pure coercion – and that can also link individuals of different status.

> A patron may have some coercive power and he may also hold an official position of authority. But if the force or authority at his command are alone sufficient to ensure the compliance of another, he has no need of patron–client ties which require some reciprocity. Typically then, the patron operates in a context in which

the community norms and the need for clients require at least a minimum of bargaining and reciprocity.[54]

In an agrarian setting in which a landlord constitutes "the major source of protection, of security, of employment, of access to arable land or to education, and of food in bad times" puts him "in an ideal position to demand compliance from those who wish to share in these scarce commodities".[55] In turn, the compliance that a patron obtains from his "clients" is important since it not only enhances his status within society but, more significantly perhaps, it also "represents a capacity for mobilising a group of supporters" when the patron cares to.[56] The capacity of the patron to mobilise support from his clients in times of need is sometimes further reinforced by the dyadic or personal nature of patron–client ties.

> The continuing pattern of reciprocity that establishes and solidifies a patron–client bond often creates trust and affection between the partners. When a client needs a small loan or someone to intercede for him with the authorities, he knows he can rely on his patron; the patron knows, in turn, that "his men" will assist him in his designs when he needs them.[57]

It should also be noted that the ties linking a client to his patron can, theoretically, be made even more enduring because of the fundamentally "diffuse" nature of the relationship. This means that unlike formal contractual relations, the link between a patron and his client (or clients) "is a very flexible one in which the needs and resources, and hence the nature of the exchange, may vary widely over time . . . [and can] persist so long as the two partners have something to offer one another".[58]

Within the larger socio-political framework, therefore, a clientelist structure can be understood to exist when the patron–client relationship expands so that: "Patrons exist at different levels of the society (national, regional, local) and the lower-level patrons are the clients of higher-level patrons who have access to greater amounts and types of resources."[59]

While the expansion of the state apparatus into society constitutes the underlying process responsible for the establishment of such linkages,[60] the difference between one clientelist system and another is arguably dependent upon who ultimately controls (or at least exerts the most influence over) the greatest resources within society. Alex Weingrod has stressed how the expansion of state power into society brings with it "the establishment of new national and regional organisations, the initiation of new agricultural programs, the recruitment of cadres of workers [and] the commitment of huge capital funds".[61] Weingrod further remarks:

> These new resources of jobs and funds are typically administered or controlled by political party members or by persons designated by the parties . . . This close association of party with government opens new possibilities for patronage; once having gained control of these resources the parties use them to serve their own electoral ends.[62]

Hence, this process, which the author refers to as "party-directed patronage", can be used to explain how certain political parties use clientelism as a means to restrict genuine electoral competition and thus protect their dominant position in the existing power structure. The party's use of patronage for such a purpose, it should be noted, can generally be distinguished on two main levels. On one level, there is the "party machine"; on the other, there is the "party of social integration".[63]

The emergence of a "party machine" (labelled by Lemarchand as the "orthodox machine")[64] is predominantly "a question of an organism responding to particular demands in exchange for votes".[65] What this means is that the "party machine" functions through the clientelist manipulation of vulnerable people, such as rural migrants and foreign immigrants, most of whom are located in crowded urban areas where unemployment is rife and means for coping with problems of economic survival are limited. In such an environment, the party is usually in the position to "buy", through brokers, the votes of these people, in return for "concrete short-run benefits".[66] Rouquié explains this with reference to the United States during the first part of the twentieth century:

> Machine politics assumed its classical form in institutional contexts of competitive pluralism, notably in the United States before and after the First World War. Founded on the power of the "boss" exercising power without responsibility, the election machine functioned thanks to the boss's services to a population that was often outcast and vulnerable. The boss brought often-indispensable assistance to immigrants and foreign minorities in crowded city areas; they used their votes as a piece of merchandise . . . When a machine was thoroughly entrenched in a ward, the opposition did not even bother to organise there. Thus, there was not only a non-competitive election, but also a single party.[67]

The same situation, the author continues, prevailed in urban Argentina, most notably in Buenos Aires:

> The isolation and anonymity of urban life resulting from atomisation and immigrant uprooting are equally responsible for the success of the Radical Party machine in Buenos Aires at the beginning of the century . . . The district chiefs (*caudillos de barrio*) provided help, charity and credit. Party committees even sold low-priced food, known as "Radical bread" and "Radical milk".[68]

While the clientelist control of the vote by the party machine is based upon the exchange short-term material benefits, the party of social integration maintains a different, more intense, type of clientelist control. This is because a party of this nature (also labelled "mass patronage machine")[69] tends to preserve its dominant position in power on a long-term, if not permanent, basis by using the resources of power to grip "the state and society in a clientele network of extreme density".[70] Thus the party of social integration "is much more in the nature of a mass organisation; its resources are far more diversified (and so is its clientele), and its ramifications to the state bureaucracy are considerably more complex and extensive".[71] The Christian Democratic Party in Italy assumes the main characteristics of this complex, all-encompassing, clientelist party. In the words of one Italian politician:

> Clientelism . . . [used to evoke] the letter of recommendation from the notable, a practice still in existence and still frequent in Sicily, though less and less so. For at least fifteen years clientelism has been changing in nature and instead of being vertical ties as before, descending from the notable to the postulant . . . it now concerns entire (social) categories, coalitions of interests, groups of (private) employees, employees of public office or of regional enterprises. It is mass clientelism, organised and efficient . . . concessions granted no longer to the individual, but to favoured groups. In order to put this powerful machine to work, through time, the Christian Democrats have had to place party men at every level of power, in each key position . . . [Today clientelism] is a relationship between large groups and public power.[72]

This type of clientelist control is even more evident, and constitutes the main reason why, the Partido Revolucionario Institucional (PRI) in Mexico has remained in power since the early part of this century. The

PRI, which was created by President Plutarco Elias Calles in 1929, was regarded initially as "little more than a façade that ratified the political status quo".[73] However, even though opposition parties have formally existed since the late 1930s and 1940s,[74] the fact that the party has managed to maintain its dominant position for so long, and with relatively little need for coercion, is largely the result of the clientelist tactics instigated on behalf of the party by President Lázaro Cárdenas (1934–40). Under his rule, new sectors within the PRI were specifically created to incorporate the military, the middle class, the workers and the peasants – all of whom he had organised into officially separate group entities. Once incorporated into party membership "each of these groups, and especially the workers and peasants, was encouraged to regard itself as a corporate entity with interests that were distinct from, and often in conflict with, those of the locally based strongmen [*caciques*]".[75]

Cárdenas further reinforced the workers' and peasants' independence from the *caciques* through the provision of various rights and rewards. The workers, for example, were provided with a reorganised and strengthened union and collective bargaining system, while at the same time their right to strike was reinforced. The peasants, on the other hand, were given property which had previously been confiscated from large landowners during the 1910–17 social revolution. Such tactics were not insignificant since they also helped to institutionalise the party's dominant position within the political arena by ensuring that "the newly-organised peasants and workers were tied to an institution, the official party, rather than the ruler".[76]

The point here, however, is that while the corporatist organisation that was created within the framework of the PRI acted "as a countervailing force against the locally based clientelist structure",[77] it helped the party build an alternate clientelist structure, which to date allows it to dominate the Mexican political scene. Purcell explains:

> [T]he manner in which the peasants and workers were incorporated made them extremely dependent on national leaders. Both groups had been organised before they had a strong sense of class identity that would have enabled them to define their true interests, select their own leaders and enter the political system on their own terms. As a result, the price they paid for the "gifts" of organisation, resources and rights, was high. Having entered the national system from a position of relative weakness, they would find it difficult,

if not impossible, to increase their power over their new national patrons.[78]

The manipulation of state resources by a political party to ensure that not only individuals, but also disparate groups depend on it, has significant implications for elections since strategies aimed at creating such patterns of dependency encourage elections to function as a means of reaffirming clientelist control. It is argued that if "the machine or the party and its parallel hierarchies guarantees a minimum of social protection, the election enables the client" to pay his debt to the party and "by paying his debt, to deserve a patronal largesse once again".[79]

The participation of opposition parties in such a context does little to lessen the clientelist grip of the dominant party over state and society. Rather, the dominant party's monopoly of state resources can further strengthen its position if such resources are also used to tempt members of the opposition into co-option. This problem was a major issue in Mexico prior to the 1979 federal Chamber of Deputies' elections. As a result of Mexico's 1976–7 economic crisis, the then President, López Portillo (1976–82), became "personally convinced" that broad reform of the "political party system and the electoral process" would help alleviate part of the crisis.[80] It was for this reason, therefore, that opposition parties were particularly encouraged to participate in the 1979 elections. However, the fact was that most opposition organisations participated with some hesitation. They were aware that participation in the reforms, of which the 1979 election was part, could "result in their co-option by the established regime".[81] The opposition, as Middlebrook explains,

> were fully aware that minority representation in the executive-dominated Chamber of Deputies offered limited opportunities to effect substantial change. Furthermore, they had misgivings concerning the corruptive effects that access to government resources and opportunities for individual political advancement might have on opposition leaders.[82]

Indeed, the 1977 political "liberalisation" reform "marked an important departure in Mexican politics" since it led to "more active [opposition] participation in the electoral process [thus] significantly improv[ing] the ability of opposition parties to articulate alternative public policies and widen their membership base".[83] Yet, as the author acknowledges, such "liberalisation" tactics also served to incorporate, under government-defined rules, "the most important unregistered opposition organisations into the existing party system without greatly increasing their real political influence".[84]

On another level, "the lack of opposition-party access to significant resources and power"[85] may indeed be regarded as a major contributor to their subsequent "limited progress" within the electoral arena.[86] But this is not a wholly unexpected conclusion in view of the fact that the opposition was participating within a framework in which electoral domination by the PRI, since the early part of the century, had been closely linked with the downward flow of state-controlled patronage. Perhaps more important from the regime's point of view than the outcome of elections is the considerable opportunity for encouraging the registered opposition parties to become clientelistically dependent upon the regime (i.e. through the resources it controls and the necessity of being allocated a share of it if electoral gains are to be achieved). Indeed, as already mentioned, the fear of co-option was in the mind of the opposition. Yet, the fact that this fear did not deter the majority from participating, may, in the regime's eyes, have been regarded as a step towards the achievement of their aims.

In situations where a political system is not only structured along authoritarian lines but is also within the framework of personal rule, non-competitive multi-party elections can also be viewed as an important mechanism of clientelist co-option and control. The nature of clientelist control, however, differs by virtue of the ruler's personal monopoly of patronage. While one particular party may dominate the electoral arena, such a party cannot be compared to the dominant party in Mexico, for example, or, until very recently, India, where the Congress Party controlled "not only the state and national governments, but most of the local governments and new quasi-governmental bodies" with the result that "the Party has been able to establish extensive control over patronage."[87] Instead, it is the individual ruler who maintains ultimate control over state resources. In other words, the dominant party is simply given access to (not control over) state resources by courtesy of the ruler.

Personal rule functions with minimum coercion only if political institutions and groupings are weak and dependent upon the ruler. In such a context, if a dominant party, of which the ruler is head, does exist (and this will be the case unless the ruler maintains a single-party system or can manage the precarious task of placing himself as an arbiter of all parties), it is in the interest of the ruler to ensure that such a party (or, indeed, any of the participating "opposition" parties) does not emerge as a strong political entity that could potentially challenge his personal power.

The role of elections as a mechanism of co-option and clientelist control in such a case can perhaps be better understood along more traditional, and thus more personal, lines. This means that because the ruler maintains ultimate control over patronage, a political party cannot be regarded as an institutionalised, independent political entity. Instead, it is more likely to be made up of a conglomerate of personalities, each possessing its own network of supporters. The traditionally personal ties on which political parties in the Philippines were based, and the way this affected the nature of elections, is typical of that found in personal authoritarian systems of rule. As Landé explains:

> Formally, each party [in the Philippines] is an association composed of those who have become party members. In practice each party, at any point in time, is a multi-tiered pyramid of personal followings, one heaped upon the other . . . If one wishes to discover the real framework upon which election campaigns are built, one must turn away from political parties and focus one's attention upon individual candidates and the vertical chains of leadership and followership into which they arrange themselves at any given point in time.[88]

The personalistic nature of these ties, and the fact that these ties were structures independent of political parties, meant that electoral victory was mainly for those with "the greatest personal wealth, . . . the most flamboyant campaign styles", and "those who are thought most likely to be able to win and thus have access to patronage and other rewards of office".[89] More importantly, one of the main consequences of this electoral system was that it led to a "preoccupation with personalities, offices and spoils, and that lack of interest in policy or ideology, which is so strikingly characteristic of Philippine politics".[90]

This preoccupation by party members and their personal followers with patronage and spoils left political parties, as unified organisations, in a weak position. Because such electoral dynamics affected the nature of party organisation, the two major parties were "poor instruments for the formulation of distinctive and consistent programmes".[91] This, in turn, left each new President who took office with the "freedom to create his own program",[92] one that was mostly "guided by his personal views, the views of his advisers, and by a variety of pressures . . . which no President can ignore".[93]

On the basis of such individualistic methods of political participation, one can understand why it was not too difficult for President Marcos (1965–86) to establish himself in office for over two decades. The fact that the electoral contest focused upon personality-directed patronage, as opposed to party policies or even party-directed patronage, meant that political parties remained disorganised, disunited and therefore weak political entities. Thus, when Marcos decided in 1972, one year before the end of his second term as President, to impose a state of emergency and suspend elections, it was virtually impossible for any of the political parties effectively to oppose him.[94]

The dynamics of elections based on patronage encouraged the emergence of personal authoritarian rule in the Philippines during the Marcos era. This is because when patronage is ultimately under the personal control of the ruler, and the ruler installs himself as head of the "ruling" party, such elections act not only as a means of distributing to the masses tangible and other forms of rewards in return for political support but also, more importantly perhaps, as a mechanism through which the dependency of political players on the ruler is maintained and reaffirmed.

In traditional society, the expansion of the government's clientelist apparatus into society facilitated the recruitment of traditional patrons, such as large landowners, into the state apparatus. This, in turn, enabled the power-holders to redefine their roles, so that "instead of being largely creatures of the locality who dealt with the centre, the patrons became increasingly creatures of the centre who dealt with the local community".[95] This type of clientelist recruitment is perhaps most prominent in an electoral arena where the manipulation of state resources to provide facilities such as piped water, paved roads or a new school, in return for support for the "right" candidate (i.e. a government-nominated candidate), can be very enticing to an impoverished public – and more so in an arena where opinion-based voting is of little significance to electoral outcome. In such a setting, the utility calculations of individual voters in a single-party, multi-candidate system, will also prevail in a non-competitive multi-party system.

> Under a competitive party system, it makes sense for citizens to pay attention to a candidate's stand on those issues affecting the entire national political system. For if a candidate is committed to a party, then [their party's] success could conceivably affect national policy; [the candidate's] performance at the polls could combine with the performance of other candidates from [the same] party and their joint performance would help to define which team would subsequently control government . . . [under a single-party, multiple-candidate system] if successful, a candidate . . . would . . . have little impact upon national policies. In the absence of a competitive party system, voters, behaving rationally . . . therefore tend to pay more attention to the ability of candidates to do things of immediate, local value than to their stands on national issues.[96]

In this respect, it is logical to view the clientelist control of the vote as a mechanism of social control derived from the satisfaction of tangible demands in return for political support. In fact, elections in such a context function as "little more than devices through which clienteles are given the opportunity to register their loyalty to competing patrons through the vote".[97] Lemarchand and Legg note:

> Without in any way denying the selectivity with which . . . members of parliament act out their roles . . . their relationships with their . . . constituents are essentially based on personalised, affective, reciprocal ties. The deputy–constituent relationship in this case is but an extension into the modern parliamentary arena of the patron–client relationships discernible at the local or regional level.[98]

The point, however, is that because it is the ruler – not the individual patrons, or the party of which they are members – who controls most of the patronage, it is difficult for these to become independent of the ruler himself. In such an environment the ruler's control of state resources contributes towards ensuring that individual patrons/politicians cannot compete against the prevailing regime and must comply with it if they are to satisfy the demands of potential clients/constituents. Furthermore, as political clientelism radiates from a single point in the political process (the ruler), potential patrons depend on patronage at the apex of the system.[99] Hence an individual entering the electoral contest with aspirations to become a patron is more inclined to seek the patronage of the ruler through high-ranking political connections, or through membership of the party that he heads. And in doing so, he must therefore comply with the ruler's definition of "rules of the game".

The same method of political control can theoretically be extended to opposition-party members. Their success in the electoral arena also depends upon the support of potential clients/voters within society, which in turn is predominantly obtained in exchange for tangible benefits. As voters come to expect benefits that can realistically be channelled only from the centre, members of the opposition, like members of the state-supported party, may not have much choice but to depend upon the power-holder if some gains are to be made in the electoral field.

Thus, if members of the opposition decide to accept the patronage of the ruler for the sake of electoral gains, the result would arguably be advantageous to the ruler from a number of angles. The first, and most apparent, advantage is that these opposition groups would be compelled to accept, at least formally, the existing political status quo. More important, however, is the increasing possibility that these opposition groups would become weaker still. What this means is that if the ruler's control of patronage ensures that his own ruling party is little more than a conglomerate of personalities each possessing his personal network of followers, then it is likely that opposition groups, through participation in this regime-defined system of political contest, would eventually function on a similar, and thus easily controllable, basis.

Thus, where opposition parties are granted permission to participate in elections where competition is not really between parties, but between rival contestants each claiming advantage in securing the interests of voters and channelling state resources into the community, it is conceivable that members of the opposition may be inclined to focus their efforts on being representative of a constituency rather than on being representative of a party ideology. Through this emphasis, their role as intermediaries between those on the periphery and the centre would be enhanced. This tends to weaken party unity as each member of the opposition – like members of the ruler's dominant party – would be more concerned with preserving and expanding his personal base of support than with participating in party politics that could potentially threaten its durability. In such a situation, the ruler's position as ultimate patron would be enhanced and expanded, while the development of organised institutions and groupings would become further hindered; thus the possibility of posing effective challenges to the system of personal rule would diminish. This would seem the main function of democratisation in Egypt.

The case of Egypt: an overview

The role of multi-party elections in Mubarak's Egypt as an instrument of clientelist co-option and control can perhaps be better understood in the context of political activity in Egypt. The nature of this activity, as Springborg notes, is not even based upon formal political groupings. He maintains that political activity in Egypt cannot be examined by relying on organised groups as key units of analysis simply because such groups are not very important in Egypt. He goes on to suggest that "groups may not be indispensable to the [Egyptian] political process".[100] Furthermore, he points to C. H. Moore's observation that "Egyptians do not act politically primarily through organised groups" because the transformations that occurred post-1952 were not radical enough to discard certain deeply embedded traditions within society.[101]

Such traditions, which have been rooted in Egyptian society over the last few centuries, include the "individualistic orientation toward economic activity", which has "hindered the formation of a 'unified and egalitarian working class'".[102] The traditions of the predominantly peasant community are considered another factor that has contributed towards the weakness of class or professional ties. As one writer discussing the political activities of Egyptian peasants prior to 1952 observes, "the most striking feature of [peasant] communal action is its lack of formal organisation or planning."[103] Communal action in Egypt, as the author elaborates, "required no formal planning, organisation, or mobilisation to occur. In a dispute with landlord or an official, a peasant could often rely on the active support of relatives."[104] The peasant in dispute depended upon and received not only the support of close relatives "but also of scores, even hundreds of relatives (close and remote), friends and associates".[105] As a result, the "[t]ies of family and friendship . . . formed the basis of community as often as did common village residence".[106] The culprit who gave cause for complaint was "viewed as an oppressor but not as a class enemy".[107]

Islam is also considered as an important factor which may have contributed to the predominance of political individualism in Egypt. This, it is argued, is because Islam, unlike Christianity, was never effectively institutionalised. "Islam had never provided a counterbalance to arbitrary rulers nor checked their ambitions by imposing a clearly delineated, theoretical guideline to circumscribe the exercise of secular power."[108] Rather, the *ulama* of Islam were divided into cliques which centred around charismatic teachers and jurists. By offering the clique leaders administrative posts and other forms of patronage, the rulers were in a position to co-opt and control them. This resulted, as one author put it, in "the entire religious structure [being] dependent upon the favours of the ruling élite".[109]

Due to the lack of developed and organised groupings "Egypt's rulers continue to exercise the prerogatives of leadership unfettered by the constraints of organised constituencies".[110] This is evident in the fact that since 1952 all political activity, including the policy-making process, remains under the exclusive control of the President. While in modern democratic systems the head of the executive branch also dominates control over the decision-making process, in Egypt, the President is not institutionally bound to formal political organisations that share in the formation of policy. As is characteristic of authoritarian regimes, the legislative branch of government plays little role in exercising political pressure or restraint on the policy decisions of the President.

While the legislature is provided with formal control over the executive in the form of constitutional authority to license or dissolve government, in reality this power is nullified by the President's constitutional right to overrule the Assembly's vote through a public referendum. Other factors, including executive patterns of appointment, the President's prerogative to enforce emergency laws and, most important, the President's position as head and patron of the ruling party, further reinforce his individual control over the decision-making process. Accordingly, the outcome of multi-party elections under Mubarak has consistently been predetermined in favour of the President's NDP. With this in mind, Springborg can understandably say:

> Mubarak's assessment of the politically active secular and semi-secular middle and upper classes is that they do not pose a significant threat to him. He can afford to indulge them by granting rights of

expression in the form of newspapers, political parties, elections
and so on, for not only are their demands limited, but the expression
of them is almost as important as their fulfilment. For [this] small
price . . . he obtains their consent to his rule and their support in
his campaign to isolate radical extremists.[111]

As these "middle" classes do not themselves control major levers of
coercion or accumulation nor even enjoy a broad social base of support
in society, it is difficult to understand why Mubarak would need their
support or even consent to his rule. One may argue that granting formal
participatory space to this group would permit it to expand its social base
of support and politicise the masses against the regime more effectively
than extremist groups.

This is why it is more logical to view the extension of political
activity to include the participation of "opposition" elements in political
life as efforts to recruit them into the government's clientelist apparatus
so as to inhibit and contain their development and prevent them from
becoming potential threats to the regime. Multi-party elections can best
illustrate the mechanisms by which the regime reaffirms its political
domination on the basis of clientelist control. The President, at the apex
of this clientelist structure and the state resources at his disposal, is in
a prime position to co-opt non-extremist opposition leaders into the
existing political system, not only by granting them the right to form
parties, establish newspapers and participate in elections, but also by
occasionally assisting them during electoral competition, and in most
cases providing them with some access to state resources. This latter
point is of extreme significance for both the government and the
opposition. The opposition is aware that in order to obtain electoral gains
it must be capable of channelling state resources into constituencies. The
government, also aware of this dependency, readily manipulates the
situation to ensure the opposition's compliance in the same manner as it
controls members of its own party.

Through clientelist control of the vote it is difficult to create a
relationship between voters and parties on the basis of programmatic or
ideological conviction as voters are more concerned with the tangible
benefits they can acquire in return for their votes. Electoral competition
is subsequently structured on a highly parochial basis with political
campaigns between rival contestants concentrating on ways to serve the

interest of voters and promote the development of the local community. Consequently, the majority of individual contestants attempt to seek membership of the NDP, since, as the ruling party, it is in a position to provide its members with direct access to the state resources required to deliver the goods and services necessary for the continued electoral support of their constituency. As a result, such attraction to the President's party has contributed towards a weak, highly decentralised party dominated by intense intra-party competition from individual activists promoting their own personal careers.

However, from the government's perspective, this situation is ideal, for not only is it easier to maintain and control a conglomerate of personalities who constitute the dominant party, but also the situation highlights and strengthens a clientelist set of linkages which starts from the President and passes through the party and the representative before eventually reaching the constituency. In short, this process not only reinforces the dependence of activists on the government and its party for their personal political careers, but also illustrates to the voters their own dependence on the state.

The same argument can be more or less applied to Assembly members representing opposition parties. While opposition parties depend upon cordial relations with the government in order simply to function, electoral competition further reinforces such dependence. The government's clientelist control of the vote ensures that representatives from opposition parties are regarded by the majority of voters as intermediaries between themselves and central government, rather than as representatives of a party ideology. Ultimately, government opponents are elected on the same principles of personal networks and services to the community as those that define the role of NDP representatives. In other words, voters very rarely support opposition representatives because of their ideological persuasion. Rather, their support is usually given because they believe that once the individuals in question enter the People's Assembly they will be in a position to influence the government to channel resources in their direction. In this respect, opposition–government relations are of great significance for they can determine the amount of state resources that will be diverted into respective constituencies, and subsequently decide the electoral prospects of individual opponents and their party in future elections.

The extent to which a multi-party electoral arena in Mubarak's Egypt performs such a role will be discussed in detail as we examine, in the following chapters, how the fidelity-reward exchange, which this electoral arena has created, permits the President to establish a four-tier clientelist structure (consisting of the President, political parties, political activists and the masses) which links those on the periphery to the centre of power and subsequently contributes towards their containment and control.

Framework of analysis

The following chapters are organised around the clientelist chain, which appears directly related to Egypt's controlled multi-party electoral system. Chapter 2 examines the role of the President, who, by virtue of his position, is the premier patron in this clientelist system. The chapter focuses predominantly upon the nature of presidential authority and, in particular, on the significance of clientelism in the context of such authority. The aim is to show how clientelist politics is an important element contributing towards the protection of personalised rule in contemporary Egypt. As President Mubarak's strategies of rule are examined, the primary focus will be on the way in which he utilises his enormous powers to define the arena of political contest in a constrictive manner which subsequently encourages the incorporation of leading participants into the existing clientelist structure of dependency and hence control.

The role of political parties, as the second tier within the clientelist system, is examined in Chapter 3. The structure and dynamics of both the NDP and the opposition are assessed. The activities of, and opportunities for, political parties within the arena of political contest are to a large degree determined by their relationship with central government. This relationship is examined in terms of clientelist relations, rewards for conformity and methods of discipline for insubordination. The main reasons why legalised political parties appear to be left with little option but to accept these "rules of the game" are also assessed to clarify and substantiate the point. The "ruling" NDP, and the six "major" opposition "parties" – the Neo-Wafd, the Tagammu', the Nasserites, the Liberal Party, the Labour Party and the formally unrecognised Muslim Brotherhood Organisation are used as examples to highlight these issues.

The fourth chapter focuses specifically on electoral candidates. The relationships between candidates and party, and between candidates and voters, are discussed to illustrate the nature of political individualism, personal networking, role expectations and clientelism. The aim is to show that for various reasons, the majority of party candidates are compelled to adopt individualistic campaign strategies which are largely independent of the parties they officially represent. Furthermore, the purpose is to illustrate how the intended role of political activists as intermediaries between central government and those on the periphery is further reinforced by the expectations that voters have of potential representatives. This process emphasises the reason why political parties, as group entities, remain weak and are thus more easily incorporated into the clientelist structure linking the centre to those on the periphery. Moreover, the short-term material rewards that the electorates have come to expect from elections not only ensure overall social order and the voters' incorporation into the existing clientelist structure, but also discreetly reinforce the government's control over them.

In the last chapter the prevailing and potential consequences of multi-party elections are assessed. A non-democratic electoral arena of this type may appear to be a useful instrument for the maintenance of the political status quo, but the chapter examines the frailties of such a system and questions its durability.

Notes

1   S.P. Huntington and C.H. Moore (1970), p. 509.
2   L. Diamond, J.J. Linz and S.M. Lipset (1995), pp. 6–7.
3   Robert Dahl prefers the term "polyarchy" to democracy when referring to contemporary political systems that allow effective popular control but not self-rule. See R. Dahl (1971).
4   S.M. Lipset (1981), p. 73.
5   L. Diamond *et al.* (1995), p. 6.
6   A. Rouquié (1978), p. 20.
7   G. Hermet (1978), p. 5.
8   J.J. Linz (1978), p. 61.
9   R.H. Jackson and C.G. Rosenberg (1982), p. 11.
10 L. Martins (1993), p. 88.
11 J.J. Linz (1978), p. 65.
12 A. Rouquié (1991), p. 128.
13 M. Palmer (1989), p. 227.
14 J. Lacouture (1970), p. 7.
15 M. Palmer (1989), p. 227.
16 J.J. Linz (1978), p. 62.
17 R. Owen (1992) p. 238. It should be noted that political groups were first permitted legal status in Jordon under the Political Parties Law of 1955. This, however, was a very short-lived affair since they were subsequently banned in April 1957 and remained so until 1991. See R. Owen (1992), pp. 233–7.
18 A. Hermassi (1994), p. 241.
19 J.J. Linz (1978), p. 64.
20 J. Waterbury (1970), p. 148.
21 L. Martins (1993), p. 77.
22 R. Springborg (1989), p. 160; R. Owen (1994), p. 186.
23 N. Chazan, R. Mortimer, J. Ravehill and D. Rothchild (1988), p. 168.
24 J.J. Linz, (1978), p. 65.
25 Ibid.
26 Ibid.
27 R.H. Jackson and C.G. Rosenberg (1982), p. 97.
28 Ibid.
29 I.W. Zartman (1990), p. 233.
30 R. Owen (1994), p. 190.
31 L. Whitehead (1991), p. 11.
32 M.C. Hudson (1977), pp. 22–4.
33 R.S. Milne (1973), p. 208.
34 K.J. Middlebrook (1993), p. 126.
35 M.H. Heikal (1983), p. 55.
36 M. Palmer (1989), p. 160.
37 M.C. Hudson (1977), p. 239.
38 Interview by the author with a voter, Helwan, Egypt, 14 November 1995.
39 J.J. Linz (1978), p. 64.
40 P.C. Schmitter (1978), p. 149.

41 R.H. Jackson and C.G. Rosenberg (1982), p. 26.
42 Ibid., p. 25.
43 M. Palmer (1989), pp. 104–11.
44 L. Anderson (1987), p. 227.
45 D.C. Levy and K. Bruhn (1995), p. 192.
46 P.C. Schmitter (1978), p. 154.
47 A. Rouquié (1978), p. 22.
48 Ibid., p. 24.
49 L. Diamond (1995), p. 5.
50 Ibid., pp. 30–1.
51 R. Lemarchand and K. Legg (1978), pp. 122–3.
52 Ibid., p. 127.
53 J.C. Scott and B.J. Kerkvliet (1977), pp. 124–5.
54 Ibid., p. 125.
55 Ibid.
56 Ibid., p. 126.
57 Ibid.
58 Ibid.
59 L. Guasti (1977), p. 423.
60 R. Lemarchand (1981), p. 18.
61 A. Weingrod (1977), p. 326.
62 Ibid., pp. 326–7.
63 A. Rouquié (1978), p. 31.
64 R. Lemarchand (1981), p. 19.
65 A. Rouquié (1978), p. 31.
66 R. Lemarchand (1981), p. 21.
67 A. Rouquié (1978), p. 31.
68 Ibid., p. 31.
69 R. Lemarchand (1981), pp. 21–3.
70 A. Rouquié (1978), p. 32.
71 R. Lemarchand (1981), pp. 21–2.
72 Cited in M. Caciagli and F.P. Belloni (1981), pp. 35–6.
73 S.K. Purcell (1981), p. 198.
74 For example, the conservative "National Action" party (PAN) was founded in 1939 and the "Socialist Popular" party (PPS) in 1948. The latter was reorganised in 1958. See K.J. Middlebrook (1993), p. 128.
75 S.K. Purcell (1981), pp. 198–9.
76 Ibid., p. 199.
77 Ibid.
78 Ibid.
79 A. Rouquié (1978), p. 34.
80 K.J. Middlebrook (1993), p. 131.
81 Ibid., p. 133.
82 Ibid.
83 Ibid., p. 143.
84 Ibid., p. 146.
85 Ibid., p. 147.
86 Ibid.

87 M. Weiner (1964), p. 21, cited in A. Weingrod (1977), pp. 326–7.

88 C.H. Landé (1977a), p. 86.

89 Ibid., pp. 86–7.

90 Ibid., p. 88.

91 Ibid., p. 87.

92 Ibid.

93 Ibid., pp. 87–8.

94 Had it not been for the combined efforts of the church and the media in mobilising the masses following the "non-competitive" elections of 1985, and the subsequent defection of two of the President's most senior men, it is possible the President could have remained in office for the remainder of his life. To prevent a recurrence of personal rule, the current Philippine constitution, like the Mexican system, now limits the presidential tenure to one six-year term.

95 J.C. Scott and B.J. Kerkvliet (1977), p. 454, cited in R. Lemarchand (1981), p. 18.

96 R. Bates (1989), p. 92.

97 R. Lemarchand and K. Legg (1978), pp. 138–9.

98 Ibid., p. 126.

99 Ibid., p. 138.

100 R. Springborg (1975), p. 83.

101 C.H. Moore (1972), p. 18, cited in R. Springborg (1975), p. 83.

102 R. Springborg (1975), p. 84.

103 N. J. Brown (1990), p. 111.

104 Ibid.

105 Ibid., p. 112.

106 Ibid.

107 Ibid., p. 80.

108 R. Springborg (1975), p. 85.

109 D. Crecelius (1972), p. 171.

110 R. Springborg (1975), p. 86.

111 R. Springborg (1988), p. 159.

2

The Presidency

That multi-party elections in Mubarak's Egypt can best be viewed as an instrument of clientelist co-option and control cannot be appropriately examined without first understanding the nature of the presidency in post-1952 Egypt and, in particular, the significance of co-option and clientelism with regard to this presidential system of rule.

The dominant position of the President constitutes the most salient aspect of Egypt's post-1952 political system. The Egyptian President, for example, maintains a virtual monopoly over the decision-making process. As Hinnebusch noted with reference to the Sadat era:

> . . . the president is above such formal constraints as law or the administrative regulations which bind his subordinates; he remains the sole source of major policy or ideological innovation; and he still defines and can change the rules of the political game – the conditions of political participation. The presidency today is no less a concentration of enormous personalised power than under Nasser.[1]

Such personalisation of power can still be detected in the Mubarak era. As will be emphasised in the first part of this chapter, it derives not only from the immense legal-constitutional powers vested in the presidency, but also to the fact that Egypt's successive Presidents have focused upon strategies of rule in which co-option and clientelist mechanisms of control play an important role. These strategies are significant predominantly in ensuring the dependence of political institutions and groupings on the individual occupying the post of President. This, in turn, allows for the preservation of this personalised system of rule.

The second section of this chapter focuses on the nature of President Mubarak's rule, and in particular on the factors which indicate that the embryonic multi-party arena he inherited from his predecessor is intended to enhance clientelistically, not transform democratically, the prevailing system of personal rule. This view will be illustrated by assessing the President's strategies of rule, his attitude towards the multi-party system inherited from his predecessor, his conception of his role within it and the utilisation of presidential powers to ensure adherence to such conceptions. The aim is to show how the arena of political contest is defined in a constrictive manner which suggests that the President's primary objective is to impede the development of genuine party competition so that the entire multi-party arena can be incorporated into the existing clientelist structure of dependency and hence control which will thereby be reaffirmed and expanded.

The Egyptian presidency: an overview

Sources of power and authority

The pre-eminent position of the Egyptian President can be observed as early as 1953 when the provisional constitution formally accorded the "leader of the Revolution" the power to take any steps deemed necessary in order to protect it.[2] Safeguarding the Revolution, or perhaps more appropriately establishing the personalised system of rule that continues to characterise Egyptian politics, was not difficult to achieve because although the 1952 Revolution began simply as a military *coup*, it arose

> out of a "time of troubles", and Nasser . . . soon emerged as a charismatic leader, embraced by Egyptians as a national hero with unmatched personal legitimacy. It was this that legitimised the regime, allowing it to transcend its purely military origins [and raise Nasser] above the rest of his colleagues – turning them, in effect, into his "staff".[3]

Nasser's personal charisma not only contributed towards legitimising the new regime and elevating his position above those of other members who made up the Revolutionary Command Council,[4] it also allowed him to construct a political system essentially devoid of institutional checks and balances. Adopting a presidential system in which the President was to be elected through popular referendum, the 1956 constitution became the first of five[5] further constitutions created by Nasser to institutionalise personalised authoritarian rule. In other words, these constitutions were utilised in the authoritarian manner, being devices "important less as constraints on the abuse of power and more as legal instruments that a personal ruler could amend or rewrite to suit his power needs".[6]

[32]

While the growth of Nasser's charisma went hand in hand with his attainment of the status of sole decision-maker, the legal-constitutional powers vested in the presidency have contributed to ensuring that the legacy of personal rule continued into the 1970s under Sadat. This was perhaps best illustrated when Sadat managed to overcome an internal power struggle which marked the first seven months of his presidency.[7] The move, labelled the "corrective revolution", coincided with the implementation of yet another constitution. The 1971 constitution, which remains in effect, was constructed upon the same tenets as the previous constitutions. To understand why, after the demise of the charismatic Nasser, personalised presidential rule remained intact, it is necessary to start by examining the manner in which this constitution (and thus the previous ones) were formulated.

President by referendum[8]

As under Nasser, the President is officially instated by referendum. According to Article 76 of the constitution, the People's Assembly nominates the President of the Republic. The "candidate" must then obtain two-thirds of the Assembly's votes before the decision is ratified through a popular plebiscite. In the event of the President's death or permanent disability, Article 84 of the constitution states that the Assembly Speaker temporarily assumes the chief executive's position until a new President is instated. Since the Assembly can only refer one person to a national plebiscite (Article 76), the President does not have to compete for his position.

Given this background, the Egyptian President's official claim to office is not formally grounded on the basis of majority support, but on the basis of near unanimous support, as reflected in the astounding percentage of "yes" votes officially declared after such plebiscites. After Mubarak's presidential election referendum in 1987, for example, the Ministry of Interior formally declared that there had been a massive 88.5 per cent turnout, with 97 per cent of voters voting "yes". As the turnout had in fact been much lower, observers were quick to note that such "government claims appeared a reversion to the false plebiscites of Nasser and Sadat". In particular, they were ". . . disturbed that Mubarak went along with this charade".[9] Indeed, like his predecessors, Mubarak has appeared to have few qualms about the dubiousness of his referendum results. Publicly embracing the results of the 1993 referendum, for example, the President declared: ". . . all I can say is that I was moved by the high percentage of the people who turned out to vote. I believe that I have never seen such massive numbers of ballots in my life."[10] While political legitimacy in an authoritarian context, as discussed in the previous chapter, tends to be determined by certain factors predominantly related to the achievements of the individual in office, the point here is that, regardless of the authenticity of referenda as an instrument for securing office, such extraordinary results allow the Egyptian President to claim formally total popular support and thus absolute legal legitimacy.

Presidential terms

Article 77 of the constitution defines a presidential term as six years, and according to the same article there are no limits to the number of terms for which a President can be renominated. This constitutional prerogative means that Egyptian Presidents can, quite legally, remain in office for life. Both Nasser and Sadat died in office, and to judge from the current situation, it appears that Mubarak will remain in power as long as he wishes.

It is worth noting that both Sadat and Mubarak initially proclaimed their reluctance to rule for more than two terms. Sadat was so adamant that he formally implemented a two-term limitation in Article 77 of the 1971 constitution. However, he subsequently changed his mind and the article was duly amended through a plebiscite in 1980 so that he could remain in office. Mubarak also initially declared his disapproval of long-term presidential rule. As he declared in 1984: "I do not conceal from you the fact that I believe that the assumption of the office of the President by any one of us should not exceed two terms." He also added: "It pleases me that I shall be the first President to whom this rule will apply."[11] However, like Sadat, the President changed his mind and accepted renomination for a third term of office. As he explained: "This high position [of the presidency], though one of distinction and splendour, means for me no more than toil, sweat and constant effort . . . There is no gain, respite or ambition, but toil and sacrifice that continue day after day to protect this dear homeland." Yet, it would seem that, as is characteristic of authoritarian rulers, the President had by then begun to perceive of himself as indispensable to the nation. Hence, in his view, "the call of duty" left him with "no other choice but to . . . assume the honour of responsibility regardless of troubles and difficulties".[12]

Significantly, although both Sadat and Mubarak initially advocated the idea of a two-term presidency, the fact that both Presidents changed their minds illustrates the difference between formal political procedures, whereby the Assembly officially chooses the President, and the reality, in which the President actually decides his own tenure in office.

The People's Assembly

It can be argued that the People's Assembly is not obliged to renominate the President at the end of a presidential term. This is legally possible. It is also possible, on the basis of a two-thirds' majority vote, for the Assembly to file charges against the President for committing high treason or any other "criminal act" (Article 85). However, the Egyptian legislature has never exercised this prerogative; nor has it ever decided against renominating an incumbent President.

The People's Assembly is granted a number of constitutional prerogatives which should, in theory, counterbalance the office of the chief executive. For example, while the President is granted the right to appoint and dismiss the entire Cabinet, which comprises the Prime Minister, his deputies, the Ministers and their deputies (Article 141), the Assembly, according to Article 124, is entitled to address questions to any of its members concerning matters within their jurisdiction. If the Assembly is not satisfied with the performance of the Cabinet or of any of its individual members, then it is entitled to withdraw its vote of confidence (Article 126). Article 128 stipulates that if the Assembly withdraws its confidence from any of the Ministers or their deputies, the individual in question is expected to resign his office. It also stipulates that if the Prime Minister is found responsible before the Assembly, then he, too, must submit his resignation. It must be noted, however, that whether under Nasser, Sadat or Mubarak's leadership, the Assembly has never exercised this right with regard to any member of the President's Cabinet. Whether a prime minister, minister or even a whole cabinet is deemed competent or not is a decision that has invariably been determined solely by the President.

Another important prerogative of the Assembly is that of formally monitoring the considerable legislative powers accorded to the Egyptian President. As Article 147 stipulates, for example, the President, in the Assembly's absence, and in situations that "cannot suffer delay", has the right to issue decisions which have the force of law. However, according to the same article, such decisions must be submitted to the Assembly within fifteen days of the date of issuance. If the Assembly is dissolved or in recess (usually from July to October), then the President is legally obliged to submit the decisions to its next meeting. If any decisions are not submitted to the Assembly, or if the Assembly declines to ratify such decisions, then "their force of law disappears with retroactive effect".

Even when the Assembly is in session, the Egyptian President can also authorise the issuing of resolutions which have the force of law (Article 108). This article, known as the "Delegation Act", has the potential to enhance the President's legislative powers considerably as it provides him with the right to rule by decree. Therefore, in efforts to present a formal distribution of power, the same article stipulates that the President can be granted such power only with the Assembly's approval and only for a defined period. Furthermore, the President must point out to the Assembly "the subjects of such resolutions and the grounds upon which they are based".

While the President enjoys the right to conclude treaties, as confirmed by Article 151, such treaties must be presented to the Assembly accompanied by suitable clarification. For the conclusion of important treaties, such as peace settlements, alliance pacts, commercial and maritime treaties and any other treaties involving the rights of sovereignty, territorial modifications or agreements involving additional charges excluded from the state budget, the President is required to first seek the Assembly's approval. The President's power to declare war (Article 150) is also formally hindered by the article's stipulation that he must first seek the approval of the People's Assembly. In reality, however, there is ample evidence that it is precisely in such important circumstances that the Egyptian President excludes the Assembly, and even his own Cabinet, from any form of participation.[13]

The powers of the Egyptian President formally extend to his exclusive right to implement a state of emergency (Article 148). The President, according to Article 1 of the prevailing Emergency Law 162 of 1958, is entitled to declare a state of emergency "whenever security or public order are jeopardised within the Republic or in any of its regions, whether due to war or circumstances threatening war, national unrest, general disasters or the outbreak of an epidemic".[14] Under such a vaguely termed declaration, the President is entitled to safeguard security and public order by restricting the freedom of movement, assembly and residence of the citizens. However, although this law can enhance presidential power through its potential to suspend the constitutional rights of all citizens of the Republic, the President's right to declare a state of emergency is officially restrained by the Assembly's supervisory role. According to Article 148 of the constitution the President can declare a state of emergency on condition that he submits such a proclamation to the Assembly for approval within 15 days. The same article also states that "in all cases" a President's decision to proclaim a state of emergency cannot extend beyond a "limited" period without the Assembly's approval.

With regard to this point, it should be noted that all three Egyptian Presidents have managed to call for, and obtain, a formal state of emergency lasting for extraordinarily long periods. During the period between 1956 and 1963, for example, Nasser ruled under a state of emergency on the pretext of the threat of an offensive against Egypt. By June 1967 another state of emergency was declared by Nasser because of the Egyptian–Israeli war of 1967. Although declaration of a state of emergency during a war is not uncommon, it is remarkable that while the 1967 war was over almost before it started, the state of emergency lasted a total of 13 years. This means that even after Nasser's death in 1970 Sadat continued to rule under emergency measures for another decade. In his last year of rule, this law was lifted, only to be reinstated upon his assassination in October 1981. Since then, Mubarak has continued to request and obtain the Assembly's approval to maintain emergency law on the grounds of the threats of violence and terrorism.[15]

Yet, one should stress that the People's Assembly is constitutionally empowered to question and even challenge presidential authority. The fact that it refrains from doing so cannot be attributed to genuine unanimous approval of presidential policies. Rather, the People's Assembly has been confined to the role of rubber-stamping presidential decisions because its powers are restricted by certain presidential powers beyond its control.

The legislative powers of the Assembly, for example, can be virtually nullified by the President's authority to bypass the Assembly. According to Article 152 of the Constitution, the President is entitled "to call a referendum of the People on important matters related to the supreme interests of the country". Consequently, if the President decides to have his proposals endorsed through referendum, then it is impossible for the Assembly to intervene or deliberate upon the subject-matter. In addition, the potential use of referenda not only weakens the Assembly's legislative role but also restrains its supervisory role. Thus, if the Assembly decides to use its constitutional prerogative to withdraw its vote of confidence from the Cabinet (Article 126), the President can refuse to endorse the decision (Article 127) and is legally entitled to take the matter to a public referendum.

It must be noted, however, that the President in Egypt generally refrains from resorting to referenda except in circumstances where it is a formal requirement, as in the case of initiating constitutional changes. Presidents have not needed to bypass the Assembly through referenda because there has been no reason to do so. The bulk of laws passed through the legislature is initiated by the President in the first place. Moreover, according to one veteran Assembly member, whose career spans all three presidential eras, almost all presidential proposals are passed by the required two-thirds' majority with little, if any, deliberation at all.[16]

The enactment of the 1990 Electoral Law amendment, for example, illustrates the extent to which the legislature's role is predominantly one of formalising presidential decisions. In May 1990 the Supreme Constitutional Court struck down a section of the 1986 Electoral Law. This case will be examined in more detail below, but for now suffice it to say that President Mubarak decided to comply with the ruling. In doing so, the President set up a "technical preparatory committee", whose task was to remove and revise the parts of the Electoral Law found unconstitutional by the Constitutional Court. This eight-member Committee comprised two constitutional law professors, two legal experts from the Ministry of Justice, two police officers from the Ministry of Interior who possessed doctoral degrees in law, the Minister of Justice and the Secretary-General of the Council of Ministers. In other words, the Committee was narrowly composed; it did not include any elected members of parliament to represent either the dominant party or the members of the opposition who had initiated the Court challenge in the first place. Moreover, the draft recommendations were promptly passed as legislation without the President even pausing to allow any "input and comment" on the matter. As the opposition emphasised in a formal statement, the revised Law was drafted "single-handedly and in absolute secrecy".[17] The swiftness with which the legislation was passed illustrates the extent to which the majority of Assembly members were willing to overlook matters, even those concerning their own interest, rather than challenge the decisions of the President.

It would have been very difficult for them to do otherwise. The Assembly's refusal to comply with the President can result in his decision to invoke his powers to dissolve the Assembly. As Article 136 of the constitution states, the Egyptian President is empowered to dissolve the People's Assembly if "necessary" and "after a referendum of the people". In such a case, the President is formally required to issue a decision terminating the sessions of the Assembly and then hold a referendum within 30 days. If, or more realistically when, the public's approval is officially announced, the President then proceeds to set a date for new legislative elections. Naturally, the power to dissolve the Assembly has enormous implications for the Assembly's conduct and ultimately for the balance of power within the decision-making process. If the Assembly decides to take on a role that extends beyond supporting and formalising presidential legislation, the President can resort to referendum and thus dissolve it. The consequence would be not only inevitable disruption and the inconvenience of new elections, but also the dissolution of the Assembly, which can then allow the President to exclude "unruly" politicians from parliament.

Presidential patronage and political participation

The President's power to exclude non-conforming politicians from the Assembly can best be understood in the context of the President's clientelist control over political participation and the way in which this has enhanced the system of personal rule while marginalising the role of political parties in post-1952 Egypt. Prior to 1952, a multi-party parliamentary system functioned within the framework of a constitutional monarchy. Yet the abolition of the monarchy was followed by a temporary suspension of multi-party activity. On the pretext that multi-partyism constituted both an obstacle to national unity and a betrayal of the regime's ideological goals of social equity and justice,[18] this temporary suspension of political parties became a total ban.

As in most developing nations during the era of nationalist fervour, Egypt's move towards a single party was primarily intended to secure an attitude of obedience to authority and acceptance of the measures enacted by the new ruler. As the author of an early study on post-independent West African states put it, "with few exceptions the trend has been for one man in each state to be elevated to a position of great power . . . Often the constitution reflects this domination of the state not only by a single party, but, within that party, by a single man."[19] Thus, while the formal purpose of this all-encompassing type of party was to provide a forum where the people would meaningfully participate in the political process, in reality this was rarely the case.

Nasser in particular feared that an organised, single party with popular participation or decision-making powers might result in a Soviet-style system which could potentially challenge his personal position as the ultimate source of legitimacy and power.[20] This fear subsequently prompted the President to use the party "more as a means of mobilising political support than as a vehicle for political participation".[21] The extent to which the single party was intended to be no more than "an extension of one and the same command structure – the President"[22] – was reflected in the nature of political participation at the time. Potential candidates for office were not only subjected to rigorous scrutiny, but also were dependent upon presidential decrees to grant them authorisation to participate.[23] In addition, electoral results were processed and announced not by an independent body, but by the Ministry of Interior. This system continues in effect to this day. The President's strategy was to ensure that those who reached the legislature were aware that their position was not acquired by independent means but by his personal will and patronage.[24] Evidently, this aim was achieved as none of the three organisations[25] created consecutively under Nasser's one-party system managed to emerge as an independent political entity that "reflected the structure of social forces" or served as a vehicle "through which the dominant social force could extend, moderate, and legitimise its power".[26]

In the context of this personalised system of governance, the decision to change "the rules" of political participation and transform the political arena from a one-party to a multi-party system in 1977 can arguably be regarded as Sadat's personal policy initiative.[27] There did, however, appear to be a need to "satisfy participatory pressures",[28] but since the expansion of formal political groupings and organised political contest could rally diverse constituencies of supporters which would potentially challenge the very existence of personalised authoritarian regimes, Sadat's move to authorise an official opposition was hardly aimed at establishing a more democratic form of government. Instead, "liberalising" the political system appears, for Sadat, to have been intended to serve other purposes. These were to differentiate his regime from Nasser's in order to appeal to his new Western allies and to cultivate an image of political democracy to coincide with the implementation of his programme to liberalise the economy. On another level, Sadat's objective was to use the multi-party arena as a means by which to enhance the strategy of "divide and rule". His aim was to encourage overt division in élite opinion, refrain from taking sides, and so acquire the role of arbiter thereby warding off any attack on his rule.[29]

As the nature of political parties will be examined in detail in the following chapter, suffice it here to note that the extent to which Sadat intended to create a weak multi-party system that could be manipulated for such purposes is reflected in the manner in which political parties emerged at the time. The "ruling" NDP, for example, was in itself a creation of Sadat. Having perceived the ASU as a potential threat to his personal power, even in the aftermath of his "corrective revolution", Sadat proceeded in 1974 to divide the party into three ideological bodies. In 1977 he then decided to disband the ASU altogether and confer upon these bodies the official status of full-fledged political parties.

However, when, a year later, Sadat decided to create his own party (the NDP), some 250 members of the People's Assembly rushed to join the President's new party.[30] This move was undoubtedly related to the fact that the President's party would ensure for its members direct access to state resources. The main point, however, is that since most of the NDP's members were originally members of the disbanded ASU, its creation was more the result of presidential instigation than of pressures from an organised constituency. Put differently, the mass conversion from "socialist" to "democratic" ideology implied not only the desire to remain under direct presidential patronage, but also that the emergence of the ruling NDP was no more reflective of constituency interests than the ASU was under Nasser's party system.

Like the NDP, the first two opposition parties were also created from above, initially in 1976 as official platforms within the ASU, and then in 1977 as independent parties. Hence, although these two opposition parties – the National Progressive Union Party (Tagammu') and the Liberal Party (al-Ahrar) – were theoretically expected to represent socialist and liberal tendencies respectively, they did not develop as a result of an independent political movement that represented certain social forces within society. Instead, both parties were also artificially created by the President who chose old associates to head them and, in attempts to signal his official stamp of approval and thus ensure their loyalty, encouraged some of his supporters to join them.

The same tactics were also employed during the formation of the Socialist Labour Party in 1978. Ibrahim Shokri, the then Agriculture Minister, was encouraged by Sadat to launch this new party after the President discovered that both Tagammu' and Ahrar leaders were not the "supportive" opposition he had expected and were critical of the Egyptian–Israeli peace efforts.[31] The revival of the Muslim Brotherhood during that period can arguably be explained in a similar context – that is, although the group was (and remains) formally unrecognised as a legal party, it was Sadat who personally encouraged its re-emergence as a counterweight to what he eventually came to regard as his opposition: sections of the élite that included "Nasserites, leftists, liberal intellectuals [and] Wafdists survivors".[32]

The Neo-Wafd's revival in January 1978 proved the exception to the rule: it was not artificially induced by the President. Yet, it must be noted that as soon as Sadat believed that support for it might pose a threat to the regime, he issued a decree forbidding those who had held prominent political positions prior to the revolution from party membership. The consequence of this was that the Neo-Wafd's veteran leaders were banned from participation and the party was forced to suspend its activities.

The stringent control over political participation even after the transformation to a multi-party system has meant that entry to the legislature in post-1952 Egypt has been primarily a consequence of presidential patronage rather than a reflection of independent political contest. It is therefore understandable that, for the majority of politicians who reach the Assembly, being subservient to the President is the only way in which they can ensure their continued incumbency. Equally important is the fact that the clientelist domination of the President appears so embedded that it extends to the other major political and state institutions.

Presidential patronage extended

The powers of appointment and dismissal accorded to the President, combined with the patterns of recruitment into these organisations, illustrate how the Egyptian President enhances his control over the major institutions of state. These powers of appointment extend from the apex of the political structure (where they cover advisors, prime ministers, ministers and provincial governors), to all the most senior posts within the ruling party, armed forces, judiciary, bureaucracy, state-owned media, public enterprises, national universities and the formal Islamic establishment. Most importantly, the consequence of this pattern of recruitment is that individuals are not appointed on the basis of superior professional merit or as a result of ethnic, linguistic or other categorical considerations, but rather on the basis of personal attributes such as trustworthiness and loyalty, which are the most important considerations for the president when making appointments.

Springborg explains how, in order to procure such loyalty, informal organisations such as the family, the *duf'a* (graduating class) and the *shilla* (group of friends) are utilised as clientelist mechanisms of élite recruitment.[33] Prior to 1952, entry into the political élite was almost exclusively from the wealthy landowning families who, through inter-marriage and extensive clientelist networks, monopolised top political posts. While the political and economic reforms that followed 1952 undermined the prominent role of the family as an informal unit of political organisation, it did not eliminate it. On the contrary, in order to obtain "administrative expertise" and "political connections to segments of the articulate public", Nasser was himself "perfectly willing to recruit into his cabinets and into the ASU *ancien régime* politicians from prestigious families".[34] Thus, what emerged within the post-1952 regime, was a pattern in which the importance of the family in the recruitment process was maintained but was more dependent upon personal contacts within the state apparatus than upon the material wealth of the family.

In other words, the prospect of an élite appointment in post-1952 Egypt depended less upon the socio-economic status of an individual's family than on whether a member of the family occupied the ranks of the upper élite strata (and could thus recommend the individual in question to the President or someone close to the President). The operation of the *duf'a* network is perhaps most clearly depicted under Nasser's rule since the officers who led the 1952 *coup*, the members of the Revolutionary Command Council which ensued, and the majority of those holding top élite posts during that period were largely members of the same military academy *duf'a*. Finally, the *shilla* as a mechanism of recruitment is more extensive in scope. Since it is based upon the concept of friendship, it incorporates a wide range of social acquaintances, some of whom may also be linked to the President through family or *dufa* ties. The disparate mixture of élites under Sadat correlates more to the *shilla* than to the *dufa* network. Since the majority of those occupying top posts under Mubarak's rule were his close associates during the vice-presidency period, it would seem that the *shilla* tie is also depicted, albeit less conspicuously, under Mubarak.

As the President, for practical reasons, focuses his appointment powers primarily on the highest positions of the state, his subordinates are provided with lower-level appointment powers which, in their roles as patrons to individuals still lower in status, they are able to distribute to their own clients. It is in attempting to understand the large, highly diffuse and opportunistic patron–client ties at that lower level of the élite structure that informal organisations such as those defined by Springborg are perhaps most useful. However, the highest level of the clientelist structure is more stable and straightforward because of two main factors.

First, the underlying importance of personal loyalty prompts the President to appoint to the top élite posts only those individuals with whom he is personally acquainted or who come with the personal recommendations of trusted confidants. Osama al-Baz, for example, acquired the position of senior presidential advisor shortly after Mubarak assumed the presidency largely because he had been his advisor on foreign affairs during Mubarak's vice-presidency. President Mubarak's decision to appoint 'Amr Musa in 1992 as Minister of Foreign Affairs is also illustrative of this clientelist pattern of élite recruitment. In other words, Musa's appointment was not based on any apparent formal considerations on the President's part but on the personal recommendation of al-Baz, one of the most trusted presidential confidants, who recommended Musa – previously a Foreign Ministry official and a client of al-Baz. In fact, it would be very difficult to find, under the presidencies of either Nasser, Sadat or Mubarak, a member of the inner élite circle whom the President or one of his closest advisors was not personally acquainted with prior to recruitment.

This leads to the second main factor regarding the stability of the patron–client ties at the apex of this clientelist structure. The individuals on this élite level are tied to one patron – the President. Hence, in the absence of a higher patron to which to attach themselves, their main objective is to preserve their existing relationship by remaining sub-servient. It is for this reason, one can argue, that this segment of the élite has a very good chance of maintaining its posts for a long time. The government of 'Atef Sidqi (1986–96), for example, was the longest serving since the first modern Cabinet was formed in 1914.[35] Yet, in the face of this static, record-breaking tenure, Mubarak's response was: "I'm not going to take the decision [to change the Cabinet] only to please those calling for change".[36] And in fact he did not. The Cabinet thus remained virtually the same, with the only significant change being the replacement of Sidqi in early 1996. Yet, even then, Mubarak did not search very far for a successor. The President's choice of Prime Minister, an inconspicuous bureaucrat, Kamal al-Ganzuri, had been an incumbent Minister throughout the entire Mubarak period.[37]

Finally, this clientelistic power structure is perhaps all the more secure in that a change of President is not followed by a massive shift in the élite personnel of the system. That is, while each President may appoint a new group of individuals personally close to him to top positions, the existing élite personnel are not forced into retirement but are largely reshuffled to other senior posts within the political and state apparatus.[38] Invariably, this process has led to "an amorphous, sprawling élite of officers, bureaucrats, professors, *ancien régime* politicians, and others . . .".[39] Yet, more significantly, such an enormous patronage network also strains the "bonds of élite cohesion"[40], which, in turn, diminishes the potential emergence of powerful and challenging factions within the regime.[41] In addition, the provision of permanent state bases to take in the pool of circulating élites not only promotes the acquiescence of these élites, but also ensures that the prospect of a powerful group of them emerging outside the state apparatus to challenge the regime remains practically unfeasible. The fact that political mobility is ultimately dependent upon personal rather than organisational loyalty has thus reduced the roles of formal organisations and institutions to little more than those of "vehicles through which personal connections are established".[42]

The personalised power of the President in post-1952 Egypt is further enhanced by the President's personal control of state funds and resources. Hence, although an annual budget is presented to the Assembly for approval at the beginning of each fiscal year, this is basically a form-ality; specific resource allocations are neither revealed to the Assembly nor pursued through formal channels. Instead, the allocation of resources to the various political and state organisations is primarily determined according to the personal and political objectives of the President. In a study on Egypt's ministerial élite, for example, El-Gamal reveals how, during the Sadat era, a slanging match took place between two ministers over the allocation of cement to their respective ministries. The scene, between the former Minister of Defence, Field Marshal 'Abd al-Halim Abu Ghazala, and the former Minister of Construction and Housing, Hasaballah al-Kafrawi, was randomly (and personally) settled by Sadat in favour of Abu Ghazala. The reason, it seems, is that Abu Ghazala was closer to Sadat than al-Kafrawi and, as El-Gamal remarked, "those closest to the President won".[43]

Given such informal and personalistic mechanisms of resource allocation, it would not be contentious to argue, as El-Gamal has done, that the extent of the President's closeness to one particular Minister would ultimately determine the outcome of such conflicts. However, even though in that particular episode Abu Ghazala happened to be personally closer to Sadat than al-Kafrawi, the fact that the Minister of Defence gained the upper hand over a civilian Minister cannot simply be attributed to the President's personal disposition, particularly if one takes into account the role of the Egyptian military and the way in which presidential patronage appears to safeguard that role.

Since the Nasser period, the military establishment has come to perform a prominent role as the protector of Egypt's post-1952 regime. It was, after all, a military *coup* that brought the post-1952 regime to power, and the fact that all three Presidents were originally military men cannot be overlooked. Securing the protection of the armed forces, however, has not been simply the result of these factors alone, but primarily the consequence of the extent of presidential patronage extended in that direction. Under Nasser, the most prominent form of patronage bestowed upon the military was in the allocation of appointments to key political and state positions, ranging from ministerial posts to top posts in the then newly nationalised economic organisations. In the post-Nasser era, the armed forces were "no longer a corporate member of the Alliance of the Working Forces of the People",[44] and the re-emergence of a multi-party arena was followed by a ban on military personnel joining political parties or voting. Presidential patronage in the form of élite political and bureaucratic appointments subsequently became less conspicuous. However, this change was compensated for through additional material benefits for officers and their families, including subsidised housing, motor cars, hospital care, sports clubs and even electrical household appliances and groceries. State-financed study programmes in Egypt and abroad also became more accessible to officers in the ensuing patronage transformation. Presidential appointment as a form of patronage was not, however, completely eliminated. As Commander-in-Chief of the armed forces, the President still allocates the top military positions, including the Cabinet posts of Minister of Defence. In addition, Nasser's tradition of reserving the presidentially appointed posts of Egypt's provincial governors for retired (military and police) officers, was diligently preserved by his successors.

It is logical to assume that, as a consequence of such patronage, the military has maintained a vested interest in protecting and upholding the personalised authoritarian system of post-1952 Egypt. Illustrative of this is the fact that since 1952 the military has never refused a President's call to combat mass riots, such as those which took place in 1968[45] and 1977,[46] or even to confront challengers from within the system, as in 1986.[47] The extent of the military's loyalty to the President and its obedience to his decisions is perhaps most poignantly reflected in the army's support of Mubarak's decision to join forces with Western nations against Iraq in the 1991 Gulf War.

The system of personalised authoritarian rule in post-1952 Egypt was constructed by Nasser and sustained by his successors as a result of several factors which ensure the absence of autonomous group entities and thus the President's direct control over all state apparatuses. The President's prerogative of appointing and dismissing the Cabinet, for example, ensures his personal control over the entire executive branch of government. In addition, his chairmanship of a party that gains no less than three-quarters of the Assembly seats while essentially having no independent power base, and his legal-constitutional authority to overrule the Assembly and even dissolve it, ensures that the legislature allows him to rule by presidential decree, enact emergency measures and, in short, dominate the entire decision-making process. Furthermore, the President's enormous appointment powers and the way in which they are utilised ensures that the top operators of the state apparatuses are tied to the President on a clientelist rather than an institutional basis. Hence, the accumulation of such powers in the hands of the President, coupled with his patronage of the armed forces and position as Commander-in-Chief, have allowed the President to sustain personal, authoritarian rule in post-1952 Egypt.

The system of personalised rule in Egypt has prevailed for nearly half a century largely as a result of the enormous legal-constitutional powers vested in the presidency and the clientelist structure which, nurtured by three successive Egyptian Presidents, has ensured the dependency of political actors and institutions on the individual occupying the office of the President. The pre-eminent position of the President in contemporary Egypt, therefore, is inherently linked to the preservation of this clientelist structure of dependency and hence control. Reaffirming and expanding this clientelist structure to incorporate potential challengers to the existing political system is thus a logical step for a President anxious to preserve the political status quo. One can thus understand President Mubarak's strategies of rule with regard to the newly constructed multi-party arena he inherited upon assuming office.

The multi-party scene under Mubarak

As Vice-President, Mubarak ascended to power on Sadat's death with relative ease. However, while both of Mubarak's predecessors came to power with a record of political activity, including being core members of the Free Officers group, Mubarak could not claim such a legacy; nor could he claim direct association with any pre-revolutionary nationalist activities. Mubarak was an officer in the air force and his main political qualification prior to assuming office was the position of Vice-President bestowed on him by Sadat in 1973. Mubarak appears to have initially justified his relative political inexperience by claiming that he received intensive "training" from Sadat, and that this gave him the opportunity to benefit and learn "a great deal from a man with more than 40 years of experience in politics".[48] However, Sadat's unpopularity in the last few years of his rule and his death at the hands of extremist Islamic opponents suggest that it was necessary for Mubarak to distance himself from his predecessor and cultivate the necessary support to consolidate his own position.

The success of such a strategy, one may argue, meant that the new President had to deal with two sources of discontent. One was the opposition for Sadat's message of liberalism had fuelled greater expectations among opposition parties than was actually intended. Shortly before his assassination by Islamic extremists in 1981, Sadat had resorted to a wholesale crack-down on political opponents. Although assassination, as one analyst notes, "is a haphazard, individual act, and its chances of success are random, not a barometer of the stability of the regime or the strength of the opposition",[49] the experience nevertheless emphasised the mounting tension between government and political opponents.

At the same time, Mubarak had inherited a potentially turbulent civil society as a result of his predecessor's economic experiment. The open-door policy (*infitah*) introduced by Sadat had stimulated little investment in productive or export-oriented industries. Instead, it produced a consumption boom that left the economy in deficit.[50] Reforms aimed at structural adjustment of economic imbalances were necessary but risked evoking overt popular hostility – as the food riots of 1977 had previously illustrated. Because of this, the new President could hardly continue the repressive tactics employed by Sadat prior to his assassination.

Mubarak's attempt to portray himself as a staunch supporter of democracy was largely influenced by efforts aimed initially at containing both sources of discontent. By advocating democracy, for example, the President might have been finding a way to distribute responsibility for the implementation of unpopular economic reforms. Soon after coming to power he said:

> The philosophy on which we should all agree and which should guide our work is that Egypt stands above all. Egypt is not a society of a privileged minority which monopolises power . . . Egypt is for all her sons who, with their thought and toil build their own country on the basis of equal opportunity and equality in shouldering burdens.[51]

The same argument was also expressed in more explicit terms a few months later: "I believe democracy is the best guarantee of our future . . . I totally oppose the centralisation of power and I have no wish to monopolise decision-making because the country belongs to all of us and we all share a responsibility for it."[52]

It should also be noted that Egypt, since the 1979 peace accords with Israel, had come to depend upon substantial aid from its Western allies, and in particular from the United States. Considering the ailing economy Mubarak had inherited, it would be fair to assert that the apparent advocacy of democracy was also a strategy designed to safeguard the flow of this much-needed aid which, from the US alone, is estimated to be approximately US$2.1 billion per annum.[53] As Roger Owen notes: "The appeal of democracy (however limited in practice) bolsters the legitimacy of the regime both internationally and domestically. As far as the former is concerned, it [makes] it easier for the [US] president and the US congress to provide aid."[54]

The President's attempt to prove his democratic intent was illustrated most prominently when he ordered the release of politicians arrested by Sadat, and the reinstatement of the university professors and journalists who had been dismissed as a result of their political activities. It may be argued that the President's apparent courting of the opposition was an attempt not only to gain their support in the face of harsh economic conditions and a potentially turbulent society but also a useful strategy to avoid a two-front war with moderate and extremist opponents. By proclaiming that terrorism would not affect his conviction that "the reliable shield of democracy is the right of every citizen" and would not shake his "belief that the problems of democracy can only be solved with greater democracy",[55] the President appeared to be hoping to cultivate support of the moderate opposition in his quest to isolate the radical Islamic groups (Gam'eyat), which mushroomed during the Sadat period.[56]

Mubarak's strategy seems to have achieved initial success when opposition turned to almost unanimous support for the new President. On behalf of the opposition, Ibrahim Shokri, leader of the Labour Party, publicly announced his optimism when he declared: "The opposition welcomes the principles set forth by President Mubarak, particularly his call for political participation, spirit of initiative [and] adherence to democracy."[57] Even more enthusiastic was Fu'ad Serag al-Din, leader of the Neo-Wafd party, who noted:

> One fact I am sure of now that I have full confidence in [President Mubarak's] courage is that we will, together with God's help, surmount the plight of our country . . . because he respects the freedom of opinion . . . speech and political parties . . . President Mubarak wants to create a civilised democratic country in accordance with internationally established concepts.[58]

Judging from the tone of statements such as these, however, the problem with Mubarak's advocacy of democracy was that – as with Sadat – it had produced higher expectations on the part of the opposition than had been intended.

The emergence of authoritarian tendencies

The fact that President Mubarak initially projected a commitment to democracy as a mechanism to stabilise the political scene and consolidate his own position rather than to expand political participation, was more evident after 1983. These years can arguably be regarded as the period when the real Mubarak era began and thus when his real political views began to emerge. That President Mubarak was consolidating his power after 1983 was evident in several ways. For example, while the President acquired the formal position of head of the NDP upon taking power, it can be said that it was not until the party won the first parliamentary elections under his leadership in May 1984 that his position as its patron was actually established. Moreover, in September and October of the year in which the President's control over the NDP, and thus the legislature, was cemented, the first food riot under his rule took place in the Delta town of Kafr al-Dawwar – following the doubling of the price of subsidised bread. According to official reports, one person died and 28 people were injured in the ensuing clashes with the security forces.[59] The fact that a riot of this nature was swiftly contained before it became nationwide undoubtedly accentuated Mubarak's confidence that he had also established himself well in control of the state's coercive powers.[60]

In such a context it is not too surprising that President Mubarak has come to believe that Egyptians perceive him as he sees himself and to assume that his personal political priorities are the same as theirs. For example, during his initial years in office, the new President was anxious to avoid portraying himself in a patriarchal light and publicly stressed that there was "no ruler and ruled" and that all citizens were "equal".[61] Yet, later, the President's perception of himself as a father figure began to take root, believing that Egyptian people saw him in this light and, like himself, they just wanted stability.[62]

President Mubarak's authoritarian inclinations and sense of self-importance, however, are more visibly reflected in the events surrounding the annual opening of parliament. Usually held in November, the official inauguration of parliament is the only occasion that brings the President to the Assembly. The Assembly's debating chamber, where the President gives his speech, is packed tight in a small space since the event is attended by both Assembly and Consultative Council members. While the occasion exudes a monarchical aura – as it is the President's sole annual visit to the Assembly – the members in their cramped position are cut down to size emphasising Mubarak's perception of his own position as President.

On the scheduled day, the deputies are expected to arrive between eight and ten o'clock in the morning. Anyone arriving later than ten o'clock is automatically turned away. For security reasons, the army takes over the role of guarding the Assembly from the police on that day. More poignantly, the army's duty includes searching each deputy thoroughly before allowing him or her into the chamber. Once inside the chamber, no one is allowed out, not even to go to the lavatory. As Mubarak's motorcade arrives at eleven o'clock, the deputies are locked inside for one long hour.

Following the presidential speech, which on average lasts an hour, the President joins the Assembly Speaker for an informal chat in the Speaker's office. In the meantime, the deputies remain incarcerated in the chamber until the President leaves the premises. Not surprisingly, the hours of confinement result in a number of casualties every year, as frail and elderly deputies faint from suffocation or bladder retention. However, even as deputies shout and bang on the chamber doors for assistance at these times, the pleas are ignored and the doors remain locked until the President's eventual departure.[63] According to one veteran politician, this annual humiliation is a new feature, not inherited from previous Presidents.[64]

It must be noted that the above security arrangements were first imposed immediately after Sadat's assassination as Mubarak stepped into the presidency. As the political situation following Sadat's assassination was initially unclear, such precautions can arguably be viewed as an isolated measure to ensure the safe accession of the new President. However, the fact that in Mubarak's second decade of power this procedure continues to be practised suggests that the President not only regards himself above the legislature, but also views it with deep mistrust. As the majority of legislature incumbents are from his own party, it would seem that such "precautions" are directed at members of the opposition, reflecting, perhaps, the authoritarian's feeling of insecurity when facing political opponents – even those playing by the formal rules.

It is a paradox, therefore, to note how President Mubarak refers to the Assembly as though it was an independent and equal force in the political system. In a speech marking the start of a new parliamentary year, for example, he thanked the Assembly audience for fulfilling the "task of legislation and control with admiration and appreciation" and for having "controlled and corrected [the] work of the executive authority".[65] On the basis of such comments, one may be led to believe that Mubarak's authoritarian perceptions are so deeply embedded that he regards the voice of a few powerless opposition members in the Assembly as genuine legislative participants.

This, however, cannot be the case, for the President is fully aware of what genuine political participation entails, and has himself remarked that it is futile to ask him to follow the same democracy as that in the UK, France, the US or Germany: "We want to reach that standard of democracy, but we cannot do so overnight."[66] Furthermore, he explained why this sort of Western democracy cannot by achieved by saying that Egypt was not a wealthy country: "If we cease economic activity and grant freedom . . . we consequently place the people in an unstable state."[67] On a subsequent occasion he said: "Without stability, there will be no democracy at all because instability leads to disorder which conflicts with democracy . . . [therefore] the first duty of those who advocate democracy is to be keen on socio-economic stability, which is the only way for democracy."[68]

Stability versus democracy

As noted previously, President Mubarak has not always been consistent about the question of whether the political system under his rule is democratic or not. There is little doubt, however, that since 1983 he has attempted to depict himself less as an advocate of democracy and more as the guardian of stability and order. This does not imply that his longer-term intention is to abolish multi-party participation altogether. This would be self-defeating for, as he himself admitted, political liberalisation is the country's "safety valve".[69] Yet, the shift of opinion can be seen in the fact that while democracy was previously proclaimed as the "most effective weapon" with which he was "resolved to meet the challenges facing" the nation,[70] the President began publicly to concede that stability was a more crucial factor "for Egypt's present and future success",[71] and that an "overdose" of democracy could be "harmful", while small doses would conform to Egypt's "ability to absorb them".[72]

The preference of socio-economic stability to political liberalisation in Egypt means that the President can argue for responsible political participation, which he defines as not "slipping into the chaos of ideas or conflicting stances which could threaten the supreme interests of the homeland".[73] In turn, the President can discount challenges to his rule by discrediting any opposition forces that do not conform to his views by accusing them of being unpatriotic "saboteurs and evildoers"[74] who "want a state of anarchy and chaos"[75] in order to "weaken the domestic front".[76]

The President's attempt to project socio-economic development as a priority above political development does not appear to have been accompanied by overtly ambitious plans. The President's first five-year plan, for example, focused on the necessary yet hardly inspiring task of "consolidating the infrastructure". As he explained in 1987:

> We developed the infrastructure of electricity, road networks, drinking water and sanitary drainage . . . Such is the importance of the infrastructure. It is impossible to build a house without water. Likewise, it is impossible to build a house without sanitary drainage . . . [or it] would flood an entire area.[77]

In 1994, he was still reminding the public of this "great achievement":

> You are all aware of what the situation was in 1982 when I took over responsibility; but now we have forgotten. There is everything now: water, sewerage, telephones, railroads, more houses being built . . . Have we forgotten that none of this existed . . . Have you forgotten the telephone problem? I am only reminding you. You are not young and you know all this; you saw all these things . . . If one can remember where we stood and where we are today, then he can see how great this achievement has been.[78]

Perhaps Mubarak's perception that socio-economic development should take precedence over political development might have generated popular support if it was conveyed through a particular vision for the future. However, the President has appeared reluctant to do this, preferring instead to find justifications for the apparent lack of economic progress.

Some of his justifications have appeared to point the blame at the Egyptian citizens, the most popular claim being, "the problem of population growth, which exceeds economic and social development rates [and which] may prove too difficult for our capabilities to handle in the near future".[79]

Egypt's economic difficulties are not simply due to population growth, but also to other factors attributed to the policies of the regime. As one American report states: "[For] many years, Egyptian economic policies, relying on state ownership, bureaucratic controls and protection from competition, stifled productivity, efficiency, and economic growth." Furthermore, the commitments of the state to provide free public services, guaranteed employment, and subsidised goods, "led to chronic fiscal and monetary indiscipline, generating excess demand, serious inflation, balance-of-payments deficits, growing international indebtedness and foreign exchange shortages".[80]

It should be noted that these "commitments", which were undertaken by Nasser, constituted a major mechanism of social control in post-1952 Egypt. It is therefore not surprising that while President Mubarak – under pressure from the World Bank and the IMF – had little choice but to follow Sadat's path of privatisation and economic liberalisation, he has done so reluctantly. One indication of this is the fact that the constitution continues to declare Egypt a socialist state with a centrally planned economy while Mubarak has shown no enthusiasm for making the appropriate amendments. Instead, when confronted with the question of constitutional amendments, he has argued that such issues were "complex" and said: "We are going through economic and social reforms, working very hard for the development of the country, looking for the stability of the country . . . When the time is suitable we will do what is needed."[81]

The absence of constitutional change, however, has made it difficult to attract significant private investment into Egypt's ailing economy. This is illustrated by the fact that of the 314 state-owned enterprises officially targeted for privatisation in 1990, only 40 had been sold to private investors by 1996.[82] It is unlikely that Mubarak is much concerned about such lack of progress for had it not been imposed by the International Monetary Fund (IMF) as part of Egypt's reform package,[83] President Mubarak would not have initiated the dismantling of the public sector with such urgency. Earlier he said:

> I wonder about those who advocate selling the public sector, because this would be a dangerous step taken at the cost of the simple citizen . . . The public sector regulates the private one, thus offering goods to the public at reasonable prices, because state control is a must. Selling the public sector would create a socio-economic problem.[84]

Mubarak constantly finds some form of justification for initiating as little change as possible on the socio-economic front, even though he maintains that political liberalisation cannot be achieved without this. Such justifications range from his proclaimed concern for "stability", which would be threatened as a result of the "workers [who] could burn things up",[85] to apparent "humanitarian" considerations, such as "the psychological aspect of the people".[86] Moreover, the President has had little hesitation in exploiting Western fears with regard to the threat of political Islam and Egypt's strategic position. For example, he justifies the virtual absence of socio-economic development by "reminding" the US and Egypt's other Western creditors (the Paris Club), of the presence of Islamic militants, who, he says, will attempt to "take advantage of the hardships caused by Egypt's economic reform".[87] He also points to Egypt's "role in the 'peace process' for concessional aid".[88] Comparing Turkey, Mexico and India with Egypt, Waterbury writes:

> Only Egypt could collect rents from the Suez Canal, and only Egypt benefited from the enormous strategic rents paid by the United States in return for the Camp David Accords of 1979 and for Egypt's continuing role in promoting overall Arab understanding with Israel. U.S. economic assistance [alone] to Egypt totalled $13.2 billion between 1975 and 1990, with an additional 3.2 billion through the Commodity Import Programme. Military assistance, begun in 1980, reached $12.6 billion by 1990. The total flow of U.S. assistance thus cumulated to $27.4 billion over fifteen years.[89]

This implies that since Egypt was in the unique position of having access to such financial assistance, some substantial developments on the socio-economic front might have been expected. That this has not been the case has led observers to question Mubarak's overall leadership ability. As Gauch noted, with Mubarak's consolidation of power and consequently "his increased confidence and pride", it seemed that Mubarak should have been moving "less cautiously" by then and "taking bigger steps".

Yet he continued to "lack the ability of Sadat and before him, President Gamal Abdel Nasser, to strategize, innovate and subsequently motivate the public".[90]

Indeed, over the years, Mubarak has lacked the lustre of a visionary leader. He has repeatedly proclaimed his intention eventually to achieve both political and socio-economic liberalisation. However, the fact that, after nearly two decades in power, he continues to claim concern for stability as justification for the lack of progress on either front, cannot be attributed simply to an inferior personal ability to strategize and innovate change. His circumspect attitude can instead be interpreted as a strategy aimed at safeguarding the system of personalised authoritarian rule. As Tripp noted with regard to contemporary Egyptian politics, "the legacy of authoritarian politics . . . has led successive governments to give priority to their requirements for maintaining order within the state", and the pursuit of this objective "has thus led them not to question the end itself, but to concentrate on the means by which that end can be achieved".[91] By this analysis, there can hardly be any intention on President Mubarak's part to transform the existing political system. That this is true is further reflected in the manner in which multi-party participation under his rule is contained and controlled.

Control of political participation

President Mubarak's decision to continue allowing some opposition in the People's Assembly may show some degree of flexibility. Yet, it is difficult to depict this apparent flexibility as a sign of any intention to emancipate the Assembly from established presidential control. The President's continuous reliance on emergency laws, for example, is a striking indication of his attempt to maintain a tight grip on multi-party participation and hence control of entry into the Assembly.

As mentioned previously, the adoption of emergency laws has been justified by President Mubarak as a necessary measure to combat terrorism and preserve the country's stability.[92] However, while he plays up the threat of Islamic fundamentalism, he has been known to concede that the Islamic threat in Egypt is not particularly serious.[93] This shows that the long-standing emergency laws are not wholly aimed at containing terrorist activities.

Under a state of emergency, censorship may be exercised over all activities and may range from monitoring political action to limiting freedom of expression. Individuals can be arrested solely on the basis of suspicion of involvement in political crimes, and the gathering of five or more people or the distribution of any political literature without official government authorisation gives the government the right to arrest all those involved. Thus, in order to hold gatherings and rallies, to distribute pamphlets, or to pursue any of the standard activities associated with the cultivation of supporters at the grass-root level, political parties are required to apply for formal authorisation at the local police station, which then passes the request on to the Ministry of Interior for a decision. Except on specific occasions, namely during the month leading up to legislative elections, such permission has automatically been denied.[94]

One particular case worth mentioning is an incident in 1992 involving a prominent opposition leader and the then Minister of Interior, 'Abd al-Halim Musa. According to the opposition leader, he attempted to organise a small rally in which members of the intelligentsia, playwrights and popular television and film personalities agreed to participate to demonstrate their support for the government following the killing of 15 Egyptian Coptic Christians in Upper Egypt by Islamist militants. Although the presence of media personalities in an anti-fundamentalist protest could have provided the government with some popular support in its fight against the Islamist extremists, the Minister of Interior rejected the application on principle (*mabda'*): "Today you are demonstrating against the Islamists but tomorrow you may demonstrate against us."[95] This appears to confirm the notion that the state of emergency is not only aimed at terrorist activities, but also perhaps more importantly at controlling political participation.

The imposition of emergency laws also seems to be a useful way limiting the role of the Egyptian judiciary in matters relating to political participation. This is because in a state of emergency the 45 days' limit on holding an accused person in custody for questioning can be extended indefinitely without a formal court hearing. If an accused person is kept out of court indefinitely the judiciary does not have any role or influence over the case. Equally important is the 1966 Law of the Military Judiciary, which rules: "During a state of emergency, the President of the Republic has the right to refer to the military judiciary any crime which is punishable under the Penal Code or under any other law."[96] Consequently, the law gives the authorities virtual *carte blanche* to detain and prosecute civilians in military courts regardless of whether their activity endangers fundamental interests. Moreover, while civilians condemned to death in a criminal court are permitted to appeal to Egypt's Supreme Court of Appeal, in a military court there is no appeal once the three military judges have passed verdict.

Once again there appears to be a pattern that suggests the use of military courts is targeted primarily at political activists whose offence is their rejection of the political status quo. The judiciary, for example, used to play an important political role in defending the right of political parties to be formed. Hence, while the government rejected the licence applications of a large number of political parties, including the Nasserites and the Neo-Wafd, once individual parties resorted to the courts, the government complied with the court rulings and granted the necessary permits. The judiciary also played a prominent role in the various disputes between the opposition and government over electoral laws. In these cases also, even though the court rulings favoured the opposition, the government obeyed the court verdicts. As President Mubarak has consistently claimed that one of his most important aims is to "establish justice and . . . champion rights and the supremacy of law",[97] the outcome of such public test cases undoubtedly contributed to his credibility. His statement, "We have no power exceeding that of the law", rang true.[98]

Yet, on closer inspection, such landmark verdicts were obeyed by the government because their implications for the political status quo were, at best, minimal. The government eventually realised that issues such as electoral laws were of little significance since it maintained complete monopoly over the state apparatus and its resources. Furthermore, all the political parties that the government licensed as a result of court rulings were relatively insignificant, unlike the religiously based political organisations which the President perceives as "very dangerous".[99]

Hence, it is in situations where the regime's fundamental interests are thought to be at stake that President Mubarak's more measured statements are replaced by forceful assertions. When the regime's interests are not directly threatened, he makes statements such as: "[C]onfrontation of terrorism cannot be achieved by security techniques alone, but requires action on the part of society as a whole with its democratic institutions to combat terrorism politically, informatively and ideologically."[100] But when the regime is more at risk he declares that he will not allow "human rights to become a slogan to protect terrorists".[101] More importantly, in such situations, the President appears to have little hesitation in bypassing the judiciary and referring the political trials of civilians to military courts. This was clearly illustrated in October 1992 when the President decreed that two such cases should be tried in the military courts. The verdict in both cases, swiftly pronounced within a month of the trials, included the death sentence for eight defendants. The harshness of the sentences was predictable since those "sentenced to death were not charged with specific acts of violence but with planning the overthrow of the government and the assassination of some leaders".[102]

All the same, it is possible to argue that emergency measures are taken to combat the activities of political extremists working outside the legal framework. The fact that such measures also constrict the participation of those working within legal prescriptions can theoretically be viewed as the price to be paid for national security. In reality these measures only affect those wanting to play by the rules. After all, legislative elections are of primary concern only to those who want to reach public office through legal channels. Hence, the decision to change the electoral laws before the first legislative elections under his rule reflected the President's conception of political liberalisation and showed that this conception does not include losing power even through legal means. This notion was virtually confirmed when the then Prime Minister, Fu'ad Mohyi al-Din, personally admitted that, under the new system, one of the clauses – which outlawed independent candidates – was intended to limit access to the legislature of individuals who "might not be 'known' to the regime".[103]

Although the effects of the electoral law amendments will be discussed in more detail in the following chapter, it is worth noting here that the unprecedented move by the opposition formally to challenge the government through the Supreme Constitutional Court and have these laws annulled reflected the extent to which the opposition viewed these laws as biased. It would seem that the opposition's reaction and, perhaps more importantly, President Mubarak's concern for his 'democratic' image, impelled him to modify the law three years later. Striving to present the modified 1986 version as evidence of his democratic intent, the President called this a venture to "consolidate democracy" and mark Egypt's arrival "at a common understanding of the role of democracy".[104]

The President's decision to amend the electoral laws and call for early elections rather than wait for a court decision or ignore the legal outcome altogether can be understood better in terms of his own political circumstances. His renomination for a second presidential term was due at the end of 1987, and although his party's domination of the legislature meant that his position was secure, an adverse court ruling could have tarnished the legitimacy of his nomination since it would have appeared that the President was elected under an unconstitutional Assembly.[105]

The electoral system did eventually revert to the old individual candidacy system in 1990. Yet, as mentioned earlier (and as will be discussed in detail later), reversion to the old electoral system was perhaps also the result of President Mubarak's eventual realisation that electoral laws were of little significance when his consolidation of power provided him with other means, such as patronage and electoral malpractice, to ensure that entry to the Assembly remained stringently controlled.

The President's personal control of the legislature in post-1952 Egypt has been highly dependent on the President's position as head and patron of the ruling party. It is difficult to identify if any profound changes in this established pattern of control have occurred under Mubarak. In the absence of clear ideological orientations or financial independence, the NDP – as will be examined in the following chapter – remains dependent on government resources to build its electoral base. Moreover, the process of selecting NDP candidates for legislative elections continues to be strictly controlled by the President. Thus, while all members of the NDP are entitled to apply personally for electoral nomination, the application short list, as NDP Assistant Secretary-General Kamal al-Shazli confirmed, is submitted to President Mubarak "so that he can make a final decision".[106]

As in most authoritarian regimes, electoral fraud in post-1952 Egypt has been a major tool used by the government to exclude certain individuals from the Assembly. More interesting, however, is that it has also been used in Egypt to control incumbent members of parliament. Under Nasser, for example, Sha'rawi Gom'a, the then Minister of Interior, regarded it as more important to back electoral favourites through vote rigging, than less popular individuals who might actually need such irregular assistance to win. As he explained to a senior politician in 1967, rigging the votes for a popular individual who was most likely to win anyway was crucial, because if that person felt that it was genuine votes that made him win, he would "develop an ego" and, he said, "we don't want anyone to develop any ideas of self-importance. This might otherwise lead to independent thought."[107]

In his capacity as Vice-President and Vice-Chairman of the NDP, Mubarak, then Vice-President of the Republic, was undoubtedly acquainted with the voting malpractices of his predecessor, Sadat. When he became President, he declared: "The formation of the People's Assembly through free and honest elections and multiple parties is the beginning of a new phase of responsibilities and duties, in which we shall renew all our capabilities and review our steps."[108] However, it is interesting to note that one of the major bones of contention between opposition and government has been the persistent manipulation of electoral results and President Mubarak's refusal to take any action. In response to claims by the opposition of government malpractices during the 1984 elections, for example, the President chose to deny the allegations by saying: "[The] people have spoken their word free of any restrictions, pressure, forgery or rigging."[109] Furthermore, he implied that it was the opposition that was at fault because it "did not accept the people's decision in a democratic spirit but sought to cast doubt on the integrity and honesty of the elections".[110]

Indeed, it is difficult to measure accurately the extent of electoral malpractices under Mubarak's rule. However, a clear indication that ballot rigging and electoral irregularities are rather widespread emerged after the elections of 1987 when the opposition filed a suit against questionable NDP winners. The Supreme Court of Appeal found enough evidence to declare the votes for 78 of the NDP's 348 winning seats null and void. More significant was the refusal of the then Assembly Speaker, Rif'at al-Mahgub, to comply with the court's ruling on the ground that "parliament was sovereign in all matters concerning its membership".[111] Since a decision of this nature cannot be taken without the President's approval in his formal capacity of party chairman, the incident clearly illustrates that President Mubarak has little hesitation in ignoring the law if he feels that some fundamental interest is at stake. In other words, it would seem that the law in Mubarak's Egypt – as with the Egypt of his predecessors – is upheld only when it serves the interest of the regime.

Another example of the government's manipulation of the law is its repression of the freedom of the opposition's press when it began to pose a challenge to the President's authority. This action, which again illustrates the divergence between Mubarak's declared views and practice, was initially prompted by a series of attacks and counter-attacks between the President and his opponents. The President had been portraying himself as an honest ruler who would not tolerate "hypocrisy, corruption or trading with the livelihood of the people",[112] one who would not "abet or cover up any corruption" even if the individual involved was his "closest aide".[113] But, when the opposition press – relying on the President's claims of having "lifted all press censorship" and provided "a free national party press that writes what it wants without control or censorship"[114] – began to pursue and publicise cases relating to government corruption, the President did not appear to take such concerns seriously. Characteristically, his reaction focused on attempts to discredit his opponents by accusing them of spreading lies.

In earlier statements, Mubarak had said that the opposition's role in the "national march" was to "offer well considered views",[115] but not "trade accusation".[116] A general understanding had been established that any criticism of the government was improper and unpatriotic. Thus when in 1993 the opposition press began to report on govern-ment corruption, Mubarak felt it his "duty to warn against those who are increasingly talking about corruption in Egypt" because they "seek to weaken the domestic front [and] want to see . . . some negative phenomena".[117]

In the summer of 1995 when President Mubarak was being interviewed for an American news magazine, the journalist brought up the subject of general public corruption in Egypt. Interestingly, the President replied: "The whole story that my sons were agents for Airbus, for instance? Never. It came from the Muslim Brothers."[118] The President's denial of such accusations while blaming the opposition for using defamation strategies, was not unexpected given his customary pattern of response. That he specifically mentioned his sons as an example shows not only that he was fully aware of the level to which such accusations had reached,[119] but also may explain why Law 93 of 1995, which provides harsh penalties, including prison sentences, for the publication of false or malicious news, was implemented at that particular time.[120] Justifying the new law, the President said: "For eight years I have listened to many complaints [and] accusations are growing unnecessarily."[121] It is curious that the decision to take direct action after such a long time coincided with a widespread corruption scandal affecting members of his immediate family.

When the President tried to justify the new law, he did not actually deny the existence of corruption, but instead asked: "Suppose someone makes a mistake, why should you involve his relatives, who might occupy respectable positions? What business do you have to do this? It is improper for you to do this."[122] On the basis of such comments, it would seem that the President was less concerned about rectifying the actual problem of corruption – which he himself admitted was there – and more concerned with tightening a law that discourages public exposure of corruption. As exposure might tarnish his rule, he opted for its suppression. "What else can I do as head of state?" he asked. "I do not want to prevent a writer from writing . . . But the law is there . . . [to] increase the punishment; nothing more and nothing less."[123]

The implementation of such a stringent media law is just one of several strategies that seems to be aimed at containing and controlling multi-party participation in Mubarak's Egypt. As discussed earlier, the reliance on emergency measures, the various attempts to restrict electoral participation, including the implementation of biased electoral laws, the prevalence of electoral malpractices and the President's personal involvement in selecting candidates for his NDP, also constitute strategies that seem intended for such a purpose. By this reasoning, there is little to indicate that President Mubarak has any intention of relinquishing the prevailing personalised system of rule.

Furthermore, the President's aim is not only to contain and control multi-party participation but also to utilise it to reaffirm and expand the clientelist structure which he has inherited from his predecessors. Like them, he continues to maintain tight personal control over the allocation of state resources. President Mubarak's control of the NDP, and hence the People's Assembly, for example, means that he has been in the position to demand (and obtain) under the Delegation Act, sole responsibility for the purchase and sale of military hardware, as well as for the entire military budget.[124] The President's monopoly of such a major part of the decision-making process, which is justified on the grounds of national security, seems to imply not only that he regards himself above accountability but also that he perceives the legislature as untrustworthy to partake in "sensitive" matters concerning national security. Considering the military's long-standing role as the ultimate protector of Egypt's post-1952 regime, it is reasonable to argue that the President's personal control over the military's budget might be based less on "national security" concerns and more on efforts to safeguard the political status quo. Indeed, if the President shared decision-making powers with an independent legislature, it would be difficult for him to justify allocating an annual budget of US$3.5 billion for the army, especially in the context of other pressing matters such as the need to reduce the foreign debt which, although reduced by US$24 billion after Egypt's participation in the Gulf War, still stood at US$26 billion in 1994.[125]

Even if Egypt's foreign debt is disregarded, the amount spent on the military is still enormous when compared, say, with the amount spent on reducing unemployment (which is estimated at between 17 and 20 per cent of the workforce). The amount allocated to alleviating unemployment, which can arguably be viewed as a breeding ground for militant extremism, is slightly less than US$750 million. With over half a million people joining the workforce every year, such a meagre allocation is "barely sufficient to provide employment for 10 percent of [these] new entrants".[126]

Paradoxically, it was President Mubarak who made this declaration shortly after assuming power:

> We opt for peace in order to prevent the continued wastage of funds used for the purchase of arms and ammunition. Such funds could now be spent for the welfare and prosperity of the Egyptian people, who have long suffered from the horrors of war in both psychological and material terms.[127]

The heavy military spending was subsequently justified by emphasising the significance of the military in protecting Egypt's "freedom, sovereignty, values and leading role in the region".[128] What seems implausible, however, is Mubarak's claim that the budget allocated to the military simply "goes to pay the wages of the men, while the other half is spent on the maintenance of military equipment, food, and lodging, and clothing".[129] A blatant example of the President's diversion of enormous funds into the military establishment for reasons other than to cover more than just the basic necessities can be found in the case of Factory 200.

Factory 200, a tank-assembly plant which, after nine years of construction, was officially opened in 1992, constitutes the largest industrial installation in the Middle East. Of questionable economic viability and described by an Egyptian banker as "a big white elephant",[130] the plant is funded and maintained primarily through foreign aid. Thus, if the President can divert US$2.5 billion worth of American aid and an estimated US$450 million worth of state funds[131] into a project such as this, then it is evident that his priority is not simply to sustain the military establishment but also to ensure that he preserves the position of the President as its ultimate patron, even if this impinges on Egypt's social and economic development.

Another lever of power is the President's control of the national budget although the People's Assembly is not excluded from overseeing it to the same extent as it is excluded from supervision of the military budget. However, while the general budget is presented annually to the Assembly for official approval, its presentation format is described, in the words of one member, as resembling "one of the President's public speeches".[132] In other words, while the Assembly is presented with a broad outline of the government's policy proposals and overall budget estimates for approval before the start of each fiscal year, details such as specific resource allocations to the various ministries have remained solely the prerogative of the President. In reserving such an important role for himself, it seems that President Mubarak's main intention is to ensure that ultimately the entire governmental and state apparatuses are no less dependent upon him than they were on his predecessors. Moreover, the retention of such an important prerogative within a multi-party context means that political opponents also have little choice but to remain dependent on the President for their allocation of state resources. Indeed, as will be examined in the following chapters, electoral participation within the government-defined area makes it almost inevitable that the participating opposition will seek a share of these presidentially controlled resources.

This chapter has aimed to show the major factors that allow the President to be the ultimate source of power and authority in post-1952 Egypt. One of President Mubarak's main concerns has been to safeguard this system of personal authoritarian rule. The President's strategy for doing this has focused upon imposing disparate constraints on the embryonic multi-party system which, as Vice-President, he inherited from Sadat. President Mubarak has attempted to justify this approach with the notion that instability would result if a greater measure of political liberalisation took priority over socio-economic development.

While there is no evidence to suggest that genuine political liberalisation would slow down socio-economic reform, the President's argument appears all the more specious in view of his reluctance to initiate major socio-economic reforms. (Such reforms would, among other things, ultimately reduce the public sector and thus a major part of his own power base.) The minor economic reforms undertaken cannot in this respect be considered government initiatives, but token gestures to the international creditors whose assistance provides the President with the necessary funds to uphold the clientelist structure which, along with the enormous legal-constitutional powers vested in the presidency, play an important role in the preservation of the prevailing system of personal rule.

The process of allowing for the continuation of multi-party participation within this tightly controlled political arena, therefore, appears to suggest that the aim is not to provide political opponents with the opportunity to emerge as potential challengers to power, but to incorporate them into the same structure of clientelist dependence as is used to control the President's own party, and indeed all the major institutions and groupings within the Egyptian polity. That transformations within the authoritarian polity inherited by Mubarak were not, realistically, on his list of priorities was indicated in one of his early interviews as President.

> Egypt would go to hell if I listened to some nervous people who say "change, change!" because then what? You run and run and then the troubles begin . . . Do you want me to change everything? Do you want me to replace an entire generation? . . . The method of electric shock is futile now. If I were to apply it, there would never be stability in the country.[133]

Whether the imposed constraints we have discussed here have actually contributed towards shaping the role of multi-party elections as a tool with which to reaffirm and expand the regime's clientelist structure cannot, however, be properly understood without first examining the effects of these constraints on political parties in contemporary Egypt, and hence their response to electoral participation as defined under the Mubarak regime. This is the main focus of the following chapter.

NOTES

1 R. Hinnebusch cited in M.Y. El-Gamal (1992), p. 107.
2 T. El-Bishri (1983), p. 38.
3 R.A. Hinnebusch (1990), p. 188.
4 The Revolutionary Command Council comprised the core Free Officers' group that had executed the 1952 *coup.*
5 The other four were implemented in 1958, 1962, 1964 and 1969 respectively (T. El-Bishri (1983), p. 39).
6 R.H. Jackson and C.G. Rosenberg (1982), p. 16.
7 Sadat was, at the time of Nasser's death, the Vice-President, and through a referendum he legally acquired executive office. In reality, however, Nasser's top men had expected to share with him some form of decision-making powers, since, at best, he was considered only first among equals. Determined to remain the ultimate source of power within the political system, he began to strengthen the presidency by removing from the élite body actual and potential opposition. The most prominent of those removed were Nasser's Minister of the Interior, Sha'rawi Gom'a, the Director (of his personal) Security Services, Sami Sharaf, his Minister of Defence, Muhammad Fawzi, and First Secretary of the Arab Socialist Union (ASU), 'Ali Sabri.
8 All articles quoted are from the *1971 Constitution of the Arab Republic of Egypt*, State Information Service Press (Egypt), 1981 edition.
9 A. Lesch (1989), p. 93.
10 BBC SWB, 7 October 1993/ME/1813/MED/8.
11 BBC SWB, 26 June 1984/ME/7679/A/1.
12 BBC MSME, 24 July 1993/307240158-YGS3Y1/9307226.
13 For example, Sayyed Mar'i, father-in-law of one of Sadat's daughters and the then Speaker of the Assembly, claimed he knew nothing of Sadat's decision to go to war against Israel in 1973. Moreover, he strongly doubted "that anyone other than Ahmed Ismael (the War Minister) knew". See M.Y. El-Gamal (1992), p. 191.
14 Emergency Law 162 of 1958, Article 1, cited in M. El-Ghamry (1995), p. 14.
15 See: *Table to Show the Declarations of a State of Emergency during the Period 1914–1995* in M. El-Ghamry (1995), p. 13.
16 Interview by the author with Assembly member, Cairo, 2 January 1995.
17 "Egypt: Electoral Concerns", *News from Middle East Watch*, New York Office, 15 November 1990, pp. 5–6.
18 A.E. Hillal Dessouki (1983), p. 11.
19 K. Post (1968), p. 96, cited in R.H. Jackson and C.G. Rosenberg (1982), p. 24.
20 In response to a private enquiry as to why the party cannot be strengthened, Nasser replied, "If I allow the party to expand, where would that leave me? We would end up like the Soviet system where every decision made has to pass through party committees and could be rejected. What a waste of time." (Interview by the author with Dr Rif'at Sa'id, 9 January 1995.)
21 A.H. Hillal Dessouki (1983), p. 15.

22 I. Harik (1974), p. 90.

23 R. Stephens (1971), p. 544.

24 Interview by the author with Dr Rif'at Sa'id, Secretary-General of the Tagammu' Party, 8 January 1996. Based on a conversation between interviewee and Nasser's Minister of Interior, Sha'rawi Gom'a.

25 The Liberation Rally (1952–6), the National Union (1956–62) and the Arab Socialist Union (1962–72)

26 S. Huntington (1968), p. 249.

27 This is reflected in the fact that high officials within both the government and the army – for disparate reasons – opposed the idea of a multi-party system. See R.A. Hinnebusch (1985), pp. 158–60.

28 Ibid., p. 159.

29 Ibid., p. 62.

30 *Al-Ahram Weekly*, 12–18 October 1995.

31 For example, see Sadat–opposition relations in J. Waterbury (1983), pp. 354–88 and R.A. Hinnebusch (1985), pp. 158–1970.

32 M. Heikal (1983), p. 128.

33 R. Springborg (1975), pp. 83–108.

34 Ibid., p. 93.

35 Even so, it is worth noting that many ministers have held their portfolios for an even longer period. The Minister of Information, Safwat al-Sharif, the Minister of Electricity and Energy, Maher Abaza, and the Minister of Agriculture and Food Security, Yusef Wali, are particularly conspicuous in having held exactly the same portfolios since Mubarak came to power.

36 *Middle East Times Egypt*, 3–9 December 1995.

37 Al-Ganzuri had held the portfolio of Minister of Planning since 1982. In 1985, he was appointed Minister of Financial Affairs and International Investment and Cooperation, while retaining the Ministry of Planning. In 1992 he was appointed Deputy Prime Minister and subsequently left the Ministry of Financial Affairs, but not the Ministry of Planning. In 1996 he was appointed Prime Minister.

38 The impact on the clients of the "reshuffled" élite is somewhat minimal since the process of maximising individual opportunities of upward mobility means that patron–client ties on that level are essentially ephemeral.

39 R. Springborg (1975), p. 92.

40 Ibid.

41 For example, although the Leftist faction that attempted to oust Sadat in 1971 comprised important ASU leaders, the Minister of Interior, the Minister of Defence and their respective clientelist power bases, it failed to achieve its objectives and was instead purged by Sadat. This "was perhaps due to its Byzantine complexity, which would have made a well-timed, carefully co-ordinated strike difficult and security leaks inevitable". (Springborg (1975), p. 95.) The Minister of Defence, General Muhammad Fawzi, who spent 1971–6 in prison for his involvement in the faction, also hinted at this probability by stating to me that "Sadat sensed we might have him for dinner, so he decided to have us for lunch". (Interview by the author with Muhammad Fawzi, Cairo, 15 November 1995.)

42 R. Springborg (1975), p. 104.

43 M.Y. El-Gamal (1992), pp. 186–7.

44 N.N. Ayubi (1991), p. 243.

45 Nasser resorted to calling in the army when in February 1968 public anger erupted in demonstrations against the system in general in the wake of the 1967 defeat.

46 Government subsidy of basic food commodities has been a policy pursued since 1952 and constitutes a huge drain on the budget. Hence, the 1977 food riots erupted when Sadat attempted to balance the budget by removing some of the subsidies.

47 Again, the military proved indispensable, this time for Mubarak, when thousands of army conscripts in the Central Security Forces wreaked havoc in Cairo on the news that their military service might be extended.

48 *Egypt: The Quest for Peace and Prosperity Continues* (Ministry of Information, State Information Service, Cairo, n.d.), p. 7.

49 I.W. Zartman (1990), p. 239.

50 See, for example R.A. Hinnebusch (1993a), pp. 159–71.

51 Address to the People's Assembly and Consultative Council, 8 November 1981 (State Information Service, Cairo).

52 Public address, April 1982, cf. *Egypt: A Decade of Peace, Development and Democracy, 1981–1991* (Ministry of Information, State Information Service, Cairo, 1991).

53 *Wall Street Journal Europe*, 15 June 1993.

54 R. Owen (1994), p. 190.

55 Address to the People's Assembly and Consultative Council, 8 November 1981 (State Information Service, Cairo).

56 See, for example, N. Guenena (1986).

57 *Mayo,* 9 December 1981.

58 *October,* 29 December 1981.

59 N.N. Ayubi (1991), p. 229.

60 This feeling was further reinforced after the 1986 Central Security Forces' insurrection was promptly suppressed by the army during the first day of riots, indicating the army's loyalty to the President.

61 For example, see Mubarak's address to the People's Assembly and Consultative Council, 14 October 1981 (State Information Service, Cairo).

62 For example, see Mubarak's interview with the *Sunday Times,* 24 April 1994.

63 Interviews by the author with Egyptian MPs, November 1994–January 1995, Cairo.

64 Interview by the author with a politician, 3 January 1995, Cairo.

65 Presidential address to the People's Assembly and Consultative Council, 12 November 1994 (State Information Service, Cairo).

66 Mubarak interview, cited in R. Owen (1994), p. 189.

67 BBC SWB, 14 February 1987/ME/8485/A/2.

68 Mubarak's speech marking National Police Day, 25 January 1993 (State Information Service, 1994, Cairo).

69 Mubarak interview, *al-Majalla,* 12–18 July 1989.

70 Address to the People's Assembly and Consultative Council, 14 October 1981 (State Information Service, Cairo).

71 BBC SWB, 7 April 1987/ME/8558/A/2.

72 Ibid.

73 BBC MSME, 31 May 1994/405310291/DPAREN/940531.
74 President's May Day Speech 1988 (State Information Service, Cairo).
75 *Financial Times*, 23 January 1986.
76 President's May Day Speech 1993 (State Information Service, Cairo).
77 BBC MSME, 12 May 1987/705127317/BINNZP/870512.
78 BBC SWB, 10 May 1994/MEW/0332/WME/3.
79 BBC SWB, 10 May 1994/MEW/0332/WME/7.
80 *United States Embassy (Cairo), Foreign Economic Trends and their Implications for the United States: Report for the Arab Republic of Egypt*, 1992, p. 1, cited in T. Parfitt (1993), p. 13.
81 Reuter News Service, REUTME, 5 October 1993, 310052713/7LSXUA/931005.
82 *Financial Times Survey: Egypt*, 13 May 1997.
83 For details on the IMF–Egypt reform package for the years 1987/8 to 1991/2 see H. Handoussa (1991), pp. 10–15. For a summary of Handoussa's work, see T. Parfitt (1993), p. 14.
84 Mubarak's words in 1987, cited in J. Waterbury (1993), p. 142.
85 Mubarak interview, *Newsweek*, 19 June 1995.
86 Mubarak interview with the *Financial Times*, 22 April 1993.
87 BBC World Service broadcast, 2 April 1993, cited in T. Parfitt (1993), p. 18.
88 J. Waterbury (1993), p. 60.
89 Ibid., p. 80.
90 S. Gauch (1991), p. 41.
91 C. Tripp and R. Owen (1991), p. 160.
92 For example, with reference to opposition objections to the continuous renewal of emergency laws, the President responded by arguing that such measures were necessary "in order to confront terrorism [and] protect democracy and stability in this country". His discomfort at the idea of ending the state of emergency is evident when he reminded critics of his position by adding, "I am in charge and I have the authority to adopt [emergency] measures . . . I am in charge of the country's stability." See the President's 1988 May Day Address (State Information Service, Cairo).
93 In an interview the President claimed that the fundamentalist problem in Egypt cannot be compared to that in Algeria and that he believed it to be so insignificant in Egypt that he expected it would be eradicated within a few months. See the *Financial Times*, London, 22 April 1993.
94 During elections candidates have been known to bypass official channels and hold gatherings and small rallies for fear that their applications would be rejected or authorisation intentionally delayed. Those who go through the formal channels tend to be more constrained in their speeches as they suspect infiltration by security personnel.
95 Interview by the author with Rif'at Sa'id, 9 January 1995, Cairo.
96 cf. *Military Courts in Egypt: Courts without Safeguards, Judges without Immunity and Defendants without Rights*, The Centre for Human Rights Legal Aid Report (Cairo, September 1995).
97 BBC MSME, 24 July 1993/307240160/GV881E/930726.
98 BBC SWB 4 May 1993/ME/1679/A/7.
99 See Mubarak's interview in *The Sunday Times*, 24 April 1994.

100 Mubarak's address before joint session of the People's Assembly and the Shura Council, 15 December 1990 (State Information Service, Cairo).

101 *Middle East Watch*, vol. 5:3 (July 1993).

102 The *Washington Post*, 4 December 1992, cited from *Middle East Watch*, vol. 5:3 (July 1993).

103 R. Owen (1994), p. 186.

104 *Middle East Contemporary Survey*, vol. XI (1987), p. 324.

105 One month after the May 1987 elections the Supreme Constitutional Court ruled that the 1983 electoral law was incompatible with the constitution, but by then a new Assembly under the amended electoral laws was already in session.

106 *Al-Ahram Weekly*, 12–18 October 1995.

107 Interview by the author with Rif'at Sa'id, 8 January 1995, Cairo.

108 BBC SWB, 3 May 1984/ME/7633/A/10.

109 BBC SWB, 26 June 1984/ME/7679/A/1.

110 Ibid., ME/7679/A/2.

111 *Al-Ahram Weekly*, 12–18 October 1995.

112 BBC SWB 15 October 1981/ME/6854/A/14.

113 BBC SWB 28 April 1993/ME/1674/A/3.

114 BBC SWB 14 October 1993. It is worth noting that in view of the imposed participatory restrictions and the fact that the entire broadcasting media and a large section of the press remained under direct government control, Mubarak must have perceived freedom of the press as relatively harmless, particularly as some in the population are illiterate and the poverty-stricken majority is unlikely to pay 50 piastres for a newspaper.

115 *Al-Ahram*, 23 October 1981.

116 Presidential speech to a joint session of the People's Assembly and Consultative Council, 8 November 1981 (State Information Service, Cairo).

117 BBC SWB, 4 May 1993/ME/1679/A/7.

118 Mubarak interview, *Newsweek*, 19 June 1995.

119 The "Airbus" affair as relayed to me was that President Mubarak's sons had, in early 1995, made a huge commission by selling some 20 airliners at inflated prices to EgyptAir on behalf the Airbus manufacturers. Interviews by the author with veteran political activists and Assembly members, November–January 1996, Cairo.

120 Moreover, to ensure that this controversial law would be passed with minimal publicity, it was rushed through the Assembly on a Saturday, when most MPs were absent, and was not even mentioned on that day's parliamentary agenda. See "Strangling the Press", *Middle East International*, 9 June 1995.

121 BBCMS ME, 30 May 1995/505300330/5VV8RC/950530.

122 Ibid.

123 Ibid.

124 Interviews by the author with various MPs and ex-MPs, Cairo, November 1994–January 1996.

125 The *Wall Street Journal Europe*, 15 June 1993.

126 Cassandra (1995), p. 12.

127 Mubarak interview, *October*, 1 November 1981.

128 BBC SWB, 1 July 1986/ME/8299/A/1.

129 Ibid.
130 Contracts to supply tanks to clients other than the Egyptian army has been very difficult to conclude because each tank costs twice as much as its US$2 million American-made counterpart. See the *Wall Street Journal Europe*, 15 June 1993.
131 Ibid.
132 Interview by the author with veteran political activists and Assembly members, 3 January 1995, Cairo.
133 Mubarak interview, *al-Sharq al-Awsat*, 22 January 1982.

3

Political Parties

The primary concern in this chapter is to examine how the arena of political contest is utilised under the Mubarak regime to co-opt and subsequently control individuals representing disparate political parties. First, the nature of the President's NDP is examined. The aim is to show that although the party is controlled by the President and his designated men to the extent that it lacks a compelling ideology, charismatic leadership and autonomous access to resources, its participation in legislative elections still allows it to attract, and hence co-opt, prominent individuals who appear to possess extensive networks of support.

As was stressed earlier, President Mubarak, like his predecessors, does not appear institutionally bound to formal political organisations which share in the shaping of policy. In such a setting, election to the People's Assembly is not intended to give members the opportunity to participate in the formulation, or the deliberation, of public policy. Instead, what is emphasised here is how the election of a member of the President's party offers the opportunity to achieve alternative gains – that is, direct access to a share of the resources that the President and his government command. These resources do not simply provide these members of the Assembly with the potential to enhance and expand their prestige and influence in their localities, but also emphasise their role as intermediaries between central authorities and their constituencies.

The implications are advantageous to the regime from two perspectives – the more obvious one being that the electoral process allows the President's party to recruit individuals and define their roles as clientelist linkages binding the periphery to the centre. On another level, his party's cohesion is hampered by the clientelist basis on which members are elected. This situation is ideal for the President since an organised and cohesive party, even if he is its chairman, still constitutes a potential challenge to his personal power.

In the second part of the chapter attention is focused on members of the opposition who participate in the political contest. As already discussed, the presence of opposition parties was seen by President Mubarak as beneficial to his rule. However, it was evident from the way in which the President imposed various impediments, such as emergency measures and stringent press laws, that their presence in the formal political arena was not intended to challenge the political status quo. In the case of elections, it seems that these, too, were intended to act as a mechanism of control. Yet, rather than blatantly suppressing the activities of opponents, such as the imposition of emergency measures, it can be argued that by granting opponents the opportunity to compete in the arena of political contest, the primary aim was to incorporate them into the same clientelist linkage as that utilised to control NDP members.

The extent to which elections have contributed to defining the role of the opposition as clientelist linkages that bind the centre to the periphery is assessed as we examine the opposition's strategies and performance during the periods of the four legislative elections of 1984, 1987, 1990 and 1995. The six "major" opposition parties – the Neo-Wafd, the National Progressive Unionist Party, otherwise known as al-Tagammu' (NPUP), the Labour Party, the Liberal Party the Nasserite Democratic Party, and the technically illegal Muslim Brotherhood – are used as examples. Before 1990 opposition parties appeared generally united in perceiving participation in electoral contest as a process that would eventually lead to genuine competition for power. To what extent this attitude has changed since 1990, however, is here assessed. In particular, the aim is to show how the function of elections as a mechanism of clientelist recruitment has become increasingly applicable to political opponents.

Elections and the National Democratic Party

The NDP has since its creation by Sadat in 1978 systematically occupied no less than three-quarters of the seats in the People's Assembly. The NDP, like the previous "organisations" under Nasser's single-party system, was not only created by a President, but was also, and continues to be, headed by the President. While the NDP was created by Sadat to replace Nasser's ASU, the majority of ASU parliamentarians and senior party members swiftly converted to Sadat's new party. Given this history and the President's pre-eminent position in the political arena, it would be too much to expect the present-day NDP to differ significantly from previous organisations in terms of autonomy.

That the NDP represented a change in its ideological outlook and socialist disposition cannot be regarded as an indication of a fundamental change. In fact, it seems the party does not actually have a clear ideological stand. The NDP's programme for example, is formally based upon the principles of promoting democracy and "fostering Egypt's affiliation to the Arab world, [and] venerating [*sic*] . . . economic liberalisation that encourages private investment".[1] As the Party's ideology has been left rather vague and open to interpretation one suspects the ambiguity to be deliberate. As Hinnebusch points out, while the Party was, by the end of the Sadat era, cleared of left-wing elements and had thus become established "firmly to the centre-right", the fact that the official programme was vague meant that the Party would be able to "accommodate a fairly heterogeneous spectrum of political attitudes".[2] Thus the President and his government can adopt any policy decision without appearing to be compromising the Party's "official" standing.

Organisational structure

Considering the NDP's overwhelming majority in the Egyptian legislature, one might imagine it to be a vastly complex organisation. In reality the ruling party appears to be structured along very simplistic lines. In terms of financial resources, for example, the NDP officially controls only £E20 million in capital. This sum was raised by Sadat in 1978 from four main sources. The National Bank of Egypt, Banque Misr and Bank of Alexandria each contributed a quarter of the amount. The remainder was donated by a few private party subscribers, probably eager to demonstrate their support of the President and his new party. At the same time, Sadat established the National Development Bank (NDB).

The purpose of the NDB was, and continues to be, primarily to invest the secured £E20 million capital, and use the proceeds to finance the NDP and its development projects. In addition to its bulk capital, the party also has a formal annual subsidy of approximately £E250,000 from the sale of its official publications, including its daily newspaper, *Mayo*. The Party's other source of known income is an annual grant of £E100,000 from the Consultative Council – an amount awarded by the Council to each registered political party in Egypt.[3] It is indeed curious that such a large party should control such a small capital and receive such a meagre income. Is this an attempt by the President to ensure that the Party does not develop into an autonomous and thus potentially challenging entity?

The President's efforts to control the NDP are (also) reflected in the nature of the Party leadership. President Mubarak, upon assuming the chairmanship of the three-year-old Party, ensured that certain members were promptly expelled. These members included NDP deputies such as Rashad 'Othman, Mustafa Khalil and Mahmoud Sulayman. Described as a breed of "parasitic bourgeoisie",[4] these members were initially encouraged by Sadat to join his new Party, reportedly as founding members. Nearly a quarter of the £E20 million capital secured for the NDP in 1978 was donated by 'Othman 'Ahmad 'Othman, the then Minister of Housing and Reconstruction, father-in-law of one of Sadat's daughters and building contractor, arguably the richest of Egypt's "parasitic bourgeoisie".[5]

It may be remembered that in 1980 'Othman published a controversial book about Nasser which caused a public outcry, forcing Sadat to remove him from office. When Mubarak came to power he had a ready-made excuse to ease 'Othman out of the NDP. Those closely connected with 'Othman also suffered a similar fate.

The potential influence of lesser "parasitic bourgeoisie" within the party was also swiftly curtailed. On the pretext that the new President would not tolerate "hypocrisy, corruption, or trading with the livelihood of the people",[6] the most discernible tactic employed almost immediately after Mubarak assumed the presidency was the removal of a number of these individuals from the Assembly, and thus the Party, on corruption charges. In December 1981, for example, Rashad 'Othman, who was at the time the NDP's deputy for Alexandria, was stripped of his parliamentary immunity and party membership to face charges of illegal profiteering from timber sales. Mahmoud Sulayman, the NDP's deputy for the electoral constituency of Rosetta, also encountered a similar fate when he found himself abandoned by the Party and accused of drug-trafficking. The NDP deputy for Kom Ombo, Salah Abu al-Magd, was yet another example of the "parasitic bourgeoisie" whom President Mubarak managed to eliminate from the Party on charges of trading in state land.[7]

If the NDP had been established for a longer period of time before Mubarak assumed the presidency, it is doubtful whether the removal of these millionaires would have been so straightforward an affair, for they would have had a better opportunity to build a clientelist base of support within the Party. While such clientelist networks do not necessarily denote protection against presidential hostility, one can argue that such bases of support would have made it difficult to arraign one person without implicating many others within the Party. Such a predicament, for example, was faced by President Sadat when he attempted to prevent the ASU leader, 'Ali Sabri and his *clique*, from using the ASU as an instrument of mobilisation and control. Indeed, Sabri was unable to use the ASU for such a purpose because of the "chain of command [being] weakened by the defection of *apparatchiks* who stayed loyal to Sadat".[8] Yet, the clientelist base of support which Sabri had cultivated over the years meant that, by removing Sabri, Sadat also had to remove Sabri's allies within the Party. This was one of the major factors leading to the eventual dismantling of the ASU.

Mubarak's swift move against the more visible members of the "parasitic bourgeoisie" shows that the new President had no intention of allowing them to become too established and have the opportunity to build a clientelist power base, which could potentially challenge his own grip on the Party. This pre-emptive strike must have served as a warning to other party members who may until then have nurtured high expectations of their role within the Party.

President Mubarak's efforts to prevent the emergence of powerful and thus potentially challenging leaders within the NDP is further reflected in the fact that all senior posts within the Party continue to be presidential appointments. This includes the 13 seats that comprise the Party's Politburo, the 23 positions that constitute the Party's General Secretariat, and the chairmanship posts of 15 Standing Committees. As seen in the previous chapter, extra insurance is provided by the type of people he appoints.

Legislative elections and the NDP
In the absence of a compelling ideology, autonomous access to resources, or even independent party leaders, the NDP depends on its links with the President as its major source of propaganda. During the period leading up to the 1995 legislative elections, for example, the official NDP posters located around Cairo and in the buildings where formal gatherings of NDP candidates took place, all depicted enlarged photographs of

President Mubarak waving (as though to the nation), with the Party's name, al-Hezb al-Watani al-Dimoqrati, printed at the bottom of the poster. By association, the message suggested that by supporting the NDP one was supporting the President and the nation.

At the individual level, NDP candidates, when officially referring to the Party they represent, also seem to focus primarily on the presidential link, in particular by stressing to the voters how grateful they should be for such an "association" and the "privileges" that are derived from it. This attitude was evident, for example, during a formal NDP gathering for the benefit of the public sector workers of the industrial governorate of Helwan wa al-Tibbin. The four NDP candidates for the governorate's two electoral constituencies were in attendance, two of whom were Cabinet ministers: the Minister of Religious Endowments, Dr Muhammad Mahgub, and the Minister of War Productions, General Muhammad al-Ghamrawi. The guest speakers comprised various senior NDP members, including the Minister of Public Enterprise, Dr 'Atef 'Obayd, and the Governor of Cairo, General 'Omar 'Abd al-Akhar. Although these prominent individuals were attending in their capacity as senior representatives of the NDP, this aspect was cast in the shade when Mahgub introduced them with these words: "Today, President Hosni Mubarak has sent his men to Helwan. This is because Helwan is an important part of Egypt. It is the production centre of Egypt . . . We thank the President and we thank our prominent guests for coming."[9] The address of the Governor of Cairo 'Omar 'Abd al-Akhar was even more direct:

> Yes the problems of Helwan continue to exist . . . what I say is that problems exist everywhere, all the time in life. This is what life is all about. However, in the last four years, the NDP has already spent 600 million pounds on Helwan wa al-Tibbin areas alone. Therefore I think that the government and the NDP deserve your respect and gratitude for what has been done for you.[10]

During a similar gathering held for the two NDP contestants in the electoral constituency of Nozha wa Almaza, the same attitude can be observed. The veteran of the two candidates, Dr Hamdi al-Sayyed, thanked the prominent party speakers for their attendance. In particular, he thanked the Deputy Governor of Cairo, General Ahmad Hasan al-Gawahirgi, who, he told the audience, refused an invitation to a five-star hotel with the Ambassador of Oman. "He refused a five-star meal and five-star entertainment to come to you."[11] That the audience, which consisted largely of factory workers whose problems included the lack of electricity in their homes, should be "grateful" for the Deputy Governor's "sacrifice", was condescending to say the least. But such an attitude illustrates how intently NDP candidates focus on emphasising their links with the most senior members of the state apparatus, especially when such links ultimately lead to the patronage of the President. As Dr al-Sayyed concluded in his address to the audience:

> You must remember that your interest lies in the government party, the National Party [NDP]. You must also remember that the State is not stingy; it helps you. It does everything it can for you and you must not forget that. Finally, I will not forget, and you must not forget, that the NDP, headed by President Mubarak, has paid for all your services.

The lack of commitment among senior party members to the Party as an autonomous entity was also evident in private conversations with NDP members and others. Muhammad al-Sayyed, NDP member for the urban constituency of Hada'iq al-Qobba since 1990, summarised his views on the significance of his Party's position as follows:

> The NDP is good. But I am not talking about ideology or anything like that. This is not important. I do not think any of us [NDP deputies] care about that. What I mean is that it provides access to the services needed by the people. This is because it is the President's Party. I or anybody else in the NDP would join any party that is in the NDP's position. This is because it would be able to provide the necessary services to the constituents.[12]

It is noteworthy that the political analysts and academics whom I interviewed also showed little hesitation in stressing the NDP's deficiencies as a party. As Wahid 'Abd al-Magid, an editor at *Al-Ahram*'s Centre for Political and Strategic Studies, noted:

> One cannot talk of a political agenda when referring to the NDP. It is evident from general elections that its overall political agenda is weak. That is why the party resorts to provincial-style politics.[13]

Indeed, the NDP, as a party, appears to depend primarily on its links with the government when attempting to attract electoral support. This, however, is arguably an intentional strategy on the part of the government. If the Party was an independent entity, it would be difficult for the regime to use elections either as a propaganda tool or as a clientelist mechanism of recruitment to link those on the periphery to the centre. In fact, it would be difficult for the government to use elections in such a manner if its hold over the Party did not include a role in the selection of candidates. This is because if elections are to perform the function that the government intends, then it is necessary not only to ensure that the Party does not emerge as an independent entity, but also that "suitable" candidates can be selected for the Party.

Electoral candidates for the NDP

Formally, NDP members who aspire to reach legislative office are required to submit an application for nomination to the Party's local secretariat, of which there is one in each of Egypt's 26 governorates. The local secretariat is subsequently expected to pass all the applications, along with the candidates' personal recommendations, to the Party's headquarters in Cairo. Before the President decides, the applications are first short-listed under the supervision of the Party's Secretary-General and Assistant Secretary-General. Formally, the short list is determined on the basis of individual merit. According to the NDP's Assistant Secretary-General, Kamal al-Shazli, for example: "[M]embers of the outgoing Assembly who are running for re-election [are] chosen on the basis of their record – the services they extended to their constituents and, more importantly, their effective participation in parliamentary debates and the legislative process."[14] In the case of new applicants, al-Shazli maintains: "The criteria for choosing NDP candidates are a good reputation, hard work and commitment to the party."[15]

The mechanism of electoral candidates being chosen by a few senior party members, led by the President in his capacity as party chairman, is indicative of the centre's attempts to maintain overall control of the Party's internal dynamics. Realistically, therefore, it would be difficult for the centre to maintain control over the Party if potential candidates actually showed signs of intending to pursue effective legislative participation and commitment to the Party as an autonomous political organisation. This is why electoral nominations appear to be determined by informal factors that relate to the personal status rather than the ideological position of an individual. In other words, it seems that NDP electoral candidates are nominated not on the basis of dedication to the party, hard work, political capability or the like, but on whether a person, because of his personal influence and social networks within the community, merits co-option into the system. As one veteran NDP deputy explained:

> The NDP depends on choosing people who have a good local reputation. Sometimes that person with a good local reputation might not be the best man for the job. But he is usually the most popular person with a lot of family support and recognition from the local people."[16]

Illustrative of such individuals is Ahmed al-Sharqawi, NDP deputy for one of Egypt's rural constituencies.

A standard NDP deputy: Ahmad al-Sharqawi[17]

The population of al-Sharqawi's consituency, he says, comprises approximately half a million people, most of whom work in agricultural production and commerce. The constituency, which is situated in the governorate of Gharbeyya, is typical of predominantly rural Egypt in that it lacks infrastructure and services, such as electricity and water supplies, paved roads and schools. The local peasant population, therefore, is inclined to turn to the established or "notable" families in the community for various forms of assistance and favours. Al-Sharqawi, who originates from an established middle-range landowning family,[18] is, in his own right, a successful businessman trading in agriculture-related equipment. In addition, al-Sharqawi holds a Ph.D. and lectures at the local state-owned university.

Among the predominantly peasant inhabitants of the constituency, al-Sharqawi's stature did not pass unnoticed. Aware that someone of his position would have better connections and access to the authorities than they, the local people sought al-Sharqawi's assistance in both personal and communal matters. It became a matter of routine, for example, for al-Sharqawi to bail out local people held in custody.[19] On a more communal level, he would be approached by local people, including village headmen (*'omdas*), to intervene on their behalf with the authorities in matters concerning, say the construction of a local school and medical centre.

The electoral law amendments implemented before the 1984 legislative elections contributed, according to al-Sharqawi, to a dramatic rise in the number of local people requiring his assistance. This was because the electoral law amendments led to the election of people not well known to the local inhabitants with the result that they became all the more dependent upon prominent local figures, such as al-Sharqawi, to act as intermediaries between them and the strangers who had come to be their parliamentary representatives. Hence, in the period between the implementation of the electoral law amendments and when election rules reverted to the original system in 1990, al-Sharqawi came to be regarded as more than a prominent member of the community. His increased involvement in local welfare meant that he had gained a considerable reputation within the area and therefore extensive personal networks.

It should also be noted that when the electoral system reverted to the original style of individual candidacy in 1990, and the number of electoral constituencies expanded again, this time from 48 to 222, al-Sharqawi's area of residence became in itself an independent electoral constituency. Al-Sharqawi, accustomed to his prestigious role as an intermediary between the local people and the authorities, was no doubt aware that a decrease in the size of electoral constituencies would adversely affect his role in that the locals would eventually become more acquainted with their new Assembly representatives. Thus his extensive personal networks cultivated over the years in the area were likely to diminish with the contraction of electoral constituencies. If this were to happen, he would in future have a smaller chance of being placed on the NDP electoral list. Al-Sharqawi decided it was in his interest to seek NDP nomination while his personal base of support in the area of Nahtay was at its peak. The NDP swiftly accepted his application.

This brings us to consider why a prominent local man such as al-Sharqawi wanted to enter elections as an NDP candidate. Acknowledging that he had no previous history of party activity and had formally applied for party membership only shortly before seeking electoral nomination, al-Sharqawi replied that he did so because he felt he could "help more people as a deputy, than as someone asking favours from deputies".[20] As this response suggests, al-Sharqawi had few illusions about what election to the Assembly would confer on an individual in his position. Election to the Assembly as an NDP member, as he was apparently aware, would provide him with direct access to resources that would assist him in maintaining his eminent position within the community. His role would be to act as a link between his community and government, not as a legislator. As he put it: "How can I criticise government policy and then ask them the next day to fund a new school in my constituency?"[21]

The above example is intended to illustrate the exchange that elections appear to represent in the middle level of the clientelist chain. Al-Sharqawi, through elections and subsequent access to governmental resources, was able to maintain and even expand his prestige and influence in his local community. In exchange, he was willing to support the government. This implied overlooking the checks on, and scrutiny of, government policy which his role as legislator formally entails. It also meant that on the parochial level, by the channelling of state resources to his constituency, he was reinforcing the clientelist ties that link those in the centre of power to those at the grass-roots.

That elections can define the role of NDP deputies on such terms appears, therefore, to depend on two important factors. First, a candidate must be of sufficient prominence within his community for his co-option into the clientelist chain to be advantageous to the regime, in the sense that he would also, theoretically, channel his supporters and personal contacts into the clientelist chain. The second important factor is that a candidate's personal economic resources are not sufficient to undermine his dependence upon state resources. This is because if the status of a local notable flowed not only from his social standing and prestige, but also from vast personal wealth, then it would be difficult to ensure that elections would define the role of NDP deputies in the manner discussed above. The following example might clarify this point.

A wealthy NDP deputy: Ibrahim Kamel

After graduating from university, Ibrahim Mustafa Kamel[22] lived abroad until 1988, first in Paris, then in New York where he followed a business course. Thereafter, Kamel resided in Switzerland where, in collaboration with Saudi and other Gulf rulers, he built an Islamic-based financial empire, with the largest of his companies being Dar al-Mal al-Islami. On his return to Egypt, Kamel and his brothers began to venture into business investments in Menufeyya, including the construction of seven clothes' factories which employ 2,000 people. Kamel's vast wealth also appears to have been useful in allowing him to build an extensive local base of support. In 1990 he set up a local *zakat*[23] fund through which, he says, he has managed, among other things, to provide medical assistance for 50,000 people, finance the repair and modernisation of several hundred local schools and mosques, and the construction and maintenance of five preparatory schools.

It should be noted, however, that the apparently rapid creation in Menufeyya of an extensive base of support was not simply the consequence of Kamel's vast wealth and subsequent charitable contributions. Kamel was already established in the area as he belonged to a prominent local family with a history dating back centuries. One of the local schools had been the family home before it was confiscated during Nasser's socialist reforms. What this means is that Kamel was neither a stranger nor an outsider to the area. His personal and family links within the community were already established before he emigrated. Hence, by investing part of the fortune accumulated abroad in his place of origin, Kamel appears simply to have strengthened and expanded personal networks that already existed.

It is not suprising therefore, that a person of Kamel's stature with such an extensive local network appeared a highly suitable electoral candidate for the NDP. It was perhaps for this reason that the Governor of Menufeyya actually approached Kamel to enquire whether he was interested in participating in the 1990 legislative elections. Kamel was indeed interested, and to the apparent good fortune of the NDP, he saw no objection in contesting the seat as the party's formal candidate.

That Kamel won the seat was no surprise but what was unexpected was that, as a member of both the NDP and the People's Assembly, he began to show signs of active legislative and party participation. As an international businessman, he had pronounced views on legislative matters concerning the economy. He believed that four decades of state control of the economy meant that genuine economic reform would not be possible unless, he said, "President Mubarak first took his big red pen to the 40,000 odd laws passed in the last 40 years. Then we'll know where we are."[24] With regard to the party's organisational structure, Kamel also made his dissatisfaction clear. His main grievance was that the party was internally structured by way of presidential appointment, rather than through elections. This criticism earned him expulsion from the party after only two years of membership.

What this case shows is that Kamel's prominent position in the Menufeyya area initially rendered him a potential asset to the President's NDP. He was, therefore, swiftly approached by the Party. Yet Kamel differed from the majority of local people of prominence and influence in Egypt not only in the size of his fortune but also in being financially independent of Egypt. This meant that Kamel was, to a large extent, able to maintain his influential position within Menufeyya with relative independence from the authorities because a proportion of his vast wealth was channelled into ensuring the employment and welfare of a large number of local people.

Moreover, the fact that Kamel's primary assets and investments were located in Switzerland meant that his means of livelihood were not subject to government interference, which, in turn, further reinforced his independence. He thus appeared unwilling to surrender active political participation as a legislator in return for access to state resources which would not necessarily increase his parochial power and influence. This shows that it is not easy to use elections to co-opt and control the participation of local notables with extensive economic resources.

Kamel's case is, however, the exception rather than the rule because the majority of NDP members who reach public office do not have the same degree of economic independence. Indeed, the NDP focuses on the social standing, influence and prestige of those it attempts to co-opt through elections. Yet, the majority of them do not have the personal wealth to be compared with an international financier such as Kamel. As a result, while their local prominence might assist the regime by providing it with a link to the masses, economic constraints virtually ensure that such individuals are willing, sometimes eager, to enter the clientelist chain.

This, as will be discussed later, is largely linked to the absence of genuine multi-party competition, an absence that appears not to concern the majority of Egyptians who judge their parliamentary representatives on the basis of the services and goods provided, both at the individual and parochial levels. The point of concern here is that in the overwhelming majority of cases provision of such goods is dependent not only on subordination to government, but also on NDP membership. This in turn appears to have advantageous consequences for the regime, the most important of which is the undermining of group cohesion within the party. The following example from the 1990 legislative elections illustrates this point.

Elections and intra-party competition

This case involves Hamdi al-Sayyed, a prominent heart surgeon, head of the doctors' syndicate in Egypt, and a member of the NDP since its creation in 1978.[25] Hamdi al-Sayyed entered the People's Assembly for the first time in 1979. He had joined the NDP and subsequently the People's Assembly as a result of Sadat's personal encouragement. According to al-Sayyed, this was because the President had, at the time, wanted to attract professionals from diverse fields into his newly constructed political forum. Hence, while visiting the headquarters of the doctors' syndicate and meeting its new head (al-Sayyed), Sadat said he "was impressed by the way we conducted our affairs and decided I would be a useful addition in parliament".[26]

Al-Sayyed thus came to fill one of the seats for the constituency of Nozha wa Almaza, and was re-elected after Sadat's death in both the elections of 1984 and 1987. The two million inhabitants of Nozha wa Almaza comprise diverse groups, including labourers connected to public sector factories, settlers in unplanned developments on the outskirts, and wealthy middle- and upper-class people residing in urban areas such as the neighbourhood inhabited by al-Sayyed and his immediate family.

Between 1979 and 1990, al-Sayyed's main preoccupation in the constituency had been the problems encountered by inhabitants of the poorer areas. As he maintained an office open twice a week, the inhabitants of Nozha wa Almaza were provided with direct access to their parliamentary representative. Factory workers, settlers and other individuals routinely turned up to ask for his assistance or enquire about the progress of their latest concern. During one of these open days, for example, a couple of workers were sent by their colleagues to enquire when the electricity supply would be connected to their new homes, which coincidentally were situated within the precincts of their factories in an isolated desert area a few miles from Cairo airport. Al-Sayyed responded by assuring them that he had information from the Ministry of Electricity that the power supply would be in working order by the end of the week. Another person, a young handicapped man, had, as a result of al-Sayyed's intervention, managed to obtain a free public transport travel pass. On that particular day, he had come not only to thank his parliamentary representative, but also to ask for a letter of reference to present to a potential employer. Al-Sayyed promptly obliged. By 1 a.m. the following morning, al-Sayyed, with the help of his assistant, had seen at least 40 people regarding individual or parochial problems of this nature.[27]

The significant point was not so much the nature of assistance that the constituents received from their representative, but that they were able to have direct access to al-Sayyed on a regular basis. This was a special case for, unlike al-Sayyed whose constituency is based in the suburbs of Cairo, the majority of deputies represent distant constituencies and are based in Cairo during the parliamentary season. They therefore cannot meet personally with constituents on such a regular basis.

Such accessibility naturally expanded al-Sayyed's personal networks within the constituency as local people and their leaders became personally acquainted with him. This was an important accomplishment considering that al-Sayyed was not himself a local man. Born in rural Egypt, he had pursued postgraduate studies in medicine in Britain and subsequently resided there until the mid-1970s. He had, therefore, little personal contact with his adopted constituency before he represented it in 1979 in the People's Assembly. In retrospect it is difficult to imagine that al-Sayyed could have won his parliamentary seat in 1979 without the encouragement and "support" of Sadat. However, while Sadat might have imposed al-Sayyed upon the constituency of Nozha wa Almaza initially – in an effort to establish the NDP and a few of its new members in the political arena – al-Sayyed managed to gain their respect and support through his accessibility and work for the constituents. One might also argue that his doing so reflected well on the NDP since it showed that the Party comprised individuals of high calibre.

It was not simply the relationship that al-Sayyed built with his constituents that appears to have rendered him an asset to the party. Since entering the legislature, he was also active in other roles, such as a member of the Health Committee, one of 18 Minister-chaired committees that discuss legislation before it is proposed to parliament.

That he reached such a position itself indicates his senior status within party ranks. The personal contacts that he maintained with Ministers and President Mubarak himself were also evidence of this.

Al-Sayyed's long-standing membership of the NDP, his active participation on its behalf both inside the legislature and outside in his constituency and his regular interaction with members of the Presidential inner circle all suggested that he was an established member of the Party. Hence, it seems curious, at least on the surface, that al-Sayyed's attempt to seek renomination for the legislative elections of 1990 was rejected. The formal reason, as expressed to him, was that the Party had simply "decided against nominating an official candidate" to compete in the constituency of Nozha wa Almaza.[28] This official reason for refusing to nominate a formal candidate in one of Egypt's largest constituencies, a candidate who was one of its most capable and prominent members who had successfully represented it for over a decade and was evidently intent on renomination, is unconvincing.

It seems that the Party's refusal to nominate its veteran member was linked to the fact that another prominent resident of the constituency had decided to contest al-Sayyed's seat. This was Badr al-Din Khattab, a lecturer at the University of Cairo who was a very wealthy businessman with a number of commercial investments, such as shops and restaurants, in the constituency. It appears that Khattab, on the basis of his status and business activities, had managed to develop a popular base of support among the local people in the area. It is alleged, for example, that Khattab's restaurants regularly donated substantial quantities of food to the impoverished citizens of the district. Through his extensive commercial activities he was also a large employer in the area.[29] In addition, as he was a well-educated member of the community, it is likely that the less-educated local people regularly approached him, as they did al-Sharqawi in Nahtay, for assistance in matters concerning the authorities.

Because of the electoral law amendments that were imposed between 1984 and 1990, al-Sayyed's constituency had expanded in size to encompass what were, and have again been since 1990, separate electoral constituencies for the areas of Madinat Nasr and Heliopolis. Al-Sayyed thus became one of six representatives in this enormous constituency, and although his regular surgeries rendered him accessible to constituents who sought his assistance, it is conceivable that the sheer number of demands on his time compelled people in the relatively distant areas to seek alternative assistance from other prominent figures, such as Khattab. In this respect, the enormous size of the constituency between 1984 and 1990 may have been advantageous to Khattab by affording him the opportunity to expand further his personal networks within the area of Nozha wa Almaza. Al-Sayyed, on the other hand, was busy attempting to meet the additional and diffuse demands resulting from the merger of Madinat Nasr and Heliopolis. That al-Sayyed did not approve of the electoral law amendments of that period appears to confirm this analysis.

The refusal of the NDP to nominate an offical candidate for al-Sayyed's seat subsequently led to several candidates – including al-Sayyed, Khattab and other less prominent individuals in the constituency – to compete with one another as independents. The official results as confirmed by the Ministry of Interior declared Khattab the winner and · he subsequently entered the People's Assembly as a member of the NDP. Al-Sayyed, however, suspicious of Khattab's victory, and without the NDP's consent, took the matter to the Supreme Court of Appeal. While Khattab's popularity in the community was not in question, al-Sayyed believed that the total number of votes for Khattab was too great to be genuine. He believed that the results had been manipulated because Khattab allegedly "bribed the chief of the election committee".[30] In court, the judge decided upon a verdict of administrative error since, in his opinion, the signatures of those who registered to vote in the constituency were unclear. The result was a court order for re-election. Al-Sayyed won, and hence retook his seat in the Assembly in August 1991, registering as an NDP member. Perhaps not wishing to witness a repeat occurrence of the 1990 events, the NDP chose to nominate officially al-Sayyed as its candidate in the legislative elections of 1995.

The rivalry between the two party members did not, however, end with al-Sayyed's official nomination in 1995. Rather, Khattab decided to register as an independent contestant, presumably with the intention of registering as an NDP member if he won the Assembly seat. In an attempt to lure al-Sayyed's supporters in the constituency, Khattab resorted to various campaign tactics, of which the most highly publicised was offering voters free meals in his restaurants in the month leading up to the elections.

Al-Sayyed won again but the incident was not without significance. On the individual level, such competition between members of the same party does little to enhance their loyalty to the party as an organisation. It is evident that the Party, or rather those appointed by the President to run it, were aware of al-Sayyed's admirable capabilities in the Assembly and as a member of the legislative committees. What they were not sure about was which of the contestants had the most extensive network of support within the constituency. Hence, it seems that the Party, by not formally nominating a candidate during the elections of 1990, wanted to leave its options open with the aim of welcoming the winner into the fold once the seat was filled. Such a strategy means that party candidates have no obligation to support each other. The post-election court battle between al-Sayyed and Khattab illustrates this well.

The above example shows that party membership cannot be viewed as binding in the categorical sense. Individual candidates are tied to the Party because their personal base of support appears conditional upon the downward flow of resources which candidates aim to receive through party membership. Yet, because of the prevailing (and not discouraged) intra-party competition, party membership appears oriented round various individual candidates and their personal followings. This is advantageous for the government because the implications are that individual candidates are preoccupied with safeguarding their own careers, which in turn are based on safeguarding their personal networks of supporters. Thus, the NDP candidates are less likely to be concerned with party programmes and policies, not only during electoral campaigns but also once elected to office, so allowing the government even more freedom in such matters. This appears to reaffirm the clientelist role of elections.

The opposition parties and elections

The use of elections as a mechanism of clientelist recruitment and control under President Mubarak's rule is also a strategy intended to incorporate political opponents. It is a successful strategy because the constraints imposed on opposition parties are not unlike the constraints that are imposed upon the President's own Party. While certain opposition parties, for example, have more distinctive ideological stances than the NDP, such ideologies are almost irrelevant in the face of the state of emergency which prevents the widespread promotion of such views.[31]

As in the case of the NDP, financial constraints are imposed in apparent efforts to ensure that opposition resources do not pose a potential challenge to the regime. It is illegal, for example, for political parties to accept donations or funding from foreign institutions or individuals. If a donation from an Egyptian individual or organisation exceeds £E2,000, the party in question is obliged by law to print notification of the exact contribution and details of the contributor in its newspaper. This provision, as 'Abd al-'Aziz Zayyan of the Neo-Wafd noted, "might encourage private donations to the NDP because the donors have nothing to fear and much to gain by publicly pledging support to the President's party". He continued: "But what businessman would want that sort of publicity for financing the opposition? He will find his business faced with a lot of bureaucratic hassle the next day."[32]

It is difficult to assess the extent of private donations received by political parties in Egypt because the parties may use covert methods to evade the law. On the formal level opposition parties depend on three sources of income: the annual £E100,000 received individually from the Shura Council by each registered party; the membership fees and donations of party members; and finally, the income derived from the sale of party newspapers. On the basis of such income, it is reasonable to assume that all opposition parties would be roughly on par in terms of economic resources. This, however, does not appear to be the case.

The headquarters of the Neo-Wafd, for example, is situated in a multimillion-pound villa in central Cairo, while the Tagammu', whose headquarters is also situated in central Cairo, occupies a run-down office. In relative terms, however, the economic disparity between all political parties is perhaps not so extensive in view of the government-imposed constraints. The difference is largely due to the fact that the NDP is granted more direct (not autonomous) access to government-controlled resources than its opposition counterparts.

The function of elections as an instrument of clientelist recruitment and control for the NDP can logically be extended to opposition parties, mainly because the opposition faces even greater participatory constraints than the President's Party. Thus the participation of the opposition in legislative elections began gradually to take a similar approach as the NDP Candidates, a phenomenon that will be examined here with reference to the period covering four legislative elections beginning in 1984.

Participating in the elections of 1984

The first legislative elections under President Mubarak's rule can be viewed as significant for opposition parties from two perspectives. First, the Tagammu', the Liberal Party and the Socialist Labour Party were joined by the Neo-Wafd and the Muslim Brotherhood in the electoral arena. The presence of these last two organisations was not insignificant because both political entities originated in pre-1952 Egypt and, more importantly, because both commanded considerable support from some sections of the population.

The origins of the Neo-Wafd can be traced back to as early as 1919. Between the 1920s and 1952, the Wafd, as it was then called, occupied a dominant role in Egyptian politics and was actually in government shortly before the Free Officers took power. The Muslim Brotherhood, on the other hand, has never actually gained formal party status. Yet, it emerged only nine years after the Wafd and also played an important role in Egyptian politics during the early decades of this century.

In terms of ideological platforms and bases of support, these two organisations were, and continue to be, at opposite ends of the political spectrum. The Muslim Brotherhood, with its belief in the implementation of an Islamic state ruled by Islamic law (shariah), has, to a large degree, depended upon the support of people at the lower end of the social scale. In contrast, the Wafd, a champion of free enterprise and political liberalisation, has systematically attracted upper- and upper-middle-class Egyptians into its ranks. Formal ideological differences aside, both organisations obtained early support at the grass-root level because of their contributions to arousing national awareness and anti-British and anti-Israeli sentiments.

To have been able to reach the masses and subsequently arouse such sentiments reflects the efficient organisational capabilities of both entities. It is therefore not surprising to find that when President Sadat decided to allow a formal multi-party system, two of the stipulations of Law 40 of 1977, the law which continues to govern the formation of political parties, was directly aimed at both organisations. One of the stipulations was that political parties could not be established on a religious basis; the second was that the re-establishment of political parties which had existed in pre-1952 Egypt was forbidden.[33]

Initially the Wafd overcame the latter stipulation by amending its pre-1952 platform and changing its name to the Neo-Wafd. Yet, the extent to which the Neo-Wafd was still considered a challenge to the regime was further reflected in President Sadat's decision to issue a decree in 1978 forbidding those who held high positions in the pre-1952 regime from holding party membership. The move produced the desired effects: the Party decided to freeze its activities in protest at the decree because several of its leaders, including its chairman, Fu'ad Serag al-Din, had held high positions in the government prior to 1952. It was not until the Neo-Wafd resorted to the courts and gained a favourable ruling in 1983 that it was able to resume its activities and hence legitimately take part in the then anticipated elections of 1984.

The fact that these potentially challenging groups were both intending to participate in the 1984 elections leads to the second reason why these elections were significant from the perspective of the opposition. President Mubarak was so apprehensive of the potential outcome of the first elections of his rule that he decided to amend the laws governing electoral competition. That the implementation of Electoral Law 114 of 1983 was influenced by the presence of these two organisations in particular can be assumed for two reasons. First, because the Muslim Brotherhood did not possess legal party status, it was intending to nominate its candidates under the independent category, which would have been possible under the previous individual candidacy system. President Mubarak's new law, however, revoked this system and replaced it with election by party list, thus preventing the Muslim Brotherhood from using that option.

It should also be noted that the party-list system meant that the small group of genuine independent candidates who depended upon the support of a local power base had to join a political party or abstain from political participation. Both options were clearly detrimental to these candidates, in particular to those with extensive power bases and previously assured seats. This was because, if they chose to abstain, they faced the possibility of losing their influence and status within the local community. However, if they chose to participate, the most assured way they could preserve their place in the Assembly under the new law would be to join the government-backed NDP, a move that would ensure their co-option into the Party on government terms. Another, less apparent, consequence of the party-list system was its role in controlling NDP members. Previously, an NDP member could enter the electoral race as an independent and then re-register as an NDP member upon taking his place in the legislature. The new law terminated this option. Hence, the law reinforced control over incumbent members of the NDP, as the risk of being dropped from the official nomination list would mean an almost certain end to the individual's political career.

Second, with the new electoral law came a reduction of the number of electoral constituencies from 176 to 48. Thus, while the average province previously had some 15 to 20 constituencies, it now had only 3 to 5.[34] Moreover, all participating parties were required to obtain a minimum of 8 per cent of the total national vote to be represented at all in the People's Assembly. If a party did not achieve the 8 per cent target, its votes were to be automatically credited to those of the largest party – in other words, the President's NDP.

President Mubarak justified the new law by claiming that the change was intended to provide voters with the "opportunity to choose among a number of different programmes and methods".[35] This comment could hardly be considered convincing in the context of the highly parochial and personalised voting patterns of the population. Rather, the adoption of such measures reflected the President's efforts to limit the electoral participation of parties which depended upon prominent candidates who, by virtue of their local standing and networks, could achieve substantial electoral gains. The opposition party that was intended to be most affected was the Neo-Wafd.

The above assumption is based on the premise that the Neo-Wafd, unlike its fellow opposition parties, has historically been linked to wealthy and influential members of society. That the party was resurrected by its veteran members on an ideological platform similar to that of the original indicated that the Party would again attract members of that category, members with favourable election prospects in their local communities. An example is the senior Neo-Wafd member, Ahmad 'Othman Abaza who originates from one of the oldest and most influential families in Egypt's governorate of Sharqiyya. Hence, if the Neo-Wafd nominated Abaza, by virtue of his family networks and standing in the area, his nomination could theoretically have provided the Neo-Wafd with a legislative representative in that area. However, the expansion of constituencies under the new law meant not only that he would have had to compete against other prominent individuals on their local territory and vice versa, but also that if he did manage to defeat his competitors, the 8 per cent minimum vote requirement could still have barred him from acquiring a seat. In this respect, it is not surprising that one opposition newspaper declared:

> The government only wants an opposition with no power so that it can boast to international public opinion and give the people at home the impression that they are being democratically represented in the Assembly . . . There will never be the chance of government alternation. The single party will forever rule.[36]

Implications of the 1983 electoral law amendments

The extent to which the new electoral system achieved its objectives is debatable. The 8 per cent hurdle prevented the relatively new Labour, Liberal and Tagammu' parties from entering the Assembly. Prominent individuals, such as the Tagammu' leader, Khalid Mohyi al-Din, were unable to provide their parties with even token representation in the Assembly, even though their personal chances of election were high in view of their local standing and networks, such as Mohyi al-Din's in his rural home constituency of Kafr Shokr.[37] In this respect, by changing the rules of political participation, President Mubarak did succeed, through what appeared to be legal and therefore theoretically legitimate means, in preventing certain sections of the opposition from entering parliament. However, they were not the opponents the President seemed to have in mind. Ahmad Abaza did in fact compete on behalf of the Neo-Wafd in his family's home constituency of Sharqiyya and won the seat. Equally important, he was able to take his seat in the legislature because his Party surpassed the 8 per cent hurdle. He was subsequently joined in the Assembly by 49 fellow Wafdist and eight Muslim Brotherhood members because the Neo-Wafd and the Muslim Brotherhood overcame the restrictive technicalities of the new law by forming an electoral alliance which entailed candidates from both entities competing under the formal Neo-Wafd banner.

The fact that this alliance overcame the restrictions of the new electoral law is symbolically significant. Rather than weaken potentially threatening opponents, the new law weakened the already fragile smaller opponents, but served to unite and strengthen the regime's two main adversaries.

It should also be noted that the new electoral law produced the unforeseen consequence of strengthening the unity of the opposition in several ways. Using their respective newspapers, the opposition parties were at one in condemning the government and its policies. Writing in *al-Sha'b*, the Labour Party's organ, Hilmi Murad, the secretary-general of the party, conceded what was apparent for a while, that "the Government needs an opposition with no power".[38] Although the Neo-Wafd went on to achieve relative electoral success in comparison with the other parties, this did not prevent it from calling the election law "an evil scheme intended to attain results contrary to the people's views",[39] and describing the government as basically a "legal heir" of the old Nasserite dicatorship because it was restricting democracy and was prepared to recognise only an opposition that was docile.[40]

Although the opposition's use of its newspapers to criticise the government did reflect the extent to which freedom of expression had expanded in comparison with both the Nasser and Sadat eras, it is worth noting that there was very little President Mubarak could do at that particular time without confirming these criticisms and, more importantly, without appearing to be an outright oppressor. In other words, because of both the state of emergency constraints on political activity and the particularly severe barriers to candidacy introduced before the 1984 elections, attempts to prevent the publication of adverse newspaper articles have more likely resulted not in containing political participation, but in blocking the main "safety-valve" for opposition expression, short of resort to underground activity.[41]

On another level, the restrictive nature of the elections did not always act as a catalyst of co-option. When the President used his prerogative to appoint ten members to the Assembly, he nominated several members of the opposition. These included Ibrahim Shokri, leader of the Labour Party (then called the Socialist Labour Party) and two of his colleagues, as well as Milad Hanna, a senior member of the Tagammu'. Dr Hanna refused the offer, in a decision that reflected both his and his party's opinion on the matter at the time, but Ibrahim Shokri and his colleagues accepted.[42]

However, one party's refusal and the other's acceptance cannot be regarded as a split in the opposition's decision to cooperate with the government. Rather, it can best be understood as a difference in strategy. The Tagammu' refused because it felt that by accepting the offer it would be sending the wrong signals to the government, that it would be indicating acceptance of the prevailing political conditions. On the other hand, the Labour Party accepted the offer with the main aim of securing an additional avenue for airing its dissatisfaction with the political situation.[43] In other words, the selection of these individuals and the constraints under which the elections were held suggest that President Mubarak intended to obstruct the political participation of opponents through formal means in an attempt to entice them into his patronage system and hence bring them under his informal control. That this attempt proved futile can be regarded as evidence of the unwillingness of opponents to adhere to the President's clientelist strategy of control.

The third and final major outcome of the 1984 electoral law amendments was that they provided the opposition with grounds to appeal to the Supreme Constitutional Court. Citing the inability of an individual to nominate himself in elections as a breach of public right, equal opportunities and equality guaranteed to all citizens by Articles 8, 40 and 62 of the constitution, the opposition contested the amendments to the election laws on the grounds that they were unconstitutional.[44]

Again, the opposition's willingness to challenge overtly the President by appealing to the Supreme Constitutional Court in order to annul the electoral amendments can be regarded as symbolically significant, for it indicated that the imposed restrictions succeeded little in pressurising opponents into accepting the political status quo. Instead, they developed the determination to demand – and be granted – change. The President was eventually impelled at the end of 1986 to amend the electoral law, dissolve the Assembly by referendum, and set a premature election date of April 1987. Indeed, President Mubarak's decision, as discussed in Chapter 2, was also influenced by considerations concerning his upcoming renomination. Nevertheless, the underlying factor was that a unified opposition front was instrumental in initiating the change.

Electoral law amendments of 1986 and the 1987 elections

The President's determination to use the electoral process as a formal instrument for containing political participation is shown by the fact that the new amendments affected the electoral law in relatively minor ways, hardly improving the chances of competitors. The most significant feature of the amendments was the amalgamation of party-list and individual-candidate systems. Independent candidates were allocated one seat in each of the 48 constituencies and the winning independent candidate was required to obtain the largest number of votes of all competing independents, a figure that should be no less than 20 per cent of the total votes cast in the constituency.

Although as many as 1,937 candidates stood for the 48 constituencies, the main beneficiaries of the independent category were not genuine independents, nor were they opposition members, like Khalid Mohyi al-Din, who decided to run under that banner to overcome the restrictive 8 per cent limit placed on participating parties. Instead, of the 48 independent places acquired in the 1987 elections, only nine were won by independents with opposition or no party affiliation. The majority of seats, 39 in total, were won by individuals identified as NDP members.[45] The large number of contestants competing in this category, therefore, suggests that the provision of an independent category inadvertently produced an additional safety-valve by providing the opportunity for disparate individuals with political aspirations to participate. Even though electoral participation expanded, the role of elections as a protective shield against a legitimate political threat remained unchanged.

Under the amended electoral law the remaining constituency representatives were elected through the old party-list system. However, the amended law stipulated that the votes of parties that did not obtain the 8 per cent vote requirement should be distributed among all the successful parties in direct proportion to their scores in the elections, rather than be credited to the largest party as under the old law.[46] The reaction of the opposition to the electoral amendments and the 1987 elections were not too dissimilar to that witnessed in the elections of 1984. However, the Neo-Wafd decided to compete in the elections without entering an alliance. Subsequently, the Muslim Brotherhood joined forces with the Labour Party and the Liberal Party to form a coalition. As a result, there was an overall increase in opposition incumbents in the legislature, as the Neo-Wafd gained 36 places and the coalition 60.

While the NDP, with 75 per cent of seats, still maintained its domination of the Assembly, the electoral outcome did appear to indicate a strengthening of the opposition in the face of adversity. Moreover, the opposition remained united in its condemnation of the electoral system which it regarded as a "fake democracy"[47] and "a horrible and violent repetition of the 1984 farce",[48] and subsequently decided to return to the Supreme Constitutional Court to contest the amendment, citing it as an "infringement upon the right to [individual] nomination and a breach of the principals of equal opportunity and equality contrary to Articles 8, 40 and 62 of the Constitution".[49] The final outcome was in May 1990 when the Supreme Constitutional Court ruled that the 1986 electoral law was unconstitutional, thus pressurising the President to issue a decree abolishing the party-list system altogether and announcing a return to the individual candidacy system of election by absolute majority for the premature elections of 1990.

Return to individual candidacy

Apart from the abolition of the party-list system, another important change in the electoral laws was the increase in the number of constituencies from 48 to 222. The implications of this were that it was then theoretically easier for non-NDP members devoid of state resources and support to compete in the elections. It must be noted, however, that the President's decision to return to the individual candidacy system was perhaps influenced more by political strategy than by the court ruling. Clearly the President was aware of the Muslim Brotherhood's electoral coalitions in the previous elections of 1984 and 1987 and its penetration into the Assembly in both instances. As he later noted: "The door is now wide open for all political forces to participate . . . certain controls have even been by-passed, letting certain groups infiltrate – groups that the constitution and laws have banned from political activity to safeguard the homeland."[50] In this context, the President perhaps considered that the individual candidacy system was after all preferable since it would put fewer restrictions on individual candidates, and consequently separate and weaken organised opposition groups.

The 1990 elections and their implications

Although it was an opposition initiative that led to the premature elections of 1990, the elections were boycotted by the Neo-Wafd, the Muslim Brotherhood, the Labour Party and the Liberals, leaving only the Tagammu' to run against the government's NDP. According to party members who boycotted those elections, the decision to stay out was related to two main issues: (1) objection to the Ministry of Interior's

tradition of supervising polling-stations and the ballot count; and
(2) the continuation of the Emergency Laws and their restrictive effect
on political participation. These issues were, and remain, genuine bones
of contention with government. However, that the majority of leading
opposition parties intended to pressurise the government into conceding
to these demands by taking the unprecedented step of withdrawing
from the elections suggests that the opposition had overrated its power
and influence in the political arena.

The opposition's success in its court battles with the government and
in obtaining a constitutional court ruling invalidating both the electoral
laws of 1983 and 1986 boosted its confidence in confronting government with these additional demands. The opposition's new perception
of its power to pressurise the government was further reinforced by
another factor. The President had decided to remove the then Minister of
Interior, Zaki Badr, in January 1990 after he publicly admitted tampering
with the results of the 1987 elections. The President's decision to remove
Badr was also influenced by another consideration: Badr began to emerge
as a political liability as a result of events such as the University of Banha
incident.[51] The opposition did not see Badr's dismissal as possibly a
mere concession by the government, but, while acknowledging that the
decision was partly influenced by the President's dissatisfaction with the
Minister's political shortcomings, it preferred to interpret Badr's removal
as a measure of its own influence over the government.

The decision of the opposition to stand firm with regard to its
stated demands appears to have been influenced by the belief that the
President would be embarrassed into making concessions if he felt that
an all-out opposition boycott would undermine his image, especially
since a boycott would mean that the President's third term renomination
in 1993 would be supported by a one-party legislature – his own party.
This impression was further confirmed when the President attempted
to persuade them to abandon the boycott. Mubarak did not actually
make personal contact with the opposition leaders during that period,
but indirect contact took place in the form of informal meetings and
telephone conversations between the senior presidential advisor, Osama
al-Baz, and representatives of the opposition. Al-Baz's attempts to mediate
and dissuade the parties from boycotting the elections did not include
promises to meet their demands.[52]

It is possible that Mubarak could have been embarrassed into some form of compromise with the opposition if the Tagammu' had not eventually decided to abandon the boycott. The party's official opinion was that boycotting the elections was not a sensible form of demonstration since emergency laws would be temporarily (and unofficially) lifted during that period, thereby providing politicians with a better opportunity to communicate with the public and recruit supporters. The Tagammu', therefore, argued that it was unwise to pursue such action as it would merely isolate the parties from the electorate.[53] On the surface, this argument seemed both practical and sensible. After all, the other parties that pursued the boycott found themselves without direct access to the Assembly and were unable to address the public for the next five years, except through their respective newspapers. The Tagammu', on the other hand, gained at least some form of direct access to both parliament and the inhabitants of the constituencies it came to represent after gaining a token five seats in the elections.

Beneath the argument put forth, however, there appears to have been another more covert issue dividing party members on the boycott issue. According to several sources within and outside party circles Khalid Mohyi al-Din, the Tagammu' leader, had resented that the Neo-Wafd leader, Fu'ad Serag al-Din, had assumed the role of opposition spokesman. The reason for this may have been a personal rivalry between the two men as a consequence of their disparate political origins. A government minister under King Faruq, and a member of one of the most prominent and aristocratic families in pre-revolutionary Egypt, Fu'ad Serag al-Din was among the pre-1952 élite who lost considerable wealth and influence under the Nasser regime and subsequently never recognised the Revolution as more than a *coup d'état*.

In contrast, Khalid Mohyi al-Din, whose origins were more modest, was one of the original Free Officers responsible for the 1952 Revolution. Moreover, under Nasser he became a member of the new ruling class which replaced the likes of Serag al-Din. In this respect, it was probably humiliating for Mohyi al-Din to find himself and his Party being represented by the same individual and Party that had been brought down by the Free Officers. On the other hand, Serag al-Din was not inclined to be conciliatory. For example, the ageing Wafd leader took the initiative to approach the government with the final decision to boycott the elections without informing the leaders of the other parties. Although the opposition was aware of the inevitability of the boycott, the fact that Serag al-Din took it upon himself to inform the government of the action without notifying them beforehand took them all by suprise.

It was at this point that Mohyi al-Din decided to inform the members of the Tagammu' Committee of his decision to participate in the elections. Almost half the Committee initially disagreed with this course of action, considering that it would be a betrayal of the other parties and would also signal defeat in their confrontation with the President. However, the Tagammu' leader insisted that he could not, in principle, allow the Party to participate in a boycott determined by Serag al-Din. The party, he argued, was independent, not a branch of the Neo-Wafd and that Serag al-Din had no right to inform the authorities of a final decision which involved other parties than his own without their prior knowledge and consent.[54]

Most of the Committee eventually came to agree with their Chairman. This incident was a turning-point for the Tagammu' leader and his Party in terms of an emergence of a clearer set of role expectations. The Tagammu' leader reached a point where a preference for mending fences with the government and accepting his party's role as a loyal opposition outweighed his inclination to do battle with a personal arch-rival.

The decision of the Tagammu' to run in the 1990 elections can arguably be regarded as a significant factor which influenced both the outcome of the boycott and the subsequent nature of President–opposition relations. The Party's presence in the electoral arena divided an opposition that had previously been united primarily on the basis of its unanimous stance against President Mubarak's form of democracy. The result of such a division was that a valid and potentially effective opposition protest became diluted to the advantage of the President. This enabled him to claim that "an opposition is part and parcel of the State system" and that any party seeking to separate itself from the system was "wasting its constitutional role".[55] As this statement shows, the participation of one opposition party in the elections took the sting out of the boycott which would otherwise have appeared as a wholesale rejection of the system.

It could be said that by participating in the 1990 elections the Tagammu' became the first opposition party to enter into the regime's clientelist structure. Prior to the 1990 elections there was little evidence to suggest the existence of clientelist relations between the regime and any of the opposition parties. Informal links between the regime and the Tagammu' began to emerge: during the elections, for example, a number of NDP candidates were allowed to collaborate with Tagammu' candidates, rather than with other NDP candidates. This collaboration basically involved vote exchange between candidates, a mechanism made possible by the one-man-two-votes' electoral procedure put in place by Nasser to ensure that workers and peasants were fairly represented in parliament. As the current constitution continues to stipulate, 50 per cent of the legislative Assembly must consist of workers or peasants (Article 87). Candidates in each electoral constituency are subsequently categorised into two groups: *fe'at* and *'omal*. Registering in the *fe'at* category is a straightforward procedure, the main requisite being that the candidate should be a university graduate or equivalent. In theory, the *'omal* comprises peasants or workers with less than degree-level education. In reality, such candidates are rarely workers or peasants, but rather wealthy landowners or merchants.

Each voter is allocated one vote to elect a representative in the *fe'at* category and one for the selection of a deputy in the *'omal* category. Subsequent vote exchange is a system whereby a candidate in the *fe'at* category cooperates with a candidate in the *'omal* category in the same constituency and the supporters of each vote for the other with the aim of doubling the number of each candidate's votes on election day.

While in theory each voter utilises the one-man-two-votes' system to choose his two representatives, in practice this procedure revokes the whole objective of the one-man-two-votes' system since supporters are exchanging their "second" vote for the opportunity to double one candidate's electoral chances. This, as will be examined further in Chapter 4, does not prevent vote-exchanging from being a common, albeit clandestine, practice. What was unusual before the 1990 elections, however, was for government-nominated candidates to contemplate pursuing electoral collaboration of this nature with opposition candidates.

In the context of this collaboration, it is interesting to note that the Tagammu' won five seats in 1990. Such token gains are not insignificant if we consider that the Tagammu' last gained entry to the legislature in 1976 when it was still confined to a platform within the ASU. Even more significant is the fact that all five winning candidates, including the Chairman of the Party, Khalid Mohyi al-Din, participated in vote exchange with their NDP opposite numbers in their respective constituencies. Senior Tagammu' members justified this informal "partnership" on the grounds that the NDP candidates sought the alliance with their party's five winning candidates because they possessed well-established power bases in their respective constituencies.[56] There is little reason to question the validity of the individual power bases of the winning Tagammu' candidates. All five were local people well known throughout the community, with long histories of political activity and at least one (Mohyi al-Din), was a national political figure. Given the Tagammu's poor electoral record, one may safely assume that it was the Tagammu' candidates who needed the alliance with the NDP in order to better their electoral chances.

The rural constituency of Kafr Shokr is one of the five places where the Tagammu' won a seat. The major competitors in the constituency were three prominent locals: an NDP candidate in the *'omal* category, and NDP and Tagammu' candidates in the *fe'at* category. Because of the boycott, the other candidates were local people of minor stature competing as independents. Illustrating the centre's indirect assistance of the Tagammu', the opposition candidate – in this case, Khalid Mohyi al-Din – was given precedence over his NDP counterpart. 'Abd al-Rahman Mosayr, the NDP *'omal* candidate, was given the freedom to join forces with Mohyi al-Din in a vote-exchange pact. Although the exact figures could not be confirmed, it is understood that Mohyi al-Din and Mosayr each had roughly the same number of supporters in the constituency. The number of voters supporting 'Abd al-Rahman Sarhan, the NDP *fe'at* and hence Mohyi al-Din's competitor, was considerably smaller, estimated at perhaps half that of Mohyi al-Din or Mosayr.

Assuming that there was no government interference during the elections, it would appear that it was Sarhan, not Mosayr, who needed a significant vote-exchange alliance in order to win a place in the Assembly. Had Mosayr joined forces with his NDP colleague, Sarhan, both NDP members would have won seats in the elections because their combined votes would have surpassed those of Mohyi al-Din and one of the minor independent candidates with whom Mohyi al-Din could have contemplated an alliance. Therefore, while it is doubtful that the government was directly involved in instigating the Mohyi al-Din–Mosayr alliance, the NDP candidate's exchange of his supporters' votes with those of the Tagammu' leader, at the expense of his NDP colleague, would have been a risky career move unless the President, in his capacity of NDP leader, had indirectly signalled his consent. Ultimately, the vote-exchange alliance of the other Tagammu' winners can be understood in the same context.

That participation in the 1990 elections eventually led the Tagammu' publicly to enter the regime's clientelist structure can be observed on another level. As we have seen, the Party refused the President's offer in 1984 to appoint one of its senior members to the legislature. In early 1995 the Tagammu' accepted the Presidential nomination of its Secretary-General, Dr Rifat Sa'id, to the Consultative (Shura) Council. This decision is indicative of the role that the Party has come to accept for itself. Prior to 1990, the Tagammu', in the words of Sa'id, "totally rejected the system".[57] Like the other opposition parties, the Tagammu' did not accept the government's dominant position, and its aim was to fight for a democratic multi-party system in the broad sense – that all parties would be given equal opportunity to compete for government. In the context of such highly ambitious expectations, opposition parties, and in particular the respective party leaders, did not accept President Mubarak as their patron. The President's efforts to appoint members of the opposition to the People's Assembly, therefore, was considered patronising and subsequently rebuffed.

The President's unsuccessful attempt to appoint Dr Hanna of the Tagammu' in 1984 illustrates this. The fate of those opposition members who were tempted to accept a presidential appointment also appears to affirm this. Mona Makram 'Obayd of the Neo-Wafd had her party membership withdrawn because in 1990 she accepted a presidentially nominated seat in the legislature. Fahmi Nashed, another Neo-Wafdist, also suffered the same fate after he accepted a presidential nomination to the Shura Council in the same year.[58]

By its decision to participate in the 1990 elections, collaborate with members of the President's Party and formally accept a presidential appointment for one of its Party leaders, the Tagammu' was evidently the first opposition Party to enter the clientelist structure of the Mubarak regime. As the Tagammu' Secretary-General Rif'at Sa'id explained, the Party changed from confrontation to cooperation in its relationship with the government because, he said: "It was crazy to isolate ourselves from the system of which we are part."[59] The comment suggests that the temptation even to nominally share power through electoral participation came to be regarded as preferable to challenging the dominant power and achieving no electoral gains in the process. By the time the People's Assembly had completed its first full five-year term under Mubarak's rule, the other opposition parties had arrived at a similar conclusion.

Return of the opposition: 1995

The boycott did not produce the widespread support the parties had expected; nor did it put enough pressure on President Mubarak even partially to concede to their demands. This meant that the parties that participated in the boycott needed to reassess both their position and political strategy in the context of their limited influence in the political arena in general. Moreover, Mubarak's insistence on maintaining a state of emergency, restricted their activities to such an extent that electioneering had become the single most important vehicle for activists to make contact with the public, and recruit new members and supporters. Thus, the parties recognised that, by withdrawing from electoral participation, they had inadvertently excluded themselves from the political scene. No longer prepared to continue the boycott and risk total obscurity, the opposition parties prepared to enter the 1995 electoral race of their own accord. While the Neo-Wafd rather meekly justified its decision on the grounds that it had participated in elections since 1924 and had no intention of stopping now,[60] the Labour Party was more to the point:

> We boycotted the last elections to pressurise the government into allowing free and fair elections. The government, however, ignored us. This time, we are participating with no illusions . . . we are aware that this time round government malpractice will be even more intense. However, we decided, in spite of their careless and short-sighted approach, not to continue the boycott. This is because we care about the constitution and the stability of the nation and we do not want to leave the government with a free rein in these elections. This can only be achieved with our participation."[61]

That Mubarak did not consider it necessasry to dispatch advisors to persuade them informally to participate indicates that the President was already aware of the opposition's predicament and of their intention of returning to the arena of political contest. On the other hand, the absence of communication between the President and the opposition before the 1995 elections may also suggest that the effects of the previous boycott on the President's image were so slight that he was not concerned about a second boycott. In either case, the decision to end the boycott indicates the extent to which the opposition had come to regard election, even in their non-competitive form, as important.

It is possibly for this reason that a shift in attitude can be observed during the 1995 electoral campaigns. To the obvious advantage of the government, several opposition parties began to proclaim a shared identification with certain goals and values of the regime. Their efforts to cultivate the local support of workers and urban poor during electoral rallies might have focused on the rejection of specific regime policies, such as the privatisation of state-owned factories or the Rent Law amendments, but general allegiance to the regime did appear to become a prominent theme among several of the leading opposition parties. For example, opposition parties made particular efforts to adopt an anti-Islamist stance, in conformity with the President's conviction that "a correct party obliges all its members to adhere to its principles and not change their slogans and principles daily for temporary gain . . . or establish an alliance with undemocratic forces that hire the party's platforms and mouthpieces to circumvent law and order".[62]

Heeding this warning was the Tagammu' Party, which used the campaign slogan "*al-din lillah wa al-watan lil jami'*" ("religion is for God and the nation is for all") throughout the 1995 elections. Evidently, this was to emphasise its rejection of those who mixed politics with religion. In fact, at a press conference held before the elections, the Tagammu' Chairman, Khalid Mohyi al-Din, stated that the participation of the other opposition parties was important not, as one would assume, to defend their position against government domination, but to defend themselves against "the threat of religious fundamentalism and terrorism".[63]

In view of the Party's link with government during the 1990 elections, it is not altogether suprising that the Tagammu' wanted to distance itself from the Islamists and reaffirm its loyalty to the system. What is interesting, however, is that the two parties whose previous association with the Muslim Brotherhood went as far as forming electoral coalitions – the Neo-Wafd and the Liberals, in 1984 and 1987 respectively – also adopted similar strategies in efforts to dissociate themselves from the Islamists.

The Neo-Wafd's shifting attitude

When in 1984 the Neo-Wafd became the first party to form an electoral alliance with the Muslim Brotherhood, both groups seem to have benefited. In defiance of the government's imposition of the party-list electoral laws, the alliance scored the only electoral victory by any opposition group. In 1990 the Muslim Brotherhood, unlike the Tagammu', supported the Neo-Wafd's initiative to announce the boycott even though it had not been informed of this move beforehand.

By 1995 such solidarity had faded. The Neo-Wafd's electoral propaganda in that year shows a deliberate move to discredit the Brotherhood to appease the government. For example, Sa'd 'Abd al-Nur, the Neo-Wafd's Secretary-General, declared in an interview during the 1995 elections: "In 1984 the Muslim Brothers were like orphans. They were a small family . . . they needed to ally themselves with a political party."[64] 'Abd al-Nur was attempting to justify the Wafd–Brotherhood alliance by hinting that it was a Brotherhood initiative and that his party agreed to the alliance because it regarded the Muslim Brotherhood as a harmless entity. More to the point was a statement by 'Abd al-'Aziz Muhammad, a prominent lawyer and senior Neo-Wafd member. During a discussion with senior party colleagues attended by an *al-Ahali* journalist, he said: "It is not in our interest to co-operate [in the 1995 elections] with an organisation [the Muslim Brotherhood] that is targeted by the authorities."[65]

The manner in which the party began overtly to endorse Muslim–Coptic ties reflected its attempt to distance itself from the Islamic tendency. 'Abd al-Nur, it should be noted, is a Coptic lawyer who was personally chosen for the post by Fu'ad Serag al-Din in early 1995. The 1995 elections also witnessed the nomination of 30 Coptic candidates, the largest number of Christian nominations by the Neo-Wafd since its revival in 1978. As if to emphasise further its non-Islamic tendencies, the illustrations on the Party's electoral posters depicted four figures who were all holding hands in unison: a peasant in *galabeyya* (full shirt); an urbanite in Western dress; and an imam and a priest wearing their respective religious garbs. The slogan above the posters read: "*al-Wafd al-Jadid: hezb al-wehda al-wataneyya*" ("the Neo-Wafd: the party of national unity"). The poster was apparently aimed at attracting four major social groups within Egyptian society: peasants; workers; Muslims and Christians.

[110]

However, on closer inspection, it is possible to argue that it was not necessary to include the characters symbolising Muslims and Christians with those representing workers and peasants since the former groups are not separate and distinct from the latter. In this respect, the Neo-Wafd's nomination of a large number of Coptic candidates, and the inclusion of symbols representing the unity of Islam and Christianity in electoral posters, were all part of the Party's attempt to denounce publicly the political ambitions of the Islamic opposition and so gain presidential favour. This interpretation is reinforced by the potentially appeasing comments of 'Abd al-'Aziz Muhammad, who claimed that his Party was not seeking, nor did it want, "power". All it wanted from the elections was "to spread the Wafd ideology".[66]

Recognition of the regime's pre-eminence is reflected in many other ways. Fahmi Nashid, who had been dismissed from the Neo-Wafd for accepting a presidential nomination to the Shura Council, was reinstated to his former position in the Party in 1995, implying that the Party no longer considered presidential appointments, and hence co-option into the regime, an unacceptable option.

The Liberal response

Although the Liberal Party's electoral efforts to distance itself from the Muslim Brotherhood were less conspicuous than those of the Neo-Wafd, certain factors indicate that the Party was also attempting to dissociate itself from the Islamic connection and publicly identify with the regime instead. Unlike the case of the Labour Party (the third member of the 1987 tripartite alliance), there was no evidence to suggest a direct association between the Liberals and the Muslim Brotherhood during the 1995 electoral campaign. According to Brotherhood spokesman, Ma'mun al-Hudhaybi, the tripartite alliance was not necessary during the 1995 elections because the change in electoral laws meant that Brotherhood members could participate as independent candidates. However, he stressed that although the three parties constituted separate entities, cooperation between them continued despite the return to the individual candidacy system. Such cooperation included "members of the coalition not running against each other in the same constituency" and a mutual exchange of "manual assistance during the electoral campaign".[67]

The precarious nature of Liberal–Brotherhood cooperation is, however, reflected in the fact that al-Hudhaybi nominated himself in the

Cairo constituency of Doqqi and was subsequently competing against (among others) Hamza De'bes, a high-ranking official of the Liberal Party. According to al-Hudhaybi, the aim of entering the electoral race in Doqqi was not to compete against any of the candidates, but simply to spread the Islamic message.[68] This remark was at odds with the publicly expressed views of De'bes, who maintained that there *was* competition and that he was not aware of any coordination between the Liberal Party and the Muslim Brotherhood.[69]

That the Liberal Party's inclination was to integrate itself in the system and distance itself from the Muslim Brotherhood can be poignantly illustrated by the election campaign of Mustafa Bakri, the then editor-in-chief of *Al-Ahrar*, the Party's official newspaper. Bakri competed in the *fe'at* category against Muhammad Mahgub, the Minister of Religious Endowments in the industrial constituency of Helwan wa al-Tibbin near Cairo. Bakri's opponent, Mahgub, originates from Helwan and is thus considered *ibn al-balad* (a term used to describe a "local son"). His family connection with the area is maintained through the large number of relatives who continue to reside there.

Moreover, since 1979 Mahgub has represented the constituency's *fe'at* category as an NDP deputy. Through his senior status in government he has been able over the years to provide much funding for his constituency from which the residents have benefited. Consequently, this working-class constituency can claim subsidised housing, surfaced roads, schools and youth centres as among the benefits obtained by Mahgub. Subsequently, through the merits of being *ibn al-balad* and because of his benevolence that was largely derived from close association with the regime, Mahgub's power base was inherently more extensive than that of the relative newcomer, Bakri. Bakri's Upper Egyptian (*Sa'idi*) origins and current residence in the middle-class suburb of Ma'di near Cairo meant that he did not have any ties with the constituency until the summer of 1995 when he helped to establish a local independent newspaper, *Sawt Helwan*.

Helwan wa al-Tibbin, however, is home to a large number of *Sa'idi* migrant workers and their families. Bakri therefore hoped he could challenge Mahgub's virtually safe seat by cultivating the support of his fellow Upper Egyptians by using *ibn al-balad* sentiments. To attract as wide an audience as possible, Bakri's electoral strategy also focused on revealing Mahgub's misappropriation of state resources and corruption.[70] What was interesting about Bakri's strategy was that he focused his attacks on his opponent without in any way implicating the regime. An excerpt from his rally speech in Helwan's 'Arab Rashed neighbourhood illustrates his cautious approach.

> The Minister attempted to prevent this rally from taking place today through bribery and blackmail [of the voters], but these methods can't work all the time . . . why hasn't he responded to my accusations [of corruption] or taken me to court? We are not afraid of him; we don't care about life or death; what we do care about is the property of the orphans and the poor ending up in his pocket [loud applause] . . . why doesn't he respect the constitution, respect the people and respect *amn al-dawla* [state security]? I was speaking to a member of *al-amn* [*al-dawla*] and he assured me election day will be clean and honest. If Muhammad Mahgub thinks the state will interfere to help him, he is insulting the Ministry of Interior, insulting the state and insulting the President.[71]

Although Bakri was denouncing a cabinet minister, he never questioned the President's disposition to appoint such a man to the cabinet nor his subsequent connection with him. Bakri elevated the President above the fray, thus indicating a public acceptance of the existing political order. Moreover, as personal communication between members of the opposition and the security apparatus would not exist without both the knowledge and approval of the President, Bakri's reference to a cordial conversation with a member of the Ministry of Interior thus indicates the development of such links.

With regard to the vote-exchange process, the same case can also be used to illustrate the extent to which the Liberal Party sought to distance itself from the Muslim Brotherhood. The main contenders in Helwan wa al-Tibbin's '*omal* category were: Muhammad Mustafa (NDP); 'Ali Fathi al-Bab (Islamist); and Mustafa 'Abd al-Ghaffar (Independent). The NDP candidate was the least popular of the three because as an employee in Sharikat al-Harir (Silk-Cloth Co.), one of the many state-owned factories in Helwan, he had begun his short political career as an Independent in 1990 to protest against the government but had defected to the NDP in that same year. The series of workers' strikes in Helwan in 1989 had resulted in the death of three workers during clashes with the police. Infuriated, the workers had taken an anti-government stance in the 1990 elections by supporting one of their own workers rather than the NDP candidate. On entering the People's Assembly, however, Mustafa joined the ruling NDP, thus letting the workers down and at the same time switching to the very party that the workers had not wanted to represent them.

Due to his betrayal of the Helwan workers, Mustafa could not cultivate popular support within the constituency during the 1995 elections despite the vast administrative and financial assistance at his disposal as an NDP candidate. As the purpose of entering a vote-exchange pact is to accumulate as many predetermined votes as possible, neither Mahgub nor Bakri wanted an alliance with the unpopular candidate. The other two candidates were considerably more popular although it should be noted that the size of their respective power bases differed substantially. The independent al-Ghaffar, was, like Mustafa before him, a public-sector employee from the same silk-cloth factory, and the 1995 elections comprised his first attempt to enter the electoral race.

According to several sources, however, 'Abd al-Ghaffar's links with fellow workers were limited primarily to those who had direct contact with him in the factory. In contrast, the Islamist al-Bab, another local figure, was in a position to claim a more extensive power base, especially in the densely populated Mayo and al-Tibbin districts of Helwan. This was largely due to the workers' loss of faith in secular co-workers following Mustafa's conduct in 1990. Moreover, unlike 'Abd al-Ghaffar, who was not associated with any particular political group, al-Bab relied upon the organisational skills of the Muslim Brotherhood to cultivate and expand his power base. Since Bakri needed a well-established partner to overcome the veteran minister's extensive power base in Helwan, he chose not to ally himself with the Islamist al-Bab but to associate himself with the relative newcomer and independent, al-Ghaffar.

While Mahgub formed a successful pact with al-Bab, the circumstances further indicated the Liberal Party's reluctance to continue its alliance with the Islamists for fear of offending the regime. Incidentally, President Mubarak removed Mahgub from the Cabinet immediately after the elections, a move possibly reflecting the President's disapproval of the minister having formed an alliance with a Muslim Brother and having thereby helped that organisation achieve its sole electoral victory.

Cooperating with the authorities

In the 1995 elections the Liberal Party won only one seat while the Tagammu' and the Neo-Wafd fared little better with five and six seats, respectively. The poor showing was not due to government interference with the three parties' electoral results. On the contrary the Liberal Party and the Neo-Wafd had followed the lead of the Tagammu's and had shifted their stand to complement rather than challenge the government's position. The government in turn had accommodated their electoral participation. Indeed, it has been noted that in some constituencies with prominent members from these parties, the NDP nominated minor, ineffective candidates. A "low-key" candidate, for example, was nominated by the NDP to compete against Yasin Serag al-Din, brother of the Neo-Wafd's Chairman, in the Cairo constituency of Qasr al-Nil.[72] Serag al-Din won the election and judging from his post-election comment that his success was "the best evidence of democracy and freedom",[73] it appears that he had decided to enter the regime's clientelist structure in return for electoral gain.

In general, however, cooperation with the authorities does not suggest that electoral competition was equal and fair. After all, the disparity between opposition and government resources remained evident, as did electoral malpractice. But as will be examined in Chapter 4, electoral malpractice was primarily the personal concern of individual candidates.

Implications for the remaining opposition

Conversely, it appears that those parties that did not adjust their roles and expectations to fit into the existing system found little freedom to participate in the 1995 elections. These included the Muslim Brotherhood, the Labour Party and the Nasserite Party. Their unwillingness to compromise their position and aspirations is evident in the manner in which they attempted to undermine the government during the electoral campaign, with the most provocative platform being that adopted by the Nasserite Party.

Given that the current regime originates from the 1952 Revolution, the Nasserites' electoral campaign has focused on trying to erode the regime's legitimacy by promoting the Nasserites as the real guardians of Nasser's ideology. The prominent electoral posters plastered around the constituencies appeared with a large photograph of Nasser beside a lengthy quotation from one of his speeches in which he warned the nation to be wary of "impostors" and "deceivers", and to protect the achievements of the Revolution: "The nation is yours. The fields are yours. The factories belong to the citizens. The national economy is your home and shelter . . . be careful not to lose it . . . be careful . . . be careful . . . be careful." The poster's message appeared intent on portraying the current regime's economic reforms and privatisation plans as incompatible with the socialist policies of Nasser, and subsequently suggesting that the Nasserite Party, not the regime, was the true guardian of Nasser's revolutionary accomplishments. As Gaber 'Abd al-'Aziz, a Nasserite electoral candidate, declared to a group of working-class voters in Cairo's Mohandesin area:

> Nasser is not dead. We are here fighting to keep his ideology alive. [The government] is causing the public sector to disintegrate. Graduates from 1984 onwards are unemployed . . . the pashas' sons get the jobs and the gap between the rich and poor is widening . . . Capitalism is not for us, it is for Europe, it is for America but it is not for us . . . America wants to eliminate the Arabs. Nasser knew this; he was not fooled by them![74]

Moreover, while the Neo-Wafd and the Liberals were refraining from allying with the Islamists in an attempt to appease the government, the Nasserites had another conception. "The general feeling in the Party at the moment," declared 'Abd al-Halim Qandil, a senior member of the Nasserite Party, "is not only that there should be much more solidarity with the Islamists, but that the Muslim Brotherhood should be allowed to operate as a political party . . . The Islamists can organise and gather people. We cannot. But after they have gathered, they will ask 'where now?' . . . They need us as we need them."[75]

The Nasserite Party was not only questioning the legitimacy of the regime in its electoral campaign but was also willing to contemplate an alliance with the Muslim Brotherhood. Under the leadership of Dhiya' al-Din Dawud, the Party applied for a formal licence in 1988, which was predictably rejected by the government-controlled party licence committee. Interestingly, Dhiya' al-Din Dawud and two other members of his yet-to-be formalised Party entered the elections of 1990 as independents, and won. Presumably, the government considered that the Nasserites were following the example of their fellow opponents, the

Tagammu', and thus left them to participate unhindered. Indeed, in 1991 the government did not contest a court ruling granting the Nasserites formal party status. The Nasserites on the other hand, did not see themselves as the government's loyal opposition – and decided to take an overtly anti-government stand in 1995. The fact that the party won only one seat in the 1995 elections shows what consequences there are for a party straying from the regime's conception of what is an acceptable opposition.

The Muslim Brotherhood and the Labour Party
The Labour Party and the Muslim Brotherhood seem to have met with more or less similar consequences for apparently the same reasons. Since the informal alliance between them continued and could thus be regarded as a more powerful challenge to the regime than the newly formed Nasserite Party, efforts to prevent fruitful participation in the elections were more evident.

One of the most conspicuous strategies employed by the government was the arrest of 83 prominent members of the Muslim Brotherhood on the grounds of initiating "illegal activities".[76] This move was apparently intended to prevent the Islamic organisation from nominating its leading candidates in the forthcoming elections. One of the detainees was 'Esam al-'Eryan, one of my first Brotherhood contacts and Secretary-General of the Doctors' Association. During an interview conducted by the author in the previous year, it had been made clear why the Brotherhood gave the government cause for concern. Al-'Eryan stressed that the reason the Muslim Brotherhood participated in legislative elections was to compete for power and that it would continue to do so regardless of the obstacles the government might place in its way. "If we are allowed to gain power through elections, we will be willing to also lose power through elections. However, if we gain power through other means, then of course we will not leave through elections," he said.[77]

The Muslim Brothers' potential for winning in competitive elections is extremely high according to Hala Mustafa, a specialist on the organisation.[78] While the government had hoped to co-opt them by allowing them to compete in previous elections, they had stood their ground with the result that the government now felt it "was not getting anything in return", according to Hala Mustafa.[79] Arrests and military trials ensued and on 22 November the military court ordered the immediate closure of the Brotherhood's official headquarters located in Cairo.[80]

Moreover, while the government attempted to accommodate some opposition figures, such as the Neo-Wafd's Yasin Serag al-Din, it manifestly made difficulties for Muslim Brotherhood members who did manage to compete in the elections. Such was the case with Ma'mun al-Hudhaybi, the Brotherhood's official spokesman, who was competing in the Cairo constituency of Doqqi. (He competed in elections for the first time in 1987 and thus came to represent Doqqi in the Assembly between 1987 to 1990.) Apart from the fact that al-Hudhaybi depended upon the support of his organisation, he also found support in Doqqi because of his family's deep roots in the area. It is said that the Hudhaybi family owns a large part of Ibn al-Walid Square, a renowned area in Doqqi. The locals presumably regarded him as one of them.

When al-Hudhaybi and most of the other opposition members boycotted the elections in 1990, al-Hudhaybi's seat was taken by Amal 'Othman, Egypt's long-standing Minister of Social Affairs. Yet, as al-Hudhaybi returned in 1995 to re-contest his seat, it seems that 'Othman wanted to be transferred to an easier seat in Khanka, Cairo. It was apparently Kamal al-Shazli, the NDP's electoral coordinator, who insisted that 'Othman remained because with a minister competing for the seat, with the resources of the ministry at her disposal, al-Hudhaybi would have little chance of re-election.[81]

Before the elections the Labour Party is said to have been targeted by the government in a similar manner. This, however, was surprising in view of the claim that the government had "warned" the Labour Party of the potential consequences of allying itself with the Muslim Brotherhood in the then forthcoming elections.[82] Not heeding such a warning the Labour Party indicated in its organ that the decision to participate in the elections was not an alliance decision only but also one based on a view guaranteed to provoke the government:

> The Muslim Brotherhood and the Labour Party are aware of the nation's support for them and it is therefore the duty of the alliance to change its strategy and participate in the forthcoming elections.[83]

The government did attempt to detain several senior party leaders, although not to the same extent as it did those of the Brotherhood.

Magdi Husayn, the editor-in-chief of the Party's organ, *al-Sha'b*, was charged in October 1995 with having published an article that accused a minister's son of impropriety. It seems that Husayn approved an article in January 1995 alleging that an unnamed son of an unnamed minister dined at a five-star hotel with friends and subsequently refused to pay the bill. When the manager approached the young man in question, he was allegedly beaten up.[84] When the charges were brought to court, it emerged that the young man was the son of Hasan al-Alfi, the then Minister of Interior. The decision to sue Husayn during the electoral period put intense pressure on the newspaper editor to abstain from competing in the elections.

Magdi Husayn's uncle, the Secretary-General of the Labour Party, also found himself in a similar situation in early 1995. Returning from a trip to Turkey, Adel Husayn was arrested at Cairo airport. It was alleged that he left on his plane seat handwritten anti-government papers, which the authorities argued constituted evidence of the anti-government propaganda he had distributed abroad. The absurdity of the charge and the Journalist Syndicate's extensive coverage of the case forced the government to back down and release Adel Husayn without charge at the end of January 1995.[85] Thus, as the government was unable to prevent Adel Husayn from participating in the elections, he proceeded to contest the *fe'at* seat in the constituency of Madinat Nasr, Cairo.

Of particular interest are the apparent efforts of the government to prevent Adel Husayn from winning. Just as it placed a minister opposite the Muslim Brotherhood's candidate, Ma'mun al-Hudhaybi, an NDP candidate, 'Abd al-Mon'im 'Imara, Chairman of the Higher Council for Youth and Sport, was positioned to compete against Adel Husayn. In a yet more blatant move to gain advantage 'Imara, using his position of authority, was allowed to register 15,000 non-resident young adults on the voting register of the constituency. Arguing that 15,000 voters "are not enough to ensure success in a constituency of 64,000 registered voters", 'Imara publicly added: "I had promised to revive young people's interest in civic action . . . Why should I deprive them of the opportunity of electing members to the People's Assembly? This is not an accusation. If I had found half a million young people to participate in electing their representative, I would have done so."[86]

Evidently, the government approved this logic, because it did nothing to prevent 'Imara's manipulation of power. This was left to the

Labour Party, which filed a lawsuit contesting 'Imara's nomination. The administrative court did not rule against 'Imara's nomination, but it did rule that the registration list of non-residents was illegal.[87] In the event, 'Imara won the seat. It is interesting to note here that while the President removed Muhammad Mahgub, the Minister of Religious Endowments, from the ministry after he collaborated in the elections with a Muslim Brotherhood member, 'Imara was not officially reprimanded by the President for what was evidently a serious abuse of power.

No doubt, elections in Mubarak's Egypt are utilised to recruit into the regime's clientelist system of control political parties other than the President's own "ruling" party. The point, however, is that multi-party elections can only perform such a role if the government can ensure that opposition parties are constrained to the extent that they become, like the President's party, dependent upon the government and its patronage. In such circumstances, they are compelled to accept the political status quo and hence to acknowledge that participation in elections is not to compete for power but to gain access to a share of the resources controlled by the centre. To a large degree, this concept appears to have emerged, albeit gradually, among the opposition.

However, if the government cannot use elections for such an advantageous mechanism of recruitment, then it seems that there is little point in allowing opponents space in the electoral arena. The Muslim Brotherhood and the Islamic-oriented Labour Party, for example, have not appeared willing to be pressurised into joining the government's clientelist chain. This, from the government's perspective, would have two disadvantageous implications. First, it means that the government is unable to use elections to persuade them to accept the existing political system. This, in turn, means that the participation of these opponents in elections provides them with the opportunity perhaps to recruit more followers – followers who, like their leaders, are unlikely to enter the clientelist chain linking the centre to the periphery. This constitutes a potentially serious threat to the regime.

It is, therefore, not suprising that the government eventually conceded, by the time of the 1995 elections, that it was not in its interest for these opponents to participate in elections. Both the Minister of Interior (Hasan al-Alfi) and the Minister of Information, (Safwat al-Sharif) publicly declared: "There will be no room [in the 1995 elections] for political groups who use religion as their platform."[88] This position was later reinforced by President Mubarak during a television interview. He said:

> Dialogue with the Islamists is no longer an option. The late President Sadat tried this and he got nowhere so he got rid of three-quarters of them. We have tried dialogue with them but as soon as they started to get strong they no longer wanted dialogue so I took the decision in 1993 to have no more of that.[89]

The importance of elections is, of course, not simply to recruit politicians into the regime's clientelist system of control but also to mobilise the followers who support them. In Chapter 4 an examination of the role of voters is presented, in particular the way in which non-competitive multi-party elections encourage an individualistic (rather than group-oriented) approach to political participation, one that lends itself best to government control.

NOTES

1 *Al-Ahram Weekly*, 12–18 October 1995.
2 R.A. Hinnebusch (1981), p. 161.
3 Information derived from interviews conducted by the author with NDP members in 1994–5 in Cairo, and from *Al-Ahram Weekly*, 12–18 October 1995.
4 The term "parasitic bourgeoisie" is used by Springborg to describe a wide range of individuals whose common ground is that they profit "principally through the subversion of the state and the conversion of its resources into private wealth" (R. Springborg, 1989), p. 81. As a group, they emerged most prominently after Sadat introduced his economic "open-door policy" (*infitah*).
5 Donations quoted from *Al-Ahram Weekly*, 12–18 October 1995.
6 BBC SWB, 15 October 1981/ME/6854/A/18.
7 *Al-Sha'b*, 18 May 1981; *Al-Ahram*, 22 May 1981.
8 R.A. Hinnebusch, 1988, p. 44.
9 Recorded at the NDP gathering for industrial workers, held at the Helwan Youth Club, 25 November 1995, Cairo.
10 Recorded at the NDP gathering for industrial workers, held at the Helwan Youth Club, 25 November 1995, Cairo.
11 Recorded at the Electoral gathering for NDP candidates, Dr Hamdi al-Sayyed and Muhammad Ragab, held at Markaz al-Sha'b, Hickstep, Nozha, 18 November 1995, Cairo.
12 Interview by the author with Muhammad al-Sayyed, 26 November 1995, Cairo.
13 Interview by the author with Wahid 'Abd al-Magid, 29 December 1994, Cairo.
14 Interview given to *Al-Ahram Weekly*, 12–18 October 1995.
15 Ibid.
16 Interview by the author with Hamdi al-Sayyed, 1 January 1995.
17 The name of the deputy has been changed here to protect his identity. The material for this example is based on interviews conducted by the author with al-Sharqawi and his brother during visits to the People's Assembly on Cairo, 3 and 4 January 1995.
18 For the purposes of this study middle-range landowners are those whose overall agricultural landholding is between 20 and 100 feddans.
19 Apart from minor crimes such as household or livestock theft, Egyptian peasants may find themselves in police custody for offences, such as fights over water distribution rights on agricultural land which result in injuries.
20 Interview by the author with Ahmad al-Sharqawi, 3 January 1995, Cairo.
21 Interview by the author with Ahmad al-Sharqawi, 3 January 1995, Cairo.
22 Information on Kamel's history is derived from an extensive profile by James Exelby entitled "Independent Delta Force" and published in *Middle East Times Egypt*, 10–16 December 1995.
23 *Zakat* constitutes one of the five pillars of Islam. It is based on the principle that Muslims should donate at least 1 per cent of their annual income to the poor.
24 Cited in James Exelby, "Independent Delta Force" in *Middle East Times Egypt*, 10–16 December 1995, p. 14.

25 Information derived from interviews by the author with various political activists, December 1994, January 1995 and November 1995.

26 Interview by the author with Hamdi al-Sayyed, 27 December 1994, Cairo.

27 Information derived from personal observation by the author at al-Sayyed's constituency office, January 1995, Cairo.

28 Interview by the author with Hamdi al-Sayyed, 27 January 1997.

29 Information derived from interviews by the author with various political activists during the 1995 electoral campaign.

30 Interview by the author with Hamdi al-Sayyed, 27 December 1994.

31 Even the Muslim Brotherhood, as will be illustrated in the following chapter, depends more on other issues than on its religious ideology to attract electoral support.

32 Interview by the author with 'Abd al-'Aziz Zayyan, 8 January 1995, Cairo.

33 Interview by the author with a senior member of the Tagammu' Party, 15 January 1996, Cairo.

34 See *Legislative Elections in Egypt: Rights and Guarantees* (the Centre for Human Rights Legal Aid, Cairo, October 1995). See also R. Springborg (1989), pp. 160–1.

35 *Middle East Contemporary Survey*, vol. VIII (1983–4), p. 357.

36 *Al-Sha'b*, 26 December 1983.

37 According to several sources within the Tagammu', the 8 per cent barrier prevented Mohyi al-Din's entry to the Assembly for the party managed to acquire only 4 per cent of the national vote.

38 *Al-Sha'b*, 26 December 1983.

39 *Al-Wafd*, 19 April 1984.

40 *Al-Wafd*, 24 April 1984.

41 It should be noted that under different circumstances (i.e. the return to the more opposition-friendly individual candidacy electoral system) the President resorted to a "penal code amendment". This vaguely worded law (implemented in May 1995) provides the government with a virtual *carte blanche* to prosecute journalists for defamation or for spreading "false information". Penalties include heavy fines and up to five years' imprisonment. See Chapter 2.

42 Interview by the author with a senior member of the opposition, 27 December 1995.

43 An indication that the Labour Party's acceptance of appointed places in the 1984 Assembly did not suggest its co-option into the President's clientelist system of control is given in its decision to form an electoral alliance with the Muslim Brotherhood during the premature elections of 1987.

44 See "The Constitutional and Legal Framework for Legislative Elections in Egypt" in *Legislative Elections in Egypt: Rights and Guarantees* (the Centre for Human Rights Legal Aid, Cairo, October 1995).

45 *Middle East Contemporary Survey*, vol. XI (1987), p. 328.

46 The law also abolished the 30 seats allocated for women in the 1983 law. See *Legislative Elections in Egypt: Rights and Guarantees* (the Centre for Human Rights Legal Aid, Cairo, October 1995) and *Legislature in Egypt* (State Information Service, Cairo).

47 *Al-Masa*, 7 April 1987, cited in *Middle East Contemporary Survey*, vol. XI (1987), p. 329.

48 *Al-Wafd*, 7 April 1987, cited in *Middle East Contemporary Survey*, vol. XI (1987), p. 329.

49 *Legislative Elections in Egypt: Rights and Guarantees* (the Centre for Human Rights Legal Aid, Cairo, October 1995), p. 4.

50 Mubarak address marking the start of his third term as President (BBC MSME, 310140275/96E982/931014, 14 October 1993).

51 A few days before his dismissal, the Minister was invited to give a speech at the University of Banha. During the speech he unleashed a stream of abuse against senior officials and public figures, including fellow ministers, resulting in an uproar as lawyers and university staff threatened to strike. See *al-Sha'b*, 9 January 1990.

52 Interview by the author with a senior Tagammu' member, 17 December 1994.

53 Interviews by the author with senior Tagammu' members, 17 December 1994, 28 December 1994, 4 January and 8 January 1995.

54 Information derived from interviews by the author with senior members of various political activists, January 1995, Cairo.

55 Mubarak's comment on the 1990 elections. See *Egypt: A Decade of Peace, Development and Democracy, 1981–1991* (State Information Service, Cairo, July 1991), p. 10.

56 Interview by the author with a senior Tagammu' Party member, 16 December 1995, Cairo.

57 Interview with Dr Rif'at Sa'id, 8 January 1995, Cairo.

58 Interview by the author with 'Ali Salama, 8 January 1995, Cairo.

59 Interview by the author with Dr Rif'at Sa'id, 8 January 1995, Cairo.

60 *Al-Wafd*, 13 July 1995.

61 *Al-Sha'b*, 29 September 1995.

62 President's address to parliament, BBC MS, BBC ME, 15 November 1994: 411150292-AM3368 941116.

63 Formal press release, Tagammu' Party, 14 October 1995.

64 Interview in *Al-Ahram Weekly*, 19–25 October 1995.

65 *Al-Ahali*, 4 October 1995.

66 Ibid.

67 Interview by the author with Ma'mun al-Hudhaybi, 11 November 1995, Cairo.

68 Interview by the author with Ma'mun al-Hudhaybi, 11 November 1995, Cairo.

69 *Al-Ahram Weekly*, 12–18 October 1995.

70 The Ministry of Religious Endowments is responsible for the distribution of property and money bequeathed (voluntarily and usually in a will) by individuals to the state for the purpose of assisting the poor and underprivileged. When an individual leaves no will, and relatives cannot be traced upon his death, the Ministry is automatically entitled to his estate. Bakri's accusations were that Mahgub distributed the Ministry's spoils to his relatives and friends rather than to the poor. In particular, he claimed that he held documentation proving that Mahgub acquired for one of his two wives an apartment overlooking the Nile worth an estimated £E1,000,000 that was in fact the Ministry's property.

71 Information obtained during the author's attendance at the 'Arab Rashed rally, 16 November 1995, Helwan, Egypt.

72 *Al-Ahram Weekly*, 9–15 November 1995.

73 The *Egyptian Gazette*, 8 December 1995.

74 Information obtained during the author's attendance at the gathering on 12 November 1995 in Cairo. Bakri also mentioned that he actually had regular contact with Hasan al-Alfi, the then Minister of Interior.

75 *Middle East Times Egypt*, 10–16 December 1995.

76 Interview by the author with Ma'mun al-Hudaybi, 11 November 1995, Cairo. See also "New Blow to Muslim Brotherhood", *Al-Ahram Weekly*, 12–18 October 1995.

77 Interview by the author with 'Esam al-'Eryan, 13 December 1994, Cairo. On 23 November 1995 the military court passed verdict on 54 of the detained Muslim Brotherhood members. Most were sentenced to three years' imprisonment with hard labour. Al-'Eryan was sentenced to five years' imprisonment with hard labour. See *Middle East Times Egypt*, 3–9 December 1995.

78 Interview by the author with Hala Mustafa, 21 December 1994.

79 Interview by the author with Hala Mustafa, 21 December 1994.

80 See *Middle East Times Egypt*, 10–16 December 1995.

81 Interview with a senior member of the Muslim Brotherhood, 11 November 1995, Cairo. As a further effort to ensure that his campaign did not run smoothly, the security services constantly monitored him. For example, during the same interview he mentioned that the previous day the Ministry of Interior had dispatched five fully packed police vans to the mosque where he was performing Friday prayers to ensure that he did nothing other than pray.

82 *Al-Ahali*, 4 October 1995.

83 *Al-Sha'b*, 29 October 1995.

84 Information obtained from various sources, including an interview by the author with Magdi Husayn, 12 November 1995, Cairo.

85 Information obtained from various sources, including an interview by the author with Adel Husayn, 13 November 1995, Cairo.

86 *Al-Ahram Weekly*, 9–15 November 1995.

87 *Al-Ahram Weekly*, 30 November–6 December 1995.

88 *Middle East Times Egypt*, 10–16 December 1995.

89 Mubarak interview, Egyptian Satellite Channel, 23 November 1997.

4

Voter Recruitment

One of the most prominent features of Egypt's multi-party electoral arena is the inclination of contestants to adopt campaign strategies that are predominantly personalistic in nature. While the relaxation of emergency laws during the one-month campaign period before elections formally offers political parties the opportunity to promote their links with the masses, party-nominated contestants appear to use this period to concentrate more on cultivating their own personal networks of electoral alliances.

The adoption of such personally oriented strategy hinders party development and hence group cohesion. In turn, multi-party participation is even less likely to constitute a threat to the prevailing system of rule because such forms of electoral participation do little to encourage the recruitment of party supporters at the grass-roots level – a necessary development if links between political parties and the masses are to expand. Instead, it reinforces the structure of political parties as controllable entities comprising conglomerates of personalities each of whom has his own personal followers. Second, and perhaps more important, the function of elections in defining the role of politicians officially representing disparate political views as intermediaries between the central authority and their respective localities appears also to be reinforced. This is because the personal assurances of support sought by electoral candidates are largely conditional upon the downward flow of patronage, most of which can realistically be channelled only from the centre. So, if a candidate is to expand his network of supporters and thereby increase his chances of success he needs to forge links with the government on which he ultimately becomes dependent. This preoccupation is bound to take precedence over party programme or ideology.

Logically, the adoption of personalistic methods of voter recruitment by party candidates is advantageous to the regime because it reaffirms the clientelist function of elections as articulated from above. Yet, in order to understand why electoral participation at the lowest tier of the clientelist structure corresponds, in general, to government's expectations, it is necessary to examine the reasons why party candidates resort to such tactics in the first place.

During the elections, NDP candidates enjoy one particular privilege unavailable to their rivals. At formal events – of which there are many – senior government officials attend as guest speakers to demonstrate their support for the NDP candidates and government employees are "encouraged" to participate as sympathetic members of the public. However, on further examination such a privilege is not as beneficial as might appear in terms of strengthening and expanding the party or the candidates' bases of support.

As for election campaigns by opposition candidates, it will be shown how government-imposed constraints prevent these candidates from organising large events on the scale of those of their NDP rivals. However, it will also be pointed out that a less obvious impediment is generally faced by opposition candidates: like their NDP rivals, they too lack support from their own parties during these campaigns. It will be argued that this is the underlying factor which leads candidates to adopt individualistic campaign strategies independent of the parties they officially represent. Such strategies, in turn, make it less difficult for the government to utilise multi-party elections as a clientelist mechanism of co-option and control.

In contrast, one of the main reasons why the Muslim Brotherhood poses a threat to the regime is that its candidates enjoy the support and assistance of their organisation. For them, electoral campaigns are opportunities for the recruitment of supporters rather than for the construction of personal networks of alliances. Thus this type of electoral participation contributes to the expansion and strengthening of group cohesion, a development that makes it difficult for the regime to use elections to pressurise the Brotherhood, and arguably those who ally themselves with it, into co-option and hence control.

Formal electoral participation: NDP candidates

As the President's party, the NDP constitutes the sole Party whose candidates have direct access to state resources. NDP candidates, therefore, are in a prime position to organise unhindered public gatherings in state-owned properties such as schools and youth clubs. As if to emphasise their prestigious connections and show that they are supported by the government, NDP candidates also have access to senior state and government personnel who attend such campaign gatherings as guest speakers. For example, in a joint gathering held by NDP candidates Hamdi al-Sayyed and Muhammad Ragab in Hickstep, Heliopolis (near Cairo), the contestants were provided not only with a newly built hall, spacious enough to hold a seated audience of about three hundred, but also with an impressive selection of prominent guest speakers. The latter included: General Muhammad Wagih, the administrative manager of the local military productions' factory; General Muhammad 'Afifi, head of security at the same factory; 'Aziz Fathallah, local treasurer of the NDP; General Karam Torraya, presidentially appointed Head of Heliopolis, and General Ahmad al-Gawahirgi, the deputy governor of Cairo.

The NDP-backed gathering attracted a big crowd that filled all the seats in the hall and all standing room, even spilling over onto the pavement outside. Judging from the atmosphere among the audience, however, the extensive turnout was less a demonstration of electoral support than the result of a need to communicate with those in authority. This was indicated, for example, when members of the audience publicly questioned the speakers on matters relating to the local community, such as the inadequate supply of water and electricity in the residential areas.

It was also clear from the large crowd that gathered around the speakers' platform that at least one hundred members of the audience had come specifically to present personal petitions to individual officials and that the majority of the audience was present mainly to question and petition the state officials on communal and personal matters rather than to listen to electoral propaganda. This led the Deputy Governor to protest angrily: "Don't expect to throw a thousand problems in my face and expect me to solve them all tomorrow!"[1]

As the community in Hickstep is newly established and relatively isolated, one can argue that it is perhaps not too surprising that the inhabitants should use NDP electoral events to communicate their personal concerns to the authorities. However, the presence of senior state and government officials at electoral events seems to attract an audience primarily for this reason even in the most well-established communities such as the one in Helwan (near Cairo), Egypt's largest industrial area where a major NDP electoral event was used in a similar way as did the community of Hickstep.

Formal NDP event at Helwan Youth Club[2]

This event was arranged for the four NDP contestants nominated for Helwan's two electoral constituencies (electoral constituencies 24 and 25). As it was an NDP event, the candidates were provided with exclusive access to the pleasant, state-owned, Helwan Youth Club. The four candidates representing the two constituencies were, in the *fe'at* category, the Minister of War Productions, Muhammad al-Ghamrawi and the Minister of Religious Endowments, Muhammad Mahgub, and, in the *'omal* category, Mustafa Mungi and Muhammad Mustafa. The guest speakers supporting these four candidates included senior government and state officials such as Mohyi al-Din 'Abd al-Latif, treasurer of the Cairo branch of the NDP, Dr 'Atef 'Obayd, the Minister of Public Enterprise, and the Governor of Cairo, General 'Omar 'Abd al-Akhar.

As at the Hickstep event, the stage where the guest speakers were seated was surrounded with people attempting to pass written petitions to the official guests. The crowd, which comprised no less than one hundred people, not only blocked the view of the front-seat audience, but also delayed the start of the electoral propaganda speeches by an hour despite efforts by security officers and members of the NDP Women's Group to collect the petitions and promising to pass them on to the relevant official. One petitioner was a worker who had been employed in a military factory for the previous fifteen years. On discovering that the Minister of War Productions would be campaigning that day, the worker decided to come and present a petition to the Minister requesting the Minister to find a job for his well-qualified, unemployed son at the same factory where he worked.[3]

In addition to individual requests, members of the audience brought up communal concerns that were not directly linked to the issue of the elections. One example was the opening hours of the local (subsidised) bakeries. These had begun a curious policy of closing at two o'clock in the afternoon, with the result that the workers were unable to buy their bread on the way home from work. Thus the formal gathering in the Helwan Youth Club was regarded by the workers as an opportunity to air their concerns before those in authority. As it turned out, the Minister of Religious Endowments promised the audience that the bakery problem "would be solved by tomorrow" and this was echoed by the Minister of Public Enterprise.

The public communication and interaction already illustrated might suggest that the privileges conferred upon NDP candidates during electoral campaigns would allow the Party to expand and strengthen its links with the masses. This, however, is not the case because the written petitions submitted to candidates and senior officials during electoral campaigns are not taken seriously. Such petitions are predominantly straightforward applications for jobs or transfers, or are simple requests that high-ranking figures cannot be bothered with.

Most of these petitions are thrown away without even being read. During the NDP gathering at the Helwan Youth Club, one member of the NDP Women's Group confided to me that the petitions which she and her colleagues helped to gather on behalf of the attending senior officials were to be discarded as soon as the event was over. When asked if they would be in trouble with their superiors for discarding the applications in their possession, she laughed, as did a colleague sitting next to her. In fact, the middle-aged bureaucrat proclaimed that this was part of their duties at such events. She said:

> Do you think we all come to these events by choice? There is no choice. We came because the organisers needed the front rows occupied so that there is a buffer between the workers and the Ministers . . . We are also here to help collect the petitions because there is always a lot of them at these election events. After we collect them we throw them away . . . We don't like doing that, but this is how it works.[4]

Securing an audience

There are two ways of luring an audience: either through pressure at the workplace or through financial inducement. In the first instance, senior public sector managers are "invited" to attend and support NDP candidates at electoral gatherings held in their respective localities. In turn, the managers expect the middle-level bureaucrats to show their support by attending. Most turn up not out of interest or choice but out of fear that their absence might be noticed by their colleagues and superiors.

An electoral event held by one NDP candidate before the 1995 elections illustrates some of the features of this situation.[5] The event took place in Hada'iq al-Qobba, the constituency that Muhammad al-Sayyed has been representing in the People's Assembly since 1990. The event was to take place in two places. At seven o'clock in the evening, al-Sayyed, an ex-football player and a local figure in the constituency, arrived at the building of Gam'eyyat Tanmeyat al-Mogtama', a state-owned and state-run institution intended to provide the local inhabitants with advice and guidance on social-service-related matters. The plan was that al-Sayyed would give a speech to the local women before moving on to the other location.

Inside the large room sat some two hundred women of mixed social classes. In the front row, sat elegantly dressed women who seemed slightly out of place in a working-class area such as Hada'iq al-Qobba. In the row immediately behind them sat women who by their outward appearance seemed to fit the category of lower-level state bureaucrats. The majority of women sat in the back rows, and judging by their dress, the black *galabeyya* (long gown), they belonged to the lower classes, those holding little more than menial jobs, if any.

These women in black gowns seemed to be returning favours to the Gam'eyya staff whose assistance they regularly sought and who had "invited" them to attend. It also emerged that the front-row women comprised both the wives of senior bureaucrats who came on behalf of their husbands, and senior bureaucrats who came in their formal capacity of representatives of the NDP Women's Group. The women located in the middle rows were indeed state employees representing both the local knitwear factory and the Gam'eyya where the event was taking place. One woman administrator at the factory said she attended the gathering because, like her colleagues, she was asked to do so by a senior manager.

> We were told that the General Manager of our factory would be a guest speaker today. We had the choice of coming here, to the women-only gathering, or going to the event where the Manager would be speaking. I chose here because it starts first and I can go home early to the children. If they weren't here [pointing at the front row women], all of us from the factory would not have come . . . What is the point of coming if nobody sees us?[26]

Perhaps because of these reasons for attendance, the atmosphere at that gathering was rather formal and strained. Indeed, most of the women, excluding those in the front row, chanted slogans such as "*hanintikhib min?* Muhammad Sayyed! *wa habibkum min?* Muhammad Sayyed!" ("Who will we elect? Muhammad Sayyed! And who do you love? Muhammad Sayyed!"). That the gathering was only a superficial demonstration of support was evident from the bored expressions on the women's faces during the address. Moreover, the chanting at the end of the gathering lasted only a few minutes before the women abruptly quietened down and swiftly made their exit.

A similar atmosphere prevailed at the second location. Held in a *khaima* (marquee) located a few minutes' walk from the Gam'eyya, the gathering was more subdued. This was because the audience (around three hundred men and women who were predominantly administrative employees from the knitwear factory) did not appear so eager to chant slogans of support for the candidate. In fact, the audience appeared very bored as it unenthusiastically acknowledged each speaker with weak applause at the start of an address.

The audience's lack of interest showed quite clearly when most of its members got up to leave before the last speaker took the microphone. (The unfortunate speaker was left with less than 50 people to address). They continued to filter out even after realising that there was a final speaker presumably because their General Manager and his entourage had slipped away and also because they had not recognised the final guest speaker, and had assumed (rightly) that he was not a senior official and therefore had no power over them.[7]

That the manual workers at the knitwear factory were conspicuous by their absence at that gathering leads one to the second point regarding the nature of formal NDP election campaigns. In contrast with bureaucrats, manual workers are less inclined to attend such events even when they are instructed to do so by their superiors. The reason for this could be that such workers have less to lose in terms of career prospects; it could also be that senior state officials do not put much pressure on them to attend for fear of provoking tension or even riots. What is clear, however, is that workers do not just have a realistic grasp of the organisation of formal election campaigns for NDP candidates but also are less willing to act as a passive audience as do their higher-ranking colleagues in the public sector. As one worker asserted following one such gathering:

All these important speakers and outsiders[8] are all here because they have to attend. They must all show support to the Party, not out of choice, but because they are all at the service of the state. We [the local workers] came because we want to know when they will provide us with some basic services in this place![9]

The social and economic problems prevailing in both old and new working-class areas ensure that a proportion of the local workers do turn up at formal NDP meetings to question officials on communal matters or to present them with personal petitions. But as the majority of manual labourers are disinclined to attend such events as passive onlookers, it is not uncommon that they are given financial inducements to ensure their attendance. This was explained by a group of workers from one of Helwan's military factories. During the month authorised for electoral campaigning, a self-appointed spokesman of the group said:

We find empty coaches waiting outside the factory after work. The other factories in the area also get coaches after work. But we do not get them every day, just two or three times a week. When we see the coaches outside we know that the government needs us to cheer for its election candidates at some place or other . . . it's up to each person to either board the coach or go home, but usually no one minds going. Actually we like going because we know that as soon as we board the coach the driver will give us ten pounds each . . . Before he drives off, he tells us where we're going and who to cheer so that we are prepared.[10]

Observing these workers chant slogans of support, cheer and clap at that gathering, one would assume that this was a genuine expression of support for the candidates and their guest speakers. It was interesting, therefore, to discover that they were effectively rented for the occasion.

Thus, while such gatherings seem to be a privilege conferred on NDP-nominated contestants, it would be wrong to regard the audience turnout as an indication of either the extent of the contestant's popularity or the size of the NDP's base of support. Indeed, the vision of hundreds of people attending an NDP electoral campaign might appear impressive and perhaps unfair compared with the more modest formal events organised by opposition parties for their candidates. Yet, the attendance of large audiences does not necessarily provide NDP candidates with a significant advantage over their opposition counterparts.

Even the NDP candidates are aware of this predicament. Indicative of this is an observation made by Muhammad al-Sayyed, the NDP's candidate for Hada'iq al-Qobba. Through personal experience and knowledge of his constituency, he expected only a fraction of those attending his gatherings actually to vote on election day. According to him, out of approximately 80,000 eligible voters residing in the constituency no more than 20,000 are registered voters. "Even with about 20,000 voters, we [implying all the candidates competing in the constituency] will be very lucky if 11,000 turned up to vote."[11]

With regard to the public sector employees who attended his formal gatherings, he was aware that not all of them resided in the constituency and that in the case of those who were registered there, no one could "force them to vote".[12] The same view is held by potential voters. One Helwan factory worker, for example, argued:

> A lot of people might be brought in to attend all these government election events. But the government can't make you turn up to vote. If they do, how can they be sure you vote for their candidates? You can vote for whoever you want; they won't know who voted for whom.[13]

The inadequacy of formal NDP events in terms of voter recruitment is perhaps better illustrated through the sceptical comments of one factory worker following the Helwan Youth Club gathering. At that gathering, the Minister of Public Enterprises concluded his speech by telling the audience: "This year we will be giving a pay rise for all our workers in Helwan . . . it is in gratitude for all the hard work we have done."[14] The workers' response was: "Who is he trying to fool by saying this at election time? We are not getting a pay rise because they are charitable or good. We are getting it because we have not had one for over two years. So it is our due. That's the law – nothing more, nothing less!"[15]

Formal electoral participation: opposition candidates

The ineffectiveness of public campaigning in recruiting voters is a predicament that candidates representing opposition parties face even more. Campaign gatherings cannot formally take place under the state of emergency without the prior permission of the Ministry of Interior. Thus, if a candidate plans to hold a public gathering, he is formally required to submit an application to the local police station stating details – such as the date and location of the intended gathering. The application is then passed on to the Ministry of Interior, where a decision is made. While NDP candidates, for obvious reasons, do not encounter difficulties in gaining permits to hold gatherings, opposition candidates find the affairs less simple and straightforward.

The most obvious way in which the authorities limit the effectiveness of opposition gatherings is in the allocation of sites. In contrast with NDP candidates, opposition candidates are rarely allowed access to youth clubs, halls or other state-owned property. Instead, they are often allocated sites, which are little more than alley-ways in relatively inaccessible areas. An example of how the allocation of such a site might affect a candidate's campaign is the formal gathering authorised for the Neo-Wafd candidate, No'man Gom'a, during the 1995 elections.

A Neo-Wafd gathering

As a contestant for the *fe'at* seat in the electoral constituency of Imbaba, No'man Gom'a, the Neo-Wafd's Deputy Chairman, had applied for permission to hold 20 formal gatherings during the month authorised for electioneering. According to one of his personal campaign assistants, one of the main problems with this arrangement was that while the authorities might not deny them permission to hold any of the gatherings, it was routine procedure not to notify them of a formal decision until the day a gathering was intended to take place.[16] So the campaign assistants had only a few hours to find the designated location, hire and erect a *khaima*, arrange the installation of microphones, and notify supporters and local people of both the event and location in Hayy al-Munira al-Gharbeyya constituency.

The haste with which the event had been arranged was evident at the hired office that Gom'a was using as his campaign headquarters in Imbaba quarter. The event was to take place that very evening. To start with, none of the people present seemed to know the directions to the intended destination. After about half an hour of uncertainty and waiting, it was eventually decided that those with cars (Gom'a and a few of his friends and supporters) would follow the minibus, which was carrying some 20 campaign assistants and supporters out of the main roads in Imbaba and into a maze of small alley-ways.

It is perhaps an understatement to note that Hayy al-Munira al-Gharbeyya was difficult to reach. Not only did the entourage get lost in many dead-end alley-ways, but also the alley-ways were so narrow that on several occasions the minibus got stuck in them. After following this maze-like and arduous route, they arrived at the *khaima* over an hour later to find it crammed in a small alley-way directly next to another *khaima* in which a local wedding celebration was taking place.[17]

The loud music coming from the neighbouring wedding meant that it was impossible for Gom'a to deliver a speech to the small audience that had gathered to listen and enjoy his hospitality of free soft drinks. Exasperated by this predicament, Gom'a eventually decided to go and introduce himself to the bride and groom, congratulate them and present them with a *noqta*[18] in the hope that this would encourage them to turn the music down. The plan seemed to work as the music was abruptly switched off, allowing Gom'a to start his speech. However, he was aware that he had to be brief so that the celebration could be resumed in full blast. Consequently, with a mixture of frustration and irony he told his audience:

> It is a pleasure to be here among you all . . . I would first like to congratulate the bride and groom next door. It must be a sign of good luck for us to be so near a happy occasion like this. We should therefore thank the Minister of Interior and the police officers for they are the reason we are here today.[19]

Almost ten minutes later, the music next door started up again, compelling Gom'a to thank his audience once more before making an exit with his assistants in tow. It was impossible, given the distractions, for Gom'a to continue any further. The fact that Gom'a was not given an opportunity to communicate at length with his audience meant that he was unable to express his views and so expand his base of support.

The obstacles Gom'a and his assistants experienced and the efforts they had to make, as well as the financial costs (which included hiring the minibus, the *khaima* and the microphone system, and also the purchase of a large quantity of soft drinks and donation of a *noqta* to the bride and groom) were out of all proportion to the result, which was little more than a tense fifteen-minute address to an audience of less than 50 people.

It should be noted, that for opposition candidates the gaining of formal permission to hold electoral gatherings largely depends on the relationship between the government and the party which the candidate represents. Hence, in the case of Gom'a, one can say that, although there were obstacles, he was not actually refused permission to hold gatherings – presumably because his party, the Neo-Wafd, had conceded that participation in elections was not to gain power but to "buy some space in the political landscape".[20]

Constraints on public interaction

In the case of opposition parties that do not particularly share the Neo-Wafd view (such as the Muslim Brotherhood, the Labour Party and the newly established Nasserite Party) the permission to hold formal election gatherings seems automatically to be denied. According to Muhammad Mahdi 'Akif, the Muslim Brotherhood's 1995 nominee for the electoral constituency of Hada'iq al-Qobba, the constituency's chief of police (al-ma'mur), had warned him at the start of the campaigning period that because of the prevailing state of emergency, he had been given specific "orders from the presidential office to prevent any candidate from holding election gatherings".[21] Obviously the implementation of these "orders" was selective. Otherwise it would be difficult to explain how, in the very same constituency, the NDP's Muhammad al-Sayyed held public electoral gatherings such as those noted earlier in the chapter.

In the electoral constituency of Doqqi, another Brotherhood candidate, Ma'mun al-Hudhaybi, encountered similar constraints. When I first interviewed him at what was then the official Muslim Brotherhood headquarters in central Cairo, he mentioned that only the previous day he and "a few young Brothers" came out of a Doqqi mosque following Friday Prayers to find five vans full of policemen parked outside. Explaining the reason for this conspicuous police presence, he said:

> Of course [the authorities] knew we must attend Friday Prayers. But they were worried because we are not allowed to hold election gatherings. They thought that we will use the mosque to hold a gathering with the congregation after the prayers . . . it was totally unnecessary to deploy five police vans but they wanted to make sure everyone dispersed immediately after the prayers . . . the message was very clear.[22]

Deploying police officers outside mosques was not aimed only at preventing Muslim Brotherhood contestants from holding unauthorised gatherings, but also at constraining contestants representing the party closely linked to the Muslim Brotherhood, the Labour Party. In the first week of November 1995, for example, 'Adel Husayn, a senior member of the Labour Party and its candidate for the electoral constituency of Madinat Nasr in Cairo, faced a similar predicament to al-Hudhaybi following Friday Prayers. In this particular case, the police decided to disperse the congregation swiftly by entering the mosque immediately after prayers – an action that resulted in a scuffle leading to six arrests. The Labour Party candidate and his assistants, it should be noted, had already become familiar with police tactics of this nature because they had previously experienced three similar incidents.

That the Labour Party and the Nasserite Party were not permitted to hold election gatherings was also reflected in the fact that, like the Muslim Brotherhood, their main method of making contact with the public at large was through personal walkabouts, coffee-house visits and the distribution of election material. The adoption of such methods, however, always carries the risk of arrest and prosecution since the prevailing state of emergency is not formally lifted during the one-month campaign period. It is simply that the government chooses to allow most contestants to ignore it. A simple illustration of this is that during the election period the streets in urban Egypt are covered with banners and posters advertising the various contestants who are competing in the respective areas.

The presence of such conspicuous material reflects the conscious decision of the authorities to ignore the publicity tactics of contestants. If the authorities chose to implement emergency measures during this period, however, it would be difficult for contestants to pursue this form of advertising because the handling or erecting of such material in public places would subject the individuals concerned to instant arrest. The point, therefore, is that despite the arrest of various assistants for putting up posters[23] (an activity that is a common procedure, does not involve personal contact with the public and is otherwise overlooked for other candidates) these contestants continue to take a considerable risk in participating in unauthorised personal communication with the public.

In view of the risk of arrest and perhaps in consequence of being forced to withdraw from electoral competition, the tactics of unauthorised personal walkabouts, coffee-house visits and the distribution of election propaganda cannot be regarded as efficient methods of voter recruitment. Contestants must remain constantly on the move to avoid being caught by the police. In turn, it is difficult for potential voters to become familiar with a candidate if he is simply "passing" through. The nature and inadequacy of these tactics are illustrated in the campaign efforts of the Labour Party candidate, 'Adel Husayn.

Shortcomings of unauthorised public interaction

From the start of the election campaign month in 1995, 'Adel Husayn, after having been denied permission to hold election gatherings, decided to use Monday and Friday evenings to walk around the constituency, meeting members of the general public. On Monday 13 November, I joined him on one such walkabouts. When I met him at his home at 6 p.m. he said that his first call was to be a mosque in Heliopolis where he would perform the early evening prayers.

After I had waited for about fifteen minutes in his car, Husayn emerged from the mosque accompanied by ten other men who turned out to be his designated guides and assistants. It later emerged that they comprised equal numbers of junior Labour Party members and junior Muslim Brotherhood members.[24]

The planned route, as it emerged, was to start near the College for Girls, continue to the Marwa Buildings' area and return to the College for Girls' area. During the three-and-a-half-hour journey, Husayn entered most of the local shops on the route, shaking hands with customers and shopkeepers while his assistants distributed leaflets. Probably because this was a predominantly upper-middle-class residential area, the atmosphere was rather subdued and the streets rather empty at that time. One of the most noticeable aspect of the walkabout was that most of the people encountered appeared to be taken by surprise. With the assistants distributing leaflets and Husayn shaking their hands as he reiterated the same words, "You must vote; use your votes against the thieves; you know what I mean; you know what is right and wrong", there was not enough time for them to gather their thoughts before the candidate and his entourage moved on.

At one point during this walkabout, Husayn and his assistants reached a coffee-shop whose owner was apparently known to them. The owner invited him to deliver a speech to his customers while he prepared some refreshments for the group. Husayn began to address the coffee-shop clients by urging them to "be united and vote on election day" so that "the polling station is kept busy and the [government] officials will not have time to fill out the empty forms". However, before he could continue, a young officer, apparently having just completed his work shift, entered the coffee-house, ordered a drink and sat in a discreet corner. Even though the coffee-shop owner assured Husayn that there would be no problems because the officer was a "local boy", Husayn abruptly ended his speech and decided it was best to move on. The remainder of the evening was spent, as it started, in a hasty tour.

As Husayn's walkabout illustrates, it is difficult for a contestant to interact effectively with potential voters when he has to be constantly vigilant of the authorities. This is best illustrated by the following example from the campaign of Muhammad Mahdi 'Akif who, as mentioned earlier, was the Muslim Brotherhood's nominee for the working-class district of Hada'iq al-Qobba in 1995.

Like Husayn, 'Akif and his assistants decided to pray at the local mosque before starting the walkabout.[25] At the approach to the mosque, there was one police officer in uniform and two in civilian clothes sitting outside drinking coffee. Acknowledging them on his departure from the mosque, 'Akif mentioned that the authorities had decided to have the mosque monitored daily because he seemed to them to be a regular visitor, and they did not want him to hold any electoral gatherings inside. To avoid trouble, he added, he had chosen to attend prayers regularly because if he stopped the police would get angry, look for him elsewhere and would never leave him alone.[26] 'Akif, therefore, appeared to view his daily attendance at that mosque as a sort of "sign-in", whereby the authorities would be reassured of his whereabouts and the fact that he was not campaigning inside.

The walkabout – which did not differ significantly from Husayn's except for the fact that the streets in Hada'iq al-Qobba were bustling with people – began once they reached a safe distance from the mosque and the police officers. 'Akif's encounters with members of the public comprised little more than handshakes and reminders that "Islam is the solution". At one particular stage, however, 'Akif entered a *makwagi*'s (clothes' ironer) workshop but before he could speak to any of the workers an aide appeared from what seemed like nowhere and told 'Akif they were being followed by police officers in civilian clothes. Within seconds, everyone dispersed, leaving a group of startled and perhaps even frightened ironers.

Fortunately for the group, the walkabout was resumed shortly afterwards because the crowded environment meant that they did not have too much trouble losing the policemen. Clearly, electoral walkabouts cannot be expected to make a significant impact on contestant–voter relations, especially when contestants have to be constantly looking over their shoulders.

Indeed, one can argue that the informal coalition between the Muslim Brotherhood and Labour Party since 1987, and their apparent refusal to accept the political status quo, renders them a sufficiently serious electoral challenge to the government for the latter to want to impose severe restrictions on their participation. This compels them to interact with the public through walkabouts and other forms of unauthorised campaigning. It is worth noting, however, that contestants representing opposition parties that are considered less challenging and possibly co-opted by the government, also appear inclined to adopt similar campaign strategies.

As previously shown in the example of No'man Gom'a, it is not uncommon for opposition contestants to be granted, at very short notice, formal authorisation to hold election gatherings at unsuitable locations. Such strategies on the part of the authorities discourage contestants from seeking formal permits. An even more discouraging strategy on the part of the authorities is to ignore completely a contestant's application. In the circumstances, the applicant is apt to cancel the planned event otherwise he would be inviting a police raid on the day.

But different candidates act in different ways. For example, Fatheyya al-'Assal of the Tagammu' who, during the 1995 elections, competed in the constituency of Imbaba, chose to abandon authorised electoral gatherings altogether and instead tried to interact with members of the public through walkabouts and informal speeches arranged at local coffee-houses. On the other hand, the editor-in-chief of *al-Ahrar* newspaper, Mustafa Bakri, focused much attention on speaking at organised gatherings which were largely unauthorised, but which attracted large audiences.[27]

Arguably, candidates such as those mentioned above did not appear to suffer dire consequences as a result of unauthorised electioneering because they represented parties that had accepted to cooperate with the government and had distanced themselves from the Muslim Brotherhood before and during the 1995 legislative elections. Nevertheless, the fact that certain candidates are not pursued by the police during unauthorised election activities does not necessarily imply that such activities are particularly advantageous in terms of voter recruitment.

Indeed, judging from personal observations throughout the 1995 election period, members of the public, especially those from urban working-class areas, generally appeared to show some interest when meeting and listening to what various opposition contestants had to say. But showing interest in the presence of a candidate and actually voting for that candidate in his absence are two different matters. Following one campaign gathering a member of the audience said:

> Every candidate promises to change the area if he gets elected . . . After work, we go home and eat and then go to the coffee-house to have a drink and chat with our friends. But during the elections we have a break from the normal routine . . . Sometimes we go and listen to an opposition candidate and sometimes they come to visit us at the coffee-house . . . Their views are sometimes very interesting. But even if we agree with the views of one contestant, this is not reason enough to vote for him. To vote for someone, you must know who he is so that if you need a favour you will know where to find him . . . it's silly to vote for a complete stranger because if he wins you will never see him again.[28]

These words bring us to arguably the most important point about the limitations of public campaigning whether authorised or unauthorised: activities of this nature are of little significance when contestants have insufficient support from their respective parties. Insufficient support includes an unassured party base in the constituency where a seat is being sought. While the need for such a base may appear obvious, it seems that it is not a foregone conclusion in Egypt's contemporary multi-party arena.

Party support systems

Party candidates, one would assume, should be in a more advantageous position than, for example, independent candidates, if only because of the material and organisational support one would expect them to secure from their parties during elections. Yet, in Egypt's multi-party arena the unrecognised Muslim Brotherhood is probably the only organisation which fits that assumption. The overall nature of Muhammad 'Akif's 1995 electoral campaign in Hada'iq al-Qobba provides an apt illustration of the type of support the Muslim Brotherhood extends to its candidates.

The Muslim Brotherhood

The constraints imposed by the authorities on Brotherhood contestants have led to the adoption of spontaneous and even futile forms of electioneering such as informal walkabouts. To compensate for this predicament the Muslim Brotherhood provides its candidates with a strong support system. In 1995 'Akif, for example, was provided with a well-appointed office in a well-presented apartment block in Hada'iq al-Qobba, the constituency in which he was competing. This office, which was spacious and contained modern equipment such as a telephone, a computer and a facsimile machine, was intended to be a base where 'Akif could discuss campaign strategies with other Brotherhood members as well as store election propaganda material.[29]

The reason for maintaining such an office during the electoral period was not to give potential voters a local site that they could easily identify and locate (which was not necessary because the presence of social projects such as the religious school, funded and run by the Muslim Brotherhood for the local people, provided the equivalent of a permanent base in the area) but to provide a base for 'Akif and the Brotherhood members specifically involved in his election campaign, who numbered at least one hundred.

These assistants were, before the start of the election campaign, personally unknown to 'Akif, and vice versa. So their participation in his campaign was not tied to any obligation or support for the candidate on a personal level but for the Muslim Brotherhood as a group entity. The intensity of support these assistants displayed for the organisation of which they are members is illustrated by the case of one assistant who, like the majority of his colleagues, was a local resident of Hada'iq al-Qobba. He suspended work on a Master's degree in engineering so that he could help with the campaign efforts of a contestant whom he did not know personally.

The role of this assistant, along with that of 79 other local Brotherhood members, focused primarily on door-to-door canvassing. As a registered candidate (formally an "independent"), 'Akif had been allowed access to police records of the names and addresses of the constituency's

80,000 adult residents. Being local residents themselves these assistants were familiar with the area and the people, and each were given a list of about 1,000 people to visit at home. The purpose of this was twofold. First, those on the electoral register were to be persuaded to vote for the Brotherhood on election day. Second, the residents who were not registered to vote (and, according to both 'Akif and the NDP's Muhammad al-Sayyed, these were the majority of residents), were to be persuaded to register and helped with the paper work involved. Since assistance of this nature would require Brotherhood members to interact several times with the potential voters, the voters' ensuing gratitude, or at least familiarity with the candidate, was intended to ensure that a proportion of them would be recruited as supporters of the organisation.

In addition to helping household members to register, discussing religious ideology and distributing election material, the Brotherhood campaigners were also expected to present each household with token gifts, such as tables inscribed with Qur'anic verses, Islamic theme calendars and Islamic theme stationery for the children.

Stationery was also provided to schools. Another smaller group of young Brotherhood members was assigned the task of waiting outside local schools as the pupils came out to distribute rulers, pencils, erasers, sharpeners and exercise books, all printed with the slogan "Islam is the Solution" and the occasional verse from the Qur'an.

Targeting children with stationery gifts, according to 'Akif, is considered an important aspect of Brotherhood campaign activities, especially in poor areas such as Hada'iq al-Qobba. This, he maintains, is because for poor parents the purchase of stationery for their children is a considerable burden on their already strained budget. Provision of these objects means that the parents still see the Brotherhood slogan and remember that the organisation is sympathetic to their circumstances. Even if the parents are not impressed by these gestures, 'Akif says, his organisation's efforts will not have been in vain. This, he argues, is because the Muslim Brotherhood also has "a programme for the recruitment of children . . . from those at primary school to those at the secondary and university level of their education".

He further explains:

> If parents do not respond to us, children are still going to remember
> who gave them goodies at the school gates and hopefully this means

our message is being slowly passed to the next generation directly . . .
We are not in a hurry, our plans are very long term.[30]

'Akif's campaign strategy outlined earlier gives a strong indication
of group cohesion. It seems that 'Akif, and arguably all Brotherhood
contestants, receive sufficient support from the Muslim Brotherhood for
campaigning not to be focused on a personalistic level but on a group
level. The fact that the Brotherhood funds all the campaign expenditure
of its candidates encourages its junior members to play an active
role in assisting the contestants, and ensures that campaign literature
describes the contestants not as individual personalities who happen
to be Brotherhood members but first and foremost as representatives
of the Muslim Brotherhood, is further evidence that this is the case.

That the legalised opposition, on the other hand, does not appear
to possess the group cohesion found within the Muslim Brotherhood
organisation can be observed in the seemingly insufficient assistance and
organisational support extended to its candidates. It is worth pointing
out that the Muslim Brotherhood does not receive or expect help from
its long-standing ally, the Labour Party, in the election campaigns of its
candidates. In contrast, the presence of Muslim Brotherhood members
during the electoral activities of Labour Party contestants is palpable.
For example, when one of the Labour Party's most senior members,
'Adel Husayn, decided to enter the electoral fray for the first time in
1995, he campaigned with the help of Muslim Brotherhood members.
If the Labour Party had provided sufficient support to its candidates,
one would assume that, as a senior member, Husayn would not have
accepted the assistance of an organisation that he does not represent.

NDP and opposition parties

That contestants representing the legalised parties lack sufficient support
from their parties is more prominently reflected in the campaign framework of these contestants. Unlike Brotherhood contestants, opposition
and NDP candidates alike seem to finance personally a large part of their
own electoral campaigns. It may be argued then that opposition parties
in particular may lack the resources to allow them to maintain local
bases in electoral constituencies where they have nominated candidates.
The truth is that it is difficult to assess accurately whether the lack of
local bases is solely the result of governmental constraints, in which

finance laws play a major part, or whether a lack of enthusiasm on the part of party leaders also contributes to this predicament. Political parties, after all, have access to some sources of finance, such as the £E100,000 that each registered party receives from the Shura Council, party membership fees and revenues derived from the sale of newspapers and other party publications both in Egypt and abroad.[31] Indeed, judging from the contrasting appearances of party headquarters, some parties are more financially secure than others. The Neo-Wafd, for example, with its headquarters in a multimillion pound villa in central Cairo, does not appear to be suffering dire financial constraints. The newspaper, *al-Wafd*, is clearly a success for it is the only daily opposition party newspaper in Egypt. Moreover, according to 'Ali Salama, the Party's Deputy Secretary-General, the more senior a member, the more he is expected to pay in membership fees. Hence, it is not uncommon for a senior member to pay between "five and ten thousand pounds" in annual membership fees.[32] One might therefore assume that an opposition party in the Neo-Wafd's position would be able to finance the establishment of a small local base outside Cairo. But this is not the case. I have witnessed a discussion in which 'Ali Salama and several other prominent Neo-Wafd members, including 'Abd al-'Aziz Zayam and Hasan Hafez, were trying hard to convince a young Neo-Wafd member to pay personally the deposit required for a new party base.

Parties and finances[33]

The young man had come from his rural home town to the party headquarters in Cairo with the news that he had found a vacant office in his locality, which he thought would be suitable as a local base for the Party. Moreover, he appeared rather excited because the property owner was demanding about £E8,000 as deposit, plus a monthly rental of £E100. Judging from the young man's description of the premises, it seemed a very good deal: the place was apparently in a good location and was well constructed with all the necessary amenities. He said that the running costs would be minimal because he was planning to run it on a voluntary basis.

The aim was to use the office as a focal point for the recruitment of unemployed young people in the area. As these unemployed people had little else to distract them, he seemed sure that he could influence them to join, thereby expand party membership at the grass-roots level.

Whether or not this would turn out to be true, Salama and his colleagues were not eager to find out. Rather, they argued that the young man should first show his commitment by paying the deposit himself. If he did, then he would have proved his commitment to the project and the matter of party material such as posters and publications, monthly rental and the annual electricity, water and telephone bills would subsequently be paid by the Party.

Since government subsidies ensure that annual electricity, water and telephone bills were low, this proposal seemed rather unfair. This was not, after all, a private enterprise project and, besides, the young man was volunteering his services for no monetary reward. Over an hour of discussion ensued during which the young man stressed several times that he could not afford to pay the deposit. Those present eventually came to a consensus that if he were to come back with half of the required deposit, then the matter would be referred to the Party Chairman for serious consideration. The result was that the young party member left Cairo with less hope than when he had arrived.

One can argue that the attitude of the Neo-Wafd may not necessarily be representative of that of other opposition parties. The majority of opposition parties may genuinely be unable to finance the maintenance of permanent or even temporary local bases. It is for this reason that their candidates are often compelled to rent their own temporary premises in their constituencies. Moreover, they often have to pay for manpower assistance. The Muslim Brotherhood not only provides volunteer members to assist its candidates but also assists those candidates representing its political ally, the Labour Party. This form of assistance is not available either to Neo-Wafd candidates or to those candidates who represent the other opposition parties.

Party manpower assistance
Confirmation of this is the apparent dependence of candidates on hired help during their electoral campaigns. One might assume that No'man Gom'a, as a senior member of the Neo-Wafd, for example, would be surrounded by junior party members eager to assist. Instead, he was aided by privately hired assistants unconnected to the party he was officially representing. Some of these assistants were participating as a favour to Gom'a – not because of party connections, but because they were junior employees of his own law firm. The majority, however, were local Imbaba

youth. Again, none were Neo-Wafd members but were apparently hired specifically for the election campaign period.

According to one of the law firm "volunteers", at least ten of these privately hired assistants were being paid the relatively enormous sum of £E500 a week to help promote Gomʿa's campaign in Imbaba. With this high figure and the fact that Gomʿa's daily expenditure on the campaign averaged £E2,500, one would assume that a candidate in his position would be only too happy to forego most of his private helpers in order to cut the cost of his campaign. But this would have been virtually impossible because the Neo-Wafd's contribution to his campaign was no more than that extended to other party candidates – that is, a few party posters and other inexpensive party propaganda material.[34]

The 1995 election campaign of Mustafa Bakri, the then editor-in-chief of *al-Ahrar*, provides another example of this predicament. Being in a similar situation to Gomʿa's, Bakri had secured the assistance of some junior journalists from the newspaper that he edited. As hired professionals at the newspaper, these young journalists were not participating in Bakri's campaign as fellow party members, but as a favour to their boss. In addition to relying on these "volunteers", Bakri also depended upon the help of his brothers who, incidentally, were Neo-Wafd members. Thus, the bulk of Bakri's help came from privately hired Helwan locals. While Bakri refused to disclose the exact amount spent on hired help, or indeed his campaign cost in general, he admitted this was not inconsiderable.[35]

On the face of it, it seems that among the candidates representing the legalised political parties it is the NDP candidates who are in the most advantageous position in terms of party support. After all, the NDP organises for its candidates formal electoral gatherings with which opposition candidates cannot compete. Yet, as discussed earlier, formal electoral gatherings, whether held on a grand scale for NDP candidates or on a more moderate scale as for opposition candidates, are not efficient mechanisms of voter recruitment. In addition, one should bear in mind that, except in cases where a candidate is also a minister and thus has direct access to the resources of his ministry, the NDP does not support more than a few such gatherings for each of its officially nominated candidates.[36]

This means that in between such gatherings NDP candidates are left to organise and finance their own campaigns. The financial and organisational burdens of running their own campaigns is reflected by Hamdi al-Sayyed:

> Election campaigns vary in cost from one candidate to another. Sometimes you get various contributions from certain members of the constituency.[37] Personally, my costs are low because of my reputation, my previous history with the constituents and the good work I have been doing on their behalf since 1979. Therefore, I usually spend in the region of 20,000 pounds. This is spent on posters, some publications and the cost of arranging meetings. Usually constituents would provide their vehicles to transport people to the meetings, but of course it would not be fair if they also paid for the fuel.[38]

To judge from this comment, it seems that al-Sayyed is suggesting that less established or unpopular colleagues are faced with personal costs exceeding those he incurs. This assumption appears to be verified by Muhammad al-Sayyed, who also maintained that his campaign costs have been "very low" because of the local people who all "help" him out. The costs incurred by less fortunate colleagues, however, can, as he points out, reach into "hundreds of thousands".[39] It seems, therefore, that during electioneering the predicament faced by NDP candidates is not too dissimilar from that faced by their (legalised) opposition counterparts. Both sides appear more dependent on their personal resources, networks and the goodwill of their constituents than on their respective parties.

On another level, one can argue that NDP candidates at least have one particular advantage not readily available to opposition candidates. If a candidate required a formal base in a particular constituency, it would not be a problem for the Party to secure one from the various state-owned properties. Hamdi al-Sayyed, for example, was provided by the NDP with access to a state-owned office, located behind a mosque in Heliopolis. Therefore, since becoming a member of the People's Assembly in 1979, al-Sayyed has been able to maintain a permanent base where his constituents can locate him, and where he can personally meet them on a regular basis.

Yet, it is worth noting that it is largely due to al-Sayyed's personal efforts – rather than those of the NDP – that the office is used so fruitfully. Al-Sayyed runs it and pays for two privately hired assistants, not NDP personnel. So if it were not for the personal efforts of al-Sayyed and his assistants, the office would be little more than an empty shell. Furthermore, as the long-running head of the Egyptian Medical Syndicate, he is able to give local people the assurance that, in cases of absolute emergency, he can also be reached at the syndicate headquarters.[40]

Since entering the People's Assembly in 1990, Muhammad al-Sayyed has also maintained an office in a local state-owned building. Like Hamdi al-Sayyed, he has been personally responsible for running the office; his assistants comprise a nephew and a couple of other local young men, none of whom are NDP members and all of whom are on al-Sayyed's personal payroll.

One can argue, therefore, that once in office, NDP candidates may be in a more advantageous position than their opposition counterparts in terms of directing state resources into their respective constituencies. But, during electoral competition, it seems that NDP candidates and legalised opposition candidates face a similar predicament – that is, insufficient financial and, more importantly, organisational support, from their parties. This state of affairs is of particular significance in explaining why candidates representing the legally authorised parties are obliged, more so than, say, the Muslim Brotherhood, to adopt individualistic campaign strategies that are almost independent of their parties. These strategies, in turn, reinforce further the role of non-competitive multiparty elections as an instrument of co-option and clientelist control.

Individualistic campaign strategies

As already mentioned in the introduction to this chapter, the two most important aspects of individualistic campaign strategies in relation to this study are, first, the way in which the dynamics of these strategies seem to do little to encourage the recruitment of party supporters at the grass-roots' level, and second, the fact that they reinforce the role of elected politicians as intermediaries between the centre and those on the periphery.

An NDP campaigner

The electoral campaign of first-time candidate Muhammad Mesiri (NDP: constituency of Kafr Ghanem)[41] in 1990, illustrates the main features of the predominantly personalistic strategies pursued by party candidates in attempts to secure voter support.

Muhammad Mesiri comes from the wealthiest business family in Tmay, the main town of the mostly rural constituency of Kafr Ghanem. Mesiri's wealth and status are well known within the community where he is considered one of the wealthiest men in the area and one of the largest private employers. Mesiri, it is said, caught the attention of the authorities in the late 1980s when his family financed the construction and equipping of a multimillion-pound technical college in Tmay, which he subsequently donated as a gift to the state. The publicity surrounding this grand gesture was further accentuated by the fact that President Mubarak had decided to open it officially himself.

On the communal level, Mesiri already laid claim to influence and networks that largely rested upon his position as one of constituency's largest employers. Moreover, the erection of a technical college undoubtedly raised his position and esteem in the community, especially with parents who had previously been faced with the hard choice of either denying their children further education or sending them to one of the Governorate's two large urban centres, Senbellawayn or Mansura. This meant that low-income people were burdened with the extra cost of separate lodgings and living expenses for their children. A technical college in Tmay, however, meant that local students from Tmay and the surrounding villages could attend their studies and return home at the end of each day.

While the above gesture on the part of Mesiri can be viewed as overtly generous in nature, it should be noted that Kafr Ghanem is a large and densely populated constituency with 174,000 registered voters.[42] So that even if one takes into account those individuals whose votes Mesiri might easily secure because of gratitude or loyalty – individuals such as employees, beneficiaries of the technical college and other social donations, family, friends and associates – these would not be sufficient to ensure a majority vote in such a large area. However, this is not to imply that a major contribution to the community such as the technical college would not benefit his campaign. Its benefit would be more symbolic in nature, indicating that he cared for the community and that, if he were to reach public office, he would be likely to ensure that sufficient state resources were channelled into the constituency.

To ensure a good turnout on election day, Mesiri proceeded to forge personal networks of electoral alliances. He travelled around the constituency visiting the *'omda*s (headmen) and the other local notables of Tmay and the surrounding villages. Behind the courteous talk, the purpose was to discuss whether these notables could use their local influence and networks to ensure sufficient voter support on election day. In other words, this process involved the recruiting of personal allies who would in turn enlist the support of as many voters as possible.

It is common for such a campaign to involve financial transactions. Misri, for example, donated an undisclosed sum to pay for a communal supper in the village *madyafa* (guest-house).[43] Such events are not festive affairs. Rather, they are subdued events to which the heads of extended households in the village would be invited.[44] The purpose of such gatherings is primarily to discuss, in a relaxed atmosphere, the elections, the absent host and the plan for election day. In this particular case, the situation was more complicated because two of the villagers had decided to compete in the elections as independents in the *fe'at* and the workers/ peasants categories respectively. This meant that the *'omda* and most family heads were engrossed in discussions on how to convince both, or at least the local *fe'at* candidate, to drop out of the electoral race. This required several other informal sittings, most of which were held in the *'omda*'s home.[45]

One may argue that the effort required to convince one or both of the local candidates to relinquish their places in order to assist Mesiri's campaign would not have been so successful if Mesiri was not such a prominent figure and had not made a substantial "donation" to the village. Moreover, neither of the local candidates was of particular prominence or wealth. One candidate was a humble village schoolteacher and the other a minor seed merchant. Neither of them was known outside the village. Such low standing does little to encourage voter support. And, in the absence of sufficient financial resources it would have been difficult for those candidates to pursue strategies to expand personal networks of support which require extensive travel across the constituency and releated expenses.

The *'omda*, therefore, felt, along with most family heads in the village, that if the local candidates dropped out, or if at least the *fe'at* candidate were to drop out, this would provide the villagers with the opportunity to support an almost certain winner in the form of Mesiri. This act would provide the villagers with the opportunity to claim additional benefits once the candidate reached office and had access to state resources. It would also save the local candidates, whom the villagers did not expect to win, a lot of wasted time, effort and, more importantly, financial resources which they could not afford to squander.

Unfortunately for Mesiri and arguably the village, neither of the local candidates agreed to drop out, and as communal ties meant that the villagers were forced – albeit reluctantly in this case – to support their own *awlad al-balad* (sons of the village), Mesiri was unable to secure any of the 6,800 votes from that village in the 1990 elections.[46] He did, however, win the overall elections mainly because there were no social barriers to overcome in the majority of other localities of the constituency. Surveying the structure of Mesiri's campaign it is clear that his party did not play a significant role in the recruitment of electoral supporters. It was due to his prominent position in the constituency that he was able to forge clientist ties and ultimately secured his admission to the People's Assembly for the first time.

Other campaigners

Use of clientelist methods of voter recruitment is not a strategy confined to NDP candidates. It is one that can also be observed in the electoral campaigns of other (legalised) opposition candidates attempting first-time entry to the Assembly. The Neo-Wafd's No'man Gom'a for example, was observed discussing with the *shaykh al-balad*[47] of Kom Bara, a rural area on the outskirts of Imbaba, the plan for Gom'a's second visit to the local inhabitants. During the discussion, the shaykh mentioned that 1,500 voters in his area not only had agreed to support Gom'a, but also had jeered Gom'a's rival when, a few days earlier, the latter had attempted to visit the area. The £E6,000 which Gom'a "donated" to the area through its *shaykh* undoubtedly contributed towards ensuring such enthusiastic electoral support.[48]

It should also be noted that during the 1995 campaign period Gom'a was in the process of establishing a branch of his law firm in Imbaba. The reason, according to one of his campaign assistants, was to provide work for some of the unemployed young law graduates in the constituency. If this venture proved successful, then it was expected that further branches would be established around the constituency at later dates.[49]

While there is no evidence to suggest that Gomʿaʾs concern for youth unemployment in Imbaba is not genuine, the fact that his decision to help tackle this problem coincided with his election campaign indicates ulterior motives. Gomʿa, after all, is not a resident of Imbaba; nor does he have family ties within the constituency. It seems, therefore, that by establishing a business in the constituency he was aiming to establish his prominence in the community, rather like Mesiri – albeit on a smaller scale. With his own law firm in the constituency he would be better placed to build and expand his clientelist ties in the community, not only as an employer, but also as an individual able to provide legal advice and assistance to needy constituents.[50]

The decision of Mustafa Bakri, a professional journalist and the editor-in-chief of the Liberal Party's newspaper, to establish personally the weekly newspaper, *Sawt Helwan* (Voice of Helwan), also points to a similar tactic. The newspaper, according to Bakri, was established with financial assistance from personal friends and associates six months before he ran for the 1995 elections. His main purpose was to provide a service to the constituents, and he accordingly considered that a newspaper focusing mainly on parochial and national issues of particular concern to the Helwan community would be of benefit.[51]

Bakri was a more strategic planner than Gomʿa since he did not wait until the elections before embarking upon his venture. The aim of the tactic appears to have been the same as Gomʿaʾs, however. Bakri, like Gomʿa, was a stranger to the constituency in which he was competing and was, through the establishment of this local newspaper, trying to make a name for himself in order to build and expand his base of support in the area. His reasoning was that as editor-in-chief of this newspaper he would build clientelist ties within the community by employing numerous local staff and that these clientelist ties would expand as aggrieved constituents approached him with social, economic and political concerns they wanted publicly aired. In this context, one could argue that his ultimate aim was to secure sufficient electoral support from grateful constituents.

To some extent, Bakri's strategy appears to have been successful. His local newspaper attained a circulation of some 20,000 a week and one assumes, therefore, that he had become a familiar name in Helwan. However, given the time scale, neither Bakri nor Gomʿa would have managed to cultivate sufficient clientelist support solely through their ventures without the extra benefit from the "services" that was provided by these candidates.

This example illustrates how far opposition candidates like their NDP counterparts, are left to their own devices when it comes to voter recruitment. The primary consequence of this is that rather than concentrating on recruiting party supporters, candidates are left with little option but to use their personal resources to build their own personal followings. This strategy, in turn, focuses predominantly on the creation and expansion of clientelist ties between candidates and voters – dynamics that further encourage the prevalence of political individualism in a multi-party arena.

Seeking re-election

With regard to candidates seeking re-election, they too face a predicament not unlike that already discussed. While these candidates may not be required to direct much effort on the establishment of a clientelist base of support, they need to expand existing clientelist ties if they want to elicit voter support on election day. This is not a simple task in view of the numerous candidates eager for the fray, some of whom may possess sufficient prominence and resources to pose a serious challenge to those seeking re-election.

It is this potential challenge that constitutes the most important factor in explaining a candidate's clientelist dependence upon government and hence the role he comes to perform in a consequence. Unlike an encumbent deputy, a new candidate competing in elections will unflinchingly use his personal resources in order to establish as large a base of voter support as circumstances will allow. Mesiri, Gomʻa and Bakri having spent a significant part of their personal resources in attempts to reach political office, and having attained that office, such individuals, would find it economically wasteful, if not impossible, to repeat this process when seeking re-election a few years later. In contrast, while the candidate seeking re-election might have depleted much of his personal resources during his initial stand for office, his new rivals, especially if they are first-time competitors, are less likely to be in the same position.

At the same time, once a candidate has attained public office voters' the expectations of him rise considerably. Thus, whereas previously a candidate might have secured electoral support on the basis of his overall recognition in a community and, on occasions, the offering of some modest donations during his campaign, once he is in office the basis of electoral support for him changes and becomes increasingly conditional upon the downward flow of state resources.

Once in office and given his desire to seek re-election, an incumbent's most logical option would be to try to channel state resources into his constituency in order to preserve and perhaps even expand his existing clientelist base of support. His dependence on the centre thus becomes established and before long he finds himself acting as an intermediary between central government and those on the periphery. This trend may be illustrated by an examination of Mesiri's 1995 re-election campaign.

Renewing NDP voter support
We have seen how Mesiri, during his initial participation in elections, depended upon the creation and expansion of a clientelist base of support. He achieved this through three main avenues: (1) traditional avenues (that is, personal/business/employment ties); (2) charitable contributions directed at the entire community (creation of a technical college); and, (3) financial contributions directed at specific individuals and communities (money directed at Mit Nas village).

The first avenue, whereby clientelist ties are formed as a direct result of Mesiri's position as a major businessman and employer in the community, is an ongoing process which does not necessarily require renewal upon his return to the arena of political contest. As for the technical college, this is a large gift to the community and Mesiri would not be expected personally to repeat a gesture of this magnitude. This leaves the third avenue. While Mesiri might have established a clientelist base of support as a result of the first two factors, during his initial campaign he was also compelled to strengthen and expand this support base by travelling around the constituency, meeting certain community heads and generally bestowing some financial contributions.

The importance of this latter avenue is not simply that it con-tributes towards strengthening and expanding Mesiri's base of support but also that the clientelist ties on which it is based appear to require renewal and reaffirmation during the electoral period. For example, when Mesiri returned to the village during his re-election campaign in 1995, new demands were presented by the villagers in return for electoral support.

At that time, the village did not have a local *fe'at* candidate running for office. However, the same seed merchant who competed (and lost) in the workers/peasants category during the 1990 elections, had decided to compete yet again as an independent in the 1995 elections.[52] The villagers, therefore, expected Mesiri not only to provide tangible rewards in return for electoral support but also to enter a vote-exchange deal with their local candidate. In other words, in exchange for giving their *fe'at* votes to Mesiri, the villagers wanted their local candidate to receive, in return, the equivalent amount of votes, but in the workers/peasants category. Such votes were logically expected to come from Mesiri's own home town of Tmay, where, because of his position as *ibn al-balad*, his most loyal supporters could be found. These were supporters who, most importantly, would be willing not only to give their *fe'at* vote to their candidate but also to "donate" their *'omal/fallahin* vote to the candidate of his choice – so as to better their candidate's electoral position.

In addition to the above vote-exchange pact, the tangible benefit agreed upon in this particular case was the paving of one of the main roads leading into the village. Moreover, it was agreed with the candidate that work on this road would finish before election day. The following comment from villagers of Mit Mas provides some explanation of the logic behind such a demand:

> We do not think that we are asking too much from Mesiri. *Al-ta'awun* [cooperation or a vote-exchange deal] with our candidate is not too much to ask. Tmay is a large place and he has a lot of support there, so giving our candidate some of the peasant votes which he controls is not a problem for him. Anyway, if we did not ask for them, some other candidate would have taken them instead. In fact Mesiri has made vote-exchange pacts with almost every competing peasant and worker in the constituency . . . Of course it is all based on how many votes they can offer him, not the other way round . . . With his supporters he can meet everyone's demands. We did ask for the road to be paved before election day because we wanted to make sure his part of the bargain was kept. I'm sure he would not deliberately ignore his side of the deal, but he is a very busy man looking after the interests of a large constituency. If it is not done now, then who's going to travel to Tmay and Cairo every day looking for him and reminding him.[53]

In answer to the question about whether paving the road was an excessive demand in view of Mesiri's 1990 "contribution" to the village and the fact that he received no electoral support in return, the same respondents argued:

> Mesiri knew two locals had put themselves up for election. He did not expect us to abandon our own and support him. He came to us then in case there was any chance they might drop out. We kept our part of the deal . . . we did everything to convince our candidates to drop out, but they were both as stubborn as mules. Even the seed merchant's wife left him because she was angry that he was squandering their life savings. Actually she's left him again because of his participation this time around . . . In the last elections we did not promise something and then not keep to it. But now we are promising something, and paving a road in return is not a big thing to ask from someone in his position . . . He must have a lot of important connections in government now; so, really, he is not expected to put his hand in his own pocket. But he is expected to offer more than the other contestants.[54]

The villagers' demands from Mesiri, and the reasoning on which they were based, illustrate how returning to the electoral arena is not a simple process. Rather, seeking re-election appears to pressurise an outgoing deputy to continue the pattern of clientelist recruitment if he is to expect re-election. Indeed, he might not depend upon his personal resources while seeking re-election, but in the reaffirmation of his clientelist base of support, the exchange of tangible benefits in the form of state resources plays an important part.

The following comment reflects the increasing pressure placed on candidates seeking re-election:

> I have competed in legislative elections eight times . . . The voters have specific expectations . . . "I'll get you the water, the school, the electricity" is all I say in my election campaign. Nobody cares what my political orientation is. Nobody bothers to ask me.[55]

This situation, in which party nomination is dependent upon the size of a candidate's assumed or established base of support and candidates are subsequently compelled to depend upon state resources in order to preserve that base of support (and thus their place in the Assembly, the party and the community) shows how the electoral arena shapes the role of NDP deputies as intermediaries between the centre and those on the periphery. It also shows how it shapes the role of opposition deputies.

In the case of opposition candidates seeking re-election the situation, one can argue, appears to be more or less the same. That is, not only is the individualistic approach to political participation reinforced as clientelist ties become renewed and reaffirmed, but also such ties appear increasingly conditional upon state-controlled resources. The base of support on which Khaled Mohyi al-Din, leader of the Tagammu', appears to have depended for re-election in 1995 illustrates this predicament.

Renewing other voter support[56]

Mohyi al-Din's role as one of the Free Officers responsible for the 1952 Revolution, and his subsequent membership of the Revolutionary Command Council, means that in contemporary Egypt he is regarded not simply as an opposition leader but also as a national figure. When he sought election in his rural home constituency of Kafr Shokr, therefore, one can argue that, as its most famous *"ibn al-balad"*, he did not have to make much effort to gain overall recognition from the inhabitants. But when it comes to seeking re-election, the process of renewing and reaffirming electoral support, and the clientelist conditions on which such support is based, do not differ significantly from first-time election campaigns.

The day I joined Mohyi al-Din on his campaign trail, he was due to visit the two villages of Kafr Abu Zahra and Kafr Shaykh Ibrahim. On arrival at each village, Mohyi al-Din and his aide were greeted by the village *'omda*, who guided him first to his home and later to the homes of the most prominent local families. These included the home of Haj Husayn Mahmoud Husayn, a 107-year-old man who, as head of eight generations comprising 182 individuals, remained one of the most influential people in Kafr Abu Zahra. On the surface, such visits might not appear overtly political. Mohyi al-Din, for example, spent no more than 20 minutes in each of the 15 households he visited on that particular day. The conversation with the hosts extended to little more than social niceties. Elections and politics were not proper topics of conversation.

Mohyi al-Din spent a large part of his re-election campaign travelling around the constituency on such visits. Hence, this was his second trip to these families. Moreover, he hoped to visit them once more before election day. This implies that conversation relating to his re-election, and the conditions of their support, is likely to have been discussed on a previous, more private occasion. If arrangements relating to these issues had not already been agreed upon, it is unlikely the candidate would have made arrangements for three visits during the relatively short one-month period designated for campaigning. Thus Mohyi al-Din's presence was most probably reaffirming the existing clientelist ties.

While the host families did not personally take part in political conversation with the candidate during that particular visit, it is worth noting that many other villagers did take this opportunity to present Mohyi al-Din with written petitions relating, among other things, to employment, water and road problems. As the nature of such petitions indicates, regardless of Mohyi al-Din's position as a respected national figure, or the fact that he heads an opposition party, his election to the People's Assembly was nevertheless viewed predominantly as a link to central government and thus to the provision of state-controlled resources. A member of one of the host families in Kafr Shaykh Ibrahim explained how he believed Mohyi al-Din was perceived in this rural community:

> Khaled Mohyi al-Din is our hero. He is Egypt's hero and we are all very proud of the things he did with Nasser for the country . . . People vote for him because they are proud of him, but also because he does a lot to help . . . Until recently, the children used to go to a secondary school outside the village but he got the government to build one here. It's things like that which are important here.[57]

Again, the above comment appears to suggest that while Mohyi al-Din was held in exceptionally high esteem, it was also the state resources he channelled into the community which ensured that his re-election efforts received sufficient voter support. With regard to party policies, the situation was more or less the same. It is the candidate's demonstrated skills at diverting state resources to the community, not his party stand, which was a decisive factor in his re-election prospects:

> The peasant will always give his support to the person or candidate that will look after his problems. It is not really important what party that person represents . . . He [Mohyi al-Din] does not talk to us about his party and nobody is bothered about that. He can do what he wants with it. As long as he continues to help solve the

people's problems, people will elect him. If he stops, then there will be no votes for him.[58]

That this reasoning is equally clear to participating candidates is reflected in the views of al-Badri Farghali, currently a second-term deputy of the Assembly and a long-term member of the Tagammu':

> My party connection is of no help at all. Actually my party is not popular in Port Said [where his constituency of Hayy al-'Arab is located] . . . I am proud of being of a member of the Tagammu' and everyone knows I am a member of that party. But in reality, they vote for me because I am able to help them with their every day problems.[59]

To acknowledge this predicament and to seek re-election on this basis is an indication of the extent to which electoral contest in Egypt's multiparty arena has influenced politicians representing disparate political views into performing the role of intermediaries between central government and those on the periphery. This role, in turn, contributes to inhibiting the expansion, and more importantly the strengthening, of political parties as group entities. At the same time, it reinforces the clientelist chain of dependence leading to government.

The government's ability to utilise non-competitive multi-party elections as a mechanism of clientelist co-option and control is strengthened largely by the government's power to impose various constraints on virtually every level of political participation. These constraints, in turn, are intended to pressurise political actors and the parties they represent into accepting the rules of this non-competitive game.

Yet, the fact that the majority of political parties accept, or have at least come to terms with, the role of elections as defined from above, cannot be attributed solely to government-imposed constraints. Political parties also contribute to this predicament. As the political parties hardly provide their candidates with any financial and organisational support there is hardly any identification with the party by the voters, a fact that in turn leaves candidates with little choice but to focus upon the promotion of themselves as the main form of voter recruitment. The clientelist base of voter support which accompanies such personalistic political behaviour further helps to reaffirm the clientelist role of elections.

[162]

NOTES

1 Deputy Governor Muhammad al-Gawahirgi to audience at Hickstep gathering, 18 November 1995.
2 The following information is derived from personal observation of the electoral event held at Helwan Youth Club on 25 November 1995.
3 Interview by the author with the petitioner "Abu Ahmad", 25 November, 1995, Helwan.
4 Interview by the author with a member of the NDP Women's Group, Helwan Youth Club, 25 November 1995.
5 Information derived from personal observation by the author of the event on 26 November 1995.
6 Interview by the author with a woman administrator, 26 November 1995.
7 The speaker was rather insignificant in that he was not an important official. He was apparently a supporter of al-Sayyed and had come simply to express his gratitude publicly to al-Sayyed for assisting him during a family crisis.
8 He was referring to the bureaucratic-looking members of the audience who include members of the NDP Women's group and their male counterparts.
9 Interview by the author with a factory worker, Hickstep, 18 November 1995.
10 Interview by the author with a factory worker attending (with colleagues) the NDP electoral event held at the Helwan Youth Club, 25 November 1995.
11 Interview by the author with Muhammad al-Sayyed, 26 November 1995.
12 Interview by the author with Muhammad al-Sayyed, 26 November 1995.
13 Interview by the author with a factory worker following an election event for Mustafa Bakri in the Mayo area of Helwan, 22 November 1995.
14 Speech by 'Atef 'Obayd, Minister of Public Enterprises, 25 November 1995.
15 Interview by the author with a group of Helwan factory workers, 25 November 1995.
16 Interview by the author with a campaign assistant, 19 November 1995.
17 In both working-class districts and rural areas of Egypt, it is common practice for wedding celebrations (and post-funeral congregations) to take place in a *khaima* in the street so that as many guests as possible can be accommodated. This is largely because the close-knit nature of such communities means that weddings and funerals are regarded as communal affairs to which the entire neighbourhood is invited or expected to attend.
18 A *noqta* is money traditionally given to a bride and groom instead of a wedding present. In this case, Gom'a presented them with £E100, a large sum considering he was a stranger to the couple.
19 Speech by No'man Gom'a, 19 November 1995.
20 Ambassador Tahsin Bashir, retired Egyptian diplomat and political analyst, describing a personal conversation with Neo-Wafd Chairman, Fu'ad Serag al-Din to the author on 14 December 1994 in Cairo.
21 Interview by the author with Muhammad Mahdi 'Akif, 11 November 1995.
22 Interview by the author with Ma'mun al-Hudhaybi, 11 November 1995.
23 In an interview with the author on 11 November 1995, Ma'mun al-Hudhaybi said that five of his assistants were in jail awaiting their lawyers because on the evening of 10 November they were arrested for "putting up posters" in his

Doqqi constituency. In another example, several assistants of Sayyed Hussayn Sha'ban, the Nasserite Party candidate for the electoral consituency of al-Manyal, including two of his brothers, were arrested for the same reason. They were, however, released from jail nine hours later. (Information derived from interview by the author with Sha'ban on 9 November 1995.)

24 Interestingly, the Muslim Brotherhood's influence on the Labour Party was apparent not only in the presence of its members, but also in the leaflets planned for distribution. The leaflets, which carried Husayn's name and picture, also carried the famous Brotherhood slogan "Islam is the Solution".

25 The description of the walkabout is derived from personal observation by the author on 15 November 1995.

26 Interview by the author with Muhammad 'Akif, 15 November 1995.

27 According to information provided to the author in an interview with Bakri on 20 December 1995, over 60 such gatherings were held during the campaign period.

28 Interview by the author with an audience member, Helwan, 14 November 1995.

29 Personal observation by the author, 15 November 1995.

30 Interview by the author with Muhammad 'Akif, 15 November 1995.

31 It has been noted that political parties receive a decent income from regular sales to Gulf states (Saudi Arabia in particular) of a set amount of newspapers for the price of US$1 a copy, compared with the price in Egypt of about 50 piastres a copy (about US¢8).

32 Interview by the author with 'Ali Salama, 8 January 1995.

33 This example was derived from personal observation by the author at 'Ali Salama's office, Neo-Wafd headquarters, Cairo, 8 January 1995.

34 Figures obtained from Gom'a's campaign assistants during interviews by the author on 19 November 1995.

35 Because Bakri was personally responsible for his entire campaign, including the payments for hired help, the costs incurred were so high that he had to seek financial assistance from a "friend in Alexandria" who also happened to be a "rich businessman". (Information derived from interview by the author with Bakri on 20 December 1995.)

36 See the discussion above concerning the "rented" audience that comprised Helwan workers (at Helwan Youth Club gathering, 25 November 1995) where, during the one month designated for electioneering, it was stated that the workers were required only two or three times a week. Moreover, the fact that the bus driver had to inform them in advance where they were going and who they should be cheering, meant that such formal NDP gatherings were usually for a different candidate each time.

37 No mention was made of contributions from the party.

38 Interview by the author with Hamdi al-Sayyed, 1 January 1995.

39 Interview by the author with Muhammad al-Sayyed, 26 November 1995.

40 According to Hamdi al-Sayyed, his two assistants saw the constituents four times a week at the office. On one of these occasions he was there too. Moreover he made "regular site visits to see their problems firsthand". (Information derived from interview by the author with Hamdi al-Sayyed, 1 January 1995.)

41 Information for the above example was derived from the local inhabitants of the village Mit Nas during the period 1995–6. Mit Nas is a pseudonym used here to protect the privacy of the village inhabitants.

42 This statistic was provided by a government-appointed supervisor at the polling-station located in Mit Nas. It was also confirmed by the village schoolteacher mentioned in the previous note. If we compare the 80,000 or so registered voters in the densely populated urban constituency of Hada'iq al-Qobba, to the 174,000 in Kafr Ghanem, we can better appreciate the size of the latter constituency.

43 Interview by the author with a village elder, 3 December 1995.

44 Family elders are invited on the grounds that their senior status within their respective families puts them in a position to ensure that whatever is agreed in such informal gatherings is subsequently implemented by the registered voters in their family on election day.

45 On the basis of the one-man-two-votes' procedure discussed above, the logic here was that if the *fe'at* candidate dropped out, the villagers could give that vote to Mesiri provided he entered a vote-exchange pact with the local candidate in the alternate category. In this way, the remaining local candidate would increase the number of votes obtained on election day and at the same time the village would also have been able to show its support for Mesiri. But as the local *fe'at* candidate did not see why he should be the one to withdraw, the village elders considered that it was perhaps better if both were to drop out so that neither would lose face; and at the same time the village votes could be freely used as a bargaining chip with Mesiri and other lesser candidates within the constituency.

46 The communal ties that lead rural villages, and to a lesser degree close-knit urban areas inhabited by poorer sections of society, to give priority to a local "son", appear to be based not only on sentimentality and loyalty but also on the clientelist logic that if, by some chance, the candidate won, then he would be likely to give priority to helping his "own" area and people before the rest of the constituency. If, upon gaining office, he does not match such expectations, then, as one villager put it, "No one will support him again". (Information derived from interview by the author with a villager from Mit Nas, 3 December 1995.) With regard to Mesiri the fact that the effort and expense he invested in that particular village did not produce the desired results on election day was not, as will be discussed later, futile.

47 *Shaykh al-balad* is the name given to a local leader who is of lesser status than an *'omda*. In large rural villages such as Mit Nas, several of these individuals are elected (and thus registered in the Ministry of Interior) in each area of the village. Their role is to assist with problems in their immediate neighbourhoods, but they are ultimately responsible to the *'omda*. On the outskirts of urban areas such as Imbaba, the situation is slightly different because the community might be rather small and thus not require an *'omda*, so one *shaykh al-balad* would usually be sufficient to head the community.

48 Also, according to several of Gom'a's campaign assistants, the candidate had, up to the time of the interview, contributed from his own money pocket no less than £E20,000 in "assistance" to various other communities in Imbaba. (Information derived from interview by the author with Gom'a's campaign assistants, 20 November 1995.)

49 Interview by the author with a campaign assistant, 19 November 1995.

50 A wealthy and highly successful law professor, Gom'a had profitable academic and business ventures through which he could subsidise the law firm.

51 Interview by the author with Mustafa Bakri, 14 November 1995.

52 His view was that he had a good chance of winning in 1995 because he felt he had built upon and expanded the networks he had built up during the 1990 elections. (Information derived from interviews by the author with villagers, 28 November 1995.)

53 Interview by the author with villagers of Mit Mas, 29 November 1995.

54 Interview by the author with villagers of Mit Mas, 29 November 1995.

55 Hamdi al-Sayyed, speaking during the conference on elections at Cairo's Research Centre for Human Rights, 25 December 1995.

56 Information for the above example includes that obtained from personal interviews and observation during a visit by the author to Mohyi al-Din at his rural constituency of Kafr Shokr, 12 November 1995.

57 Interview by the author with a member of the Salim family to which the late 'omda of Kafr Shaykh Ibrahim belonged, 12 November 1995.

58 Interview by the author with a member of the Khattab family (whose head was the shaykh al-balad of Kafr Abu Zahra), 12 November 1995.

59 Interview by the author with al-Badri Farghali, 31 December 1994.

5

Reflections
on Party Politics

It seems that the personalised system of rule established by Nasser following the 1952 *coup d'état* has remained intact until today. Indicative of this is the fact that following Nasser's death his personally appointed successor, Anwar Sadat, managed to dominate the political arena for ten years until his violent death in 1981. At that time, Sadat's personally appointed Vice-President smoothly assumed office and remains, until today, President of the Egyptian Republic. On the basis of the powers he inherited, President Mubarak, like his predecessors, Nasser and Sadat, has thus remained the ultimate source of power and authority in contemporary Egypt.

The personal authoritarian rule can never be fully institutionalised, however. Regimes of this nature are characterised by an "inherent uncertainty" based on "vulnerability to, or dependency on, the wills, wiles, and abilities of others".[1] In other words, because an institutionalised system "in which individuals and organisations engage publicly to win the right to govern or to influence a government's policies within an overall and legitimate framework of agreed-upon rules"[2] does not exist in personal authoritarian regimes, the ruler's position in power is inherently influenced by a number of factors, the two most important of which are the positions of the armed forces and of other political players.

In the case of post-1952 Egypt, the extensive patronage bestowed by Egypt's Presidents on the armed forces, along with the President's clientelist powers of appointment at the highest level of this establishment, have shaped the role of the Egyptian armed forces as the ultimate protectors of the post-1952 political system. Furthermore, the enormous powers of the presidency, including control over the coercive powers of the state, overall control of the resources of the state and a president-friendly legal-constitutional framework, are all major factors which have contributed towards weakening the position of political actors and organisations, while preserving the pre-eminent position of the Egyptian President.

In such a context, non-competitive multi-party elections in Mubarak's Egypt can best be viewed as an additional mechanism for hindering the development of organised political participation and thus further contributing to the consolidation of presidential power and the preservation of the political status quo.

The electoral system as an instrument of control

This study began by questioning the role of non-competitive multi-party elections in Mubarak's Egypt. Since these elections do not affect the replacement or succession of government, then it is necessary to examine the role they play for the government rather than for the individual voter. As a means of legitimising the regime's rule, non-competitive multi-party elections in Mubarak's Egypt have a limited role. Instead, non-competitive multi-party elections in contemporary Egypt function predominantly as a tool for the Mubarak regime to reaffirm and expand the clientelist structure which links central authorities to those on the periphery.

Multi-party elections within the government-defined arena seem to have encouraged and expanded an overall pattern of participation in which intra-party rivalry, political individualism, patronage and parochialism all play important roles. The expansion of links between political parties and voters on the basis of programmatic and ideological stands is consequently an issue that is overlooked by voters in favour of both received and anticipated rewards that are predominantly channelled from the centre. In other words, these rewards further encourage the clientelist chain of dependence leading to the centre. This clientelist chain of dependence, in turn, has made it less difficult for the government to define the role of political players officially representing disparate political parties as intermediaries between central government and those on the periphery.

The development of political parties as organised group entities in such a context is not a process that Egypt's multi-party arena of political contest has aimed to produce. Participation within the prevailing political scene has greatly contributed to ensuring that the President's own party, the NDP, comprises little more than a conglomerate of personalities each possessing their own personal network of supporters. Indeed, a dominant party structured along such lines is easier to control, especially when government-initiated legislation needs to be formalised in the People's Assembly. Yet, in the absence of group organisation, party cohesiveness and strong links binding supporters to the party itself rather than to personalities who also happen to be party members, the NDP cannot be viewed as an institutionalised political entity that can maintain its current position without the President's chairmanship and patronage.

Moreover, the utilisation of the electoral arena to entice opposition parties to enter the same system of clientelist co-option and control as that practised on the NDP does not appear to have been difficult for the Mubarak regime. The behaviour of the "major" legalised opposition parties (apart from the Labour Party and the Nasserite Party) demonstrates that this is the case.

The various constraints imposed on political participation, in addition to the limited resources accessible to these parties, can be regarded as the two major factors that have contributed to their weak position and hence induced them to enter the electoral chain of clientelist dependence and control. In fact, it might be suggested that if it was not for the support it receives as a result of its alliance with the Muslim Brotherhood Organisation, the Labour Party would also have been tempted to follow suit. In the absence of such an ally, the Nasserite Party would be in a rather vulnerable position.

It is not inconceivable that the Nasserite Party might also join forces with the Muslim Brotherhood in order to strengthen its position. In addition to the Labour Party, the Neo-Wafd and the Liberals previously pursued this avenue. However, as these parties later discovered, it is difficult to maintain separate and equal identities within a political partnership. As the Neo-Wafd's Deputy Secretary-General explained following the 1984 electoral alliance:

> Shaykh Salah Abu Isma'il, who was the main connection in the operation between the Wafd and the Muslim Brotherhood, tried to convince us to join his organisation in more than an election partnership. He wanted to push the Wafd into Islamist thought and ideology . . . but this was not possible because Wafd ideology is too different from the Muslim Brotherhood ideology.[3]

The decision of the Labour Party to relinquish its socialist stand in favour of a more Islamic-oriented party largely explains why since 1987 the Party has managed to maintain an alliance with the Muslim Brotherhood.[4] The point here, therefore, is that the Nasserite Party could enter an alliance with the Muslim Brotherhood. But the government's crack-down on the Muslim Brotherhood before the 1995 elections, and the fact that the Muslim Brotherhood is an organisation whose ideology and political history are totally incompatible with the Nasserist legacy which the Nasserites believe they represent, makes it more likely that the Party might instead be induced into covert government co-option.

The vulnerable position which the Nasserite Party has found itself in following the legislative elections of 1995, when it won only one seat, makes this possibility even more likely. The Party's Chairman, Dhiya al-Din Dawud, for example, was, according to his personal assistant, showing signs of depression after losing the seat he had previously won in 1990 (which he competed for as an independent during the 1990 elections) in his home constituency of Sariskur.[5] While this might appear an exaggerated observation, the fact that Dawud's personal assistant noticed that her boss was spending long hours alone in his office, refusing to meet anyone except in the most urgent circumstances, indicates that low morale existed at the highest level of the Party. This is arguably regarded as a positive sign by the government since it suggests that the Party is experiencing a sense of weakness and defeat – especially since it had won three seats in the previous elections even before it became an officially recognised party – that could induce it to reconsider entry into the government's clientelist system of co-option and control sooner rather than later.

The utilisation of the electoral arena as a clientelist mechanism with which to co-opt and control political parties is a tactic aimed at ensuring that these parties remain weak and thus unable to challenge the existing political order. It is probably reassuring for the government, therefore, that the participation of opposition parties in elections has produced an overall pattern of activity not too dissimilar to that of the NDP – in other words, a parochial-oriented, individualistic means of cultivating voter support. Patterns of participation have thus hindered the development of political parties as strong, cohesive group entities that could potentially challenge the political status quo. It is not too surprising that the prevalence of such a form of activity within the multi-party electoral arena seems to be encouraged by the President. Illustrative of this is the fact that the President publicly urged voters during the elections of 1995 to "go to the polling-stations and vote for the candidate best able to shoulder the responsibility, regardless of his or her party orientations and commitments".[6]

The President's encouragement to voters to ignore party politics and concentrate upon the candidate's personal abilities may indeed be beneficial to the regime in so far as it further hinders the expansion of party links with the masses. But encouraging allegiance to candidates on a personal level may appear encourage electoral violence.

The problem of electoral violence

Carl Landé notes that conflict tends to emerge when participating parties and groups are characterised by "unstable membership, uncertain duration, personalistic leadership, a lack of formal organisation, and by a greater concern with power and spoils than with ideology or policy".[7] Landé explains that conflict emerges because the aim of participants is to bring benefit to leaders and adherents. Yet, the problem is that, "The losers in such zero-sum games are likely to be resentful, to hope for a turn-about in which they can 'put down' their opponents as they have been put down themselves. This leads to the related subject of feuding."[8] In contrast with group feuding, in which individual "conflicts of obligation do not arise", feuds within the confines of personality-based politics "are more easily begun and harder to contain".[9] This is because in such a setting, he says:

> An injury to any individual leads to the clustering around him of those upon whom he has claims for support, minus those who have conflicting obligations to the other side. A similar cluster forms around his opponent. The ensuing violence which others than the primary rivals may suffer – especially if vengeance is inflicted on substitute victims – creates new persons with grievances . . . the result . . . may be an endless succession of killings between shifting groups of partisans whose composition at any point in time depends upon the identity of the latest victim and the next victim to be.[10]

It is possible to identify similar patterns emerging in Egypt. By the 1995 legislative elections, electoral violence had escalated for "the first time in the history of [Egyptian] parliamentary elections" to an unprecedented level which left, according to the Centre for Human Rights Legal Aid, 51 people dead and 878 others wounded.[11] One example was in the electoral constituency of Naga' Hammadi in Upper Egypt where an unidentified person fired shots that killed a supporter of al-Sayyed al-Menufi, a prominent independent candidate. On the assumption that the hit man was probably linked to Fahmi 'Omar, the NDP's official candidate, and al-Menufi's biggest rival, an armed confrontation erupted between the supporters of both candidates. By the end of that day the confrontation had claimed the lives of seven people and left more than double that number wounded. Included in the fatalities were the son and nephew of 'Omar (who did eventually win the elections).[12]

The fact that electoral violence prevails between independent candidates and official NDP candidates can be regarded as another, more extreme, reflection of the individualistic intra-party rivalry that exists (and is encouraged) within the NDP.[13] This view is further reinforced by the fact that of the 111 seats won by independents during the 1995 election, 99 were won by NDP members who were "not nominated by the party in the election battle".[14] As one prominent political analyst notes:

> It is hard to explain how, after claiming so many victims, the electoral battle ended in such a sweeping victory for one party. No one can believe that these casualties were the result of confrontations between one party which won over 90 per cent of the votes and 14 opposition parties which together managed to win only 14 seats! They are seen rather as reflecting the vicious in-fighting among the candidates of the National Democratic Party (NDP) itself, or among its candidates and defectors from the NDP who ran as "independents" when not nominated by the party and who, on being elected, returned to its ranks.[15]

The prevalence of electoral violence between NDP candidates and opponents representing the opposition parties cannot, nevertheless, be ignored. In fact, the supporters of Mustafa Bakri were, on several occasions, involved in physical confrontations with the supporters of Muhammad Mahgub (NDP), the Minister of Religious Endowments and Bakri's main rival.

During one such incident, I had just attended a major campaign gathering held jointly by Mahgub and three other senior NDP candidates in Helwan's youth club. Shortly after leaving the club, I met one of Bakri's aides in the street who informed me that Bakri was at the local police station filing a complaint against Mahgub. Joined by the aide, I made my way to the police station in order to join Bakri and enquire about the problem. However, since the Minister of Religious Endowments Mahgub had reached the police station before us, the place was sealed off for security reasons. Yet, it was not too long before the Minister left with his extensive entourage in tow, and I was thus allowed to join Bakri in the office of the *ma'mur* (chief of police).

As it turned out, some of Mahgub's supporters had apparently been sent to disrupt an electoral gathering that Bakri was holding that same evening in a marquee (*khaima*) in Helwan. Mahgub's supporters were not simply content with smashing the parked vehicles belonging to Bakri's entourage, but also decided to throw stones at the constituents attending Bakri's gathering. Paradoxically, a van full of police which had been sent on that particular occasion to ensure that Bakri's supporters did not disrupt the important NDP gathering held by Mahgub and his NDP counterparts, resulted in the police shooting bullets in the air to ward off Mahgub supporters. Those who continued the violence were subsequently arrested. The Minister, therefore, had gone to the police station immediately after his gathering in order to bail out his arrested supporters.[16]

It is worth noting that the violence that broke out between Mahgub and Bakri supporters was the main reason why Bakri pulled out of the race on the second election day. The first election day was Wednesday 29 November 1995. However, since neither Mahgub or Bakri managed to gain an absolute majority (that is, over 50 per cent of the total votes), the candidates, like hundreds of others nationwide, were compelled to compete in the second round of elections on Wednesday 6 December. In contrast with the first round of elections, the second round did not require any candidate to gain over 50 per cent of the vote, but to gain only the most votes.

During the first round of elections, it became clear that violence might erupt when Mahgub's brother Isma'il, surrounded by a personal army of bodyguards wearing Mahgub T-shirts, arrived along with a group of Mahgub supporters at one of the main polling-stations, and started hurling indecent slogans at Bakri and his supporters. Since this group appeared very intimidating, Bakri's supporters had little choice but to ignore these insults. However, at that same polling-station, one of Mahgub's wives, Saleha Sa'id, was noted by a female poll-watcher as having voted four times (the polling-station was in fact a girls' school of which Saleha Sa'id was headmistress). As she confronted Sa'id, the young woman found herself on the floor, being punched and kicked by Isma'il's bodyguards.[17] It is perhaps the helplessness that Bakri's supporters felt during the first election round that led some of these individuals to attend the second and final election round better equipped to deal with Mahgub supporters.[18] However, by 1.30 that afternoon Bakri had decided to pull out of the race.

It is unlikely, for various reasons discussed above, that Bakri would have beaten the Minister. In fact, Bakri was aware that critics might accuse him of trying to save face by pulling out before it was officially confirmed that he had lost the election. This, indeed, could be true. According to Bakri, however, his main concern was to prevent the bloodshed he felt would become inevitable as the events of that morning unfolded: "What other sensible choice was there? Isma'il [Mahgub's brother] had arrived with no less than 600 *baltageyya* [thugs] and they looked ready for war."[19]

While Bakri may have had the sense to direct his supporters out of potential danger at the last moment, the fact remains that both Mahgub and Bakri held senior positions within the NDP and the Liberal Party respectively, yet were competing against each other as rival personalities, not as candidates representing different party points of view. Their supporters were bound to them by personal ties of loyalty. Violent confrontations between the supporters of both men were not totally unexpected. What was unexpected, though, was President Mubarak's comment on the subject of electoral violence:

> In the pre-revolution era there were some battles in certain constitu-
> encies during the election races as feudal families, who dominated
> these areas, insisted on entering the parliament. Now the outbreak
> of violence is quite strange after feudalism was abolished.[20]

It has been noted that the President himself has urged voters to choose a candidate on the basis of personal qualities rather than party con-
siderations. Moreover, it appears that his government is determined, through the enforcement of formal and informal barriers, to hinder the development of genuine multi-party competition, preferring instead to

utilise elections as a mechanism of reaffirming and expanding its clientelist grip over political participation. Electoral violence, therefore, should not really be regarded by the President as "strange". Rather, it should be seen as one of the major consequences of his reluctance to allow, after he has been nearly two decades in power, genuine multi-party elections to develop.

Indeed, the President has frequently justified his actions by pointing to his concern for Egypt's stability. "There is a very thin line between democracy and anarchy," he said.[21] Yet, one can also argue that the prevailing electoral system is not particularly conducive to Egypt's long-term stability. Of course, the electoral violence, which appears to be on the increase, may not be regarded as an immediate threat to the stability of Egypt because it is mainly confined to political rivalry between individual players and their personal networks of supporters. But one should not overlook the fact that such violence is largely a consequence of the individualistic, parochially confined, clientelistically oriented patterns of participation that the regime seems to encourage through its "multi-party" electoral arena. Such a strategy on the part of government is arguably more detrimental to Egypt's long-term stability than the "anarchy" that President Mubarak maintains is so closely linked to democracy. These patterns of participation in Egypt's multi-party system cannot be regarded as beneficial in terms of eradicating the winner-takes-all mentality, which is currently reflected on the parochial level through violent confrontations between individual candidates and their supporters.

It may be suggested that the regime's efforts to encourage political parties to view participation in elections as a process through which its members and their supporters can become part of the existing political system and thus gain access to some of the resources it controls, can also contribute towards potential violence on another level. This is because those parties and groups (namely the Muslim Brotherhood and its long-term ally, the Labour Party) that do not want to accept the rules of this game appear to be increasingly excluded from the prevailing "multi-party" arena. The government's overt crack-down on Muslim Brotherhood members and their allies before the 1995 elections, as discussed in Chapter 3, illustrates this. The point is that the government, in pursuing this strategy, is not so much eradicating the Islamic organisa-tion as pushing it away from the electoral contest and into clandestine and illegal channels of participation. This, in turn, increases the possibility of further political violence in contemporary Egypt.

Other potential problems

Since multi-party elections appear to be used by the regime to contain rather than strengthen party organisation and develop multi-party participation, political parties, whether the presidentially chaired NDP or any of the legalised opposition parties, have been unable to "become the buckle which binds one social force to another . . . [thus creating] a basis of loyalty and identity transcending more parochial groupings".[22] Consequently, Egypt's formal multi-party arena is, in reality, no more institutionalised than a weak single-party system. Huntington writes:

> In a strong multi-party system a one-to-one relationship tends to exist between social forces and political parties . . . Such a strong system can exist only with a high level of mobilisation and political participation. If the latter are limited, the social forces active in politics are limited, and the social base for a strong multi-party system thus does not exist. If a multi-party system does exist in these circumstances it typically reflects differences of clique and family within a restricted élite. The poor institutionalisation and narrow support for the parties in such a multi-party system makes that system extremely fragile. The step from many parties to no parties and from no parties to many parties, consequently, is an easy one. In their institutional weakness the no-party and the multi-party system closely resemble each other.[23]

Along these lines, one can argue that under the Mubarak regime efforts to prevent high levels of mobilisation do not mean simply that multi-party participation is subsequently limited to the desired role of reinvigorating and expanding the vertically based clientelist structure of dependence and domination. It also means that the multi-party arena of political contest is not sufficiently institutionalised to continue functioning without further increasing the demands on resources from the centre.

The question of resources

The multi-party system in Mubarak's Egypt does not (nor is it intended to) function as a mechanism through which political parties compete for control of government. But the inclusion of opposition elements in the electoral arena produces in the long term a significant expansion in the number of competing candidates for any one legislative seat. This is illustrated, by the Minister of Interior's announcement that nearly 4,000 candidates competed for the 444 available seats in the 1995 legislative elections.[24] An average of nine candidates therefore competed at the time for each seat in the Assembly. The 1977 legislative elections, on the other hand, saw 1,660 candidates representing the then newly created right, left and centre platforms, along with independent candidates, compete for 342 Assembly seats,[25] that is an average of less than five contestants per seat. While the increase in the number of candidates competing in elections continues to have no effect on the choice of government or its replacement, it would be difficult to argue that it has not affected the choice of those who reach public office.

In view of the increasing number of competitors in elections, those who reach the People's Assembly are even more compelled actually to seek to fulfil the demands of their constituents with regard to the channelling of state-controlled resources. This is because the increase in the number of electoral contestants logically implies that the bargaining position of voters increases, and hence the social approval of the con-stituents becomes more important for an incumbent deputy. He becomes more aware of the necessity of proving the superiority of his abilities over those of his rivals; consequently, he must focus on channelling as much as possible state-controlled resources into his constituency in order to maintain his local power base, status and prestige within the community. It seems, judging from the campaign strategies of outgoing deputies, that this dilemma is already being encountered.[26]

The increase in demand for resources from the centre may indeed serve to reinforce the role of incumbent deputies as predominantly intermediaries between those on the periphery and central government. The clientelist chain linking those on the periphery to the centre is theoretically strengthened as a result. The problem, nevertheless, is that an electoral system which as is the case in Mubarak's Egypt, functions mainly on the basis of "concrete material incentives rather than ties of affection or deference" is, in the long run, more inclined to produce what James C. Scott terms "inflationary patron–client democracy".[27] This means that the distributive pressures, and hence the expense entailed in the maintenance of such a system, are largely beyond the economic capacity of the regimes which hold them, thus making it even more difficult for them to avoid running into budget deficits and other forms of financial crisis.

In the case of Egypt's contemporary electoral system, the informal nature of distribution, as well as the lack of detailed government expenditure reports, make it impossible to determine the amount of financial and material inducements used by the Mubarak regime to sustain itself. Nevertheless, such a patronage-based electoral system is the only "multi-party" system the Mubarak regime has been willing to consider. And at the lowest (and hence largest) tier of the clientelist structure, voters have also come to expect the material inducements it offers in return for their support, or at least their acquiescence. In such a context, it would be very difficult for the government to attempt altering the nature of such elections without taking a risk with the basis of its own domination in the process.

It is possible that as demands on the centre increases, the centre's inability to meet such demands will mean that the electoral system which is designed to strengthen and expand the government's clientelist control over political participation may, in the long term, lead to an erosion of the domination it was originally intended to reaffirm. In such a context, there is a big question mark over the issue of whether Egypt's current "multi-party" arena can survive in the post-Mubarak era. This is not simply because of the drain on resources which these elections entail, but also because of several other factors which should be taken into account. The first of these is the political orientation of the individual who assumes the presidency.

Reflections on the post-Mubarak era

Since President Mubarak has not appointed a Vice-President, an apparent successor does not exist. If the President were to die in office without an heir apparent, the formal procedure would be for the Assembly Speaker to assume the presidency temporarily until three-quarters of the Assembly, that is the NDP, agrees on a new President to present to the people through referendum. However, if a power struggle ensues between certain members of the élite for the position of President, the weakness of the NDP as an organised group strongly suggests that its role in the decision would be very limited indeed. Moreover, the weakness of the NDP, and the fact that as the dominant party it has little, if any, experience in mobilising mass support, means that should Mubarak's successor decide, for one reason or another, to disband the NDP and create his own party, or indeed, to suspend elections indefinitely, the NDP, regardless of its current status, would hardly be in a position to oppose him.

Should the arena of electoral contest remain intact for the foreseeable future, thus allowing Mubarak's successor to continue with the same electoral strategy of control, the issue of opposition parties cannot be overlooked. At the moment, the formal and informal constraints imposed on the opposition parties have enabled the Mubarak regime to co-opt them into the patron–client structure discussed in this study. Yet, as we have also discussed, particularly in Chapter 4, the use of elections to co-opt members of the opposition has also been made easier as a result of the weak organisational structure of these parties, one that compels individual candidates to organise their own electoral campaigns and in consequence recruit personal, rather than party-based support.

In this environment, it is difficult to overlook the fact that all five "major" opposition parties in Egypt have been managed in a rather personalistic manner by now elderly individuals whose political careers have spanned no less than three decades. It would not be unreasonable, therefore, with the demise of these leaders in the foreseeable future, to expect – as a consequence of the emergence of new, younger leadership – some significant changes in the organisational structure, and hence attitude, of at least some of these parties. Put differently, the personalistic cliques which currently appear to characterise the nature of opposition parties in contemporary Egypt cannot, in reality, continue to function in the same way in the absence of their "founders". New opposition leaders might be more inclined than their predecessors to establish a more effective organisational structure which would strengthen their respective parties as cohesive groups and help to expand their links to larger sectors of society on a more binding basis.

Divisions between old and young party members with regard to party direction and structure can already be observed. A few younger members of the Nasserite Party, for example, have begun to air their discontent with existing Party leadership. Indicative of this are the blunt views expressed before the 1995 legislative elections by Hamdi Sabahi, a member of the Party's political bureau, who questioned the legitimacy of the Party's current leadership. He asked: "What did they do for the movement? Their only qualification is that they were state employees under Nasser, but this doesn't give them legitimacy."[28] Amin Iskandar, the Party's secretary for cultural affairs, was even more to the point. He said: "I believe it is time for all these declining figures to disappear, leaving the stage for the younger generation."[29] While this younger generation of party members has yet to take control of the Party, such attitudes nevertheless reflect the potential emergence of an opinionated set of opposition leaders who might actually possess sufficient ambitions and energy to challenge the political status quo.

The relative absence of personalistic leadership within the contemporary Muslim Brotherhood, and its organisational efficiency, as discussed in Chapter 4 illustrate how, under enormous government-imposed constraints, it is still possible for political organisations to function within the prevailing political system, as cohesive, and thus potentially challenging, group entities. It is worth stressing, therefore, that a potentially strong political party which appears to have some appeal to certain sectors of the population, and indeed possesses the capability to bind these masses to it through an effective organisational structure, already exists in the form of the "illegal" Muslim Brotherhood Organisation. It is not, therefore, impossible that at least one or two of the legalised political parties might also develop along similar lines in contemporary Egypt. The potential development of opposition parties in this direction would mean, as is currently the case for the Muslim Brotherhood, that they would have difficulty in accepting an electoral system that continues to be structured along the lines discussed in this study.

Even in the unlikely event that none of the formal opposition parties manages to develop into much more than the weak entities they currently are, the Muslim Brotherhood on its own constitutes, and is most likely to remain, a big thorn in the side of Egypt's existing political system. The regime's crack-down on the Muslim Brotherhood in recent years, and in particular before the 1995 legislative elections, is a clear indication that the participation of those who reject the prevailing political system is not tolerated in the "multi-party" arena of political contest. One main point that appears to be overlooked by the government with regard to this strategy is that the Muslim Brotherhood is much more organised and structured than the personalistic cliques which continue to characterise the other (legalised) political parties in contemporary

Egypt. Consequently, it would be rather naive of the authorities to expect the organisation to be irrevocably destroyed by repressive tactics such as the imprisonment of a number of Muslim Brotherhood personalities.

Moreover, the tactic of utilising multi-party elections as a mechanism of clientelist co-option and control rather than as a way of promoting party development and the expansion of genuine party competition means that the threat of religious radicalism cannot be effectively challenged. President Mubarak himself has aired his concern about a repetition in Egypt of the Algerian experience.[30] Yet he is anxious to pursue a strategy of hindering the development of organised political participation within a legal-constitutional framework in order to preserve the political status quo.

The Muslim Brotherhood thus remains the main challenger to power in Egypt's "multi-party" system even though it is not officially recognised as a political party. This is not because the Muslim Brotherhood is so strong that the only means of keeping it at bay is by repression. Rather, it is because the legalised, secular political parties, including the President's own NDP, are neither encouraged by the regime nor provided with sufficient opportunity to develop into strong political entities that could legitimately challenge and ultimately marginalise such a threat. The reluctance to pursue such a less obtrusive and more positive strategy is due to the regime's conviction that this would spell the end of this type of "multi-party" system, one that allows centralised governance to proceed in the guise of democracy. The development and institutionalisation of a strong multi-party electoral arena, after all, cannot be expected to guard against religiously inspired politics while at the same time keeping the existing system of personal authoritarian rule intact. Consequently, non-competitive multi-party elections are more beneficial to the existing regime in contemporary Egypt when used as a means by which to reaffirm and expand the regime's clientelist structure of dependency and control. It is unlikely, therefore, that a significant change with regard to the role of these elections will be witnessed in the near future.

The adoption of a formal democratic framework can, at the international level, provide an authoritarian regime with (limited) legitimacy insofar as such a move signals "its good conduct to the outside world"[31] and in some cases makes it easier for Western democracies to provide it with aid.[32] At the national level, however, non-competitive multi-party elections are less significant as a tool of legitimisation. This is so in view of the absence of a dominant party based on a strong ideological or programmatic position, the reluctance of rulers to endorse wide-ranging mobilisation and, most importantly, the fact that elections of this nature do not affect the replacement or succession of government. Thus the fact that an authoritarian regime can preserve the political status quo while at the same time holding multi-party elections with minimal use of the state's coercive apparatus, highlights the power of patronage as a mechanism of clientelist co-option and control.

The importance of patronage lies largely in the fact that its mechanisms appear to hinder the development and expansion of potentially challenging parties and groupings which are based upon categorical ties such as socio-economic interests or conceptions. This is because, with patronage ultimately under the direct control of the ruler and his government, it is possible to distribute to the masses tangible and other forms of reward in return for regime-directed support. In fact, the prospect of obtaining a share of government-controlled resources in return for political support, or at least acquiescence, can be very enticing in societies where authoritarian regimes tend to thrive – in other words, societies where there is a general scarcity of resources and where reliable means for ensuring economic survival do not exist. As a mechanism of social control therefore, patronage performs an important role in reinvigorating and reaffirming the vertical patterns of clientelist dependency.

This, in turn, makes it very difficult for categorical bonds of social solidarity to develop. When voters come to expect benefits that can realistically only be channelled from the centre, and when opinion-based voting is of little significance to the outcome of elections, political actors, whether members of the "ruling" party or the opposition, are more tempted to seek the patronage of the power-holder. This means having to accept, at least publicly, the rulers' definition of "the rules of the game" if some electoral gains are to be made. As political actors accept this, their role as representatives of a party point of view remains insignificant in comparison with their main role as intermediaries between the centre and those on the periphery. Thus, while the clientelist chain linking those on the periphery to central government is strengthened and expanded as a result, it is difficult for political parties and groupings to develop into well-organised and autonomous group entities. A multi-party elections system where patronage radiates from a single point in the political system (that is, the ruler) is first and foremost advantageous to the regime that holds them.

The importance of patronage for the long-term survival of certain authoritarian regimes is well illustrated within the context of non-competitive multi-party elections. It may even be suggested that in the absence of government-directed patronage an authoritarian regime would find it extremely difficult to maintain peacefully for very long its dominant position within the framework of a multi-party arena. Indeed, as the case of Mubarak's Egypt illustrates, an authoritarian regime's monopoly of various forms of patronage can provide it with the flexibility to utilise even a potentially threatening process such as multi-party elections very much to its own advantage.

NOTES

1 R.H. Jackson and C.G. Rosenberg (1982), p. 26.
2 Ibid., p. 1.
3 Interview by the author with 'Ali Salama, 8 January 1995.
4 The decision of Ibrahim Shokri, Chairman of the Labour Party, to adopt an Islamic stand was not without problems. Members loyal to the ideology of socialism, for example, vented their frustration during a party conference held in 1989 by shouting slogans such as: "Shoukry sold the party to the Muslim Brothers" and "How much were you paid, Shoukry?" (H.F. Singer (1993), p. 19).
5 Interview by the author with Dawud's personal assistant, 19 December 1995.
6 The *Egyptian Gazette*, 17 December 1995.
7 C.H. Landé (1977b), p. xxxii.
8 Ibid.
9 Ibid., p. xxxiii.
10 Ibid.
11 *Final Report on the Legislative Elections in Egypt 1995* (Centre for Human Rights Legal Aid, Cairo, December 1995), p. 50.
12 *Al-Ahram Weekly*, 14–20 December 1995.
13 As discussed in Chapter 3.
14 *Al-Ahram Weekly*, 14–20 December 1995.
15 Muhammad Sid Ahmad in *Al-Ahram Weekly*, 14–20 December 1995.
16 Personal observation by the author at Helwan Police Station, 25 November 1995.
17 *Middle East Times Egypt*, 3–9 December 1995.
18 One of Bakri's supporters was arrested that day for possessing 68 Molotov cocktails. See *Middle East Times Egypt*, 10–16 December 1995.
19 Interview by the author with Mustafa Bakri, 20 December 1995.
20 The *Egyptian Gazette*, 15 December 1995.
21 The *Egyptian Gazette*, 17 December 1995.
22 S.P. Huntington (1968), p. 405.
23 Ibid., pp. 423–4.
24 *Al-Ahram Weekly*, 14–20 December 1995.
25 M.N. Cooper (1982), p. 205.
26 See Chapter 4.
27 J.C. Scott and B.J. Kerkvliet (1977), p. 142.
28 *Al-Ahram Weekly*, 9–15 November 1995.
29 Ibid.
30 For example, in the course of a personal discussion with Muhammed Sid Ahmad on the limitations of electoral participation in Egypt, President Mubarak justified his crackdown on the Muslim Brotherhood by citing the Algerian experience. (Information derived from an interview by the author with M.S. Ahmad, 8 December 1994, Cairo.)
31 G. Hermet (1978), p. 15.
32 As pointed out in the case of Egypt, for example. See R. Owen (1994), p. 190.

Appendix

National Democratic Party (NDP)

History
The NDP was established by President Sadat in 1978 to succeed the Arab Socialist Misr Party – initially the Centre Platform that succeeded the Arab Socialist Union in 1976. The pre-revolutionary Nationalist Party, which was established by nationalist-patriot Mustafa Kamel in 1907, was the inspiration behind the NDP's name. Since it is the ruling party, its official programme is predominantly a reflection of the official rhetoric and policies of government: productive *infitah* (open-door policy); agricultural development leading to self-sufficiency in food production; public sector revitalisation leading to a strong state within a market-oriented economy; upholding of democracy and the multi-party system.

Membership
Technocrats, rural notables, government officials, businessmen, contractors and the like.

Leadership
The NDP's Chairman is President Mubarak.

Newspaper
Mayo

The Liberal Party (al-Ahrar)

History
The Liberal Party started political life in 1976 as one of the three platforms created by President Sadat. With an ideology similar to that of the Neo-Wafd, it upholds the principle of presidential elections, and advocates political and economic liberalisation. The Party reversed its liberal policies when, during its 1987 coalition with the Muslim Brotherhood, it used the Islamic slogan "Islam is the Solution". Now no longer linked to the Muslim Brotherhood, it has reverted to its liberal stand.

Membership
Has little grass-roots' support, although it is meant to represent the national bourgeoisie. This is perhaps a result of its shifting views and the fact that its leader fully supported all of Sadat's initiatives, including the 1979 peace treaty with Israel.

Leadership
Until his death in 1998, the party was headed by Mustafa Kamel Murad, an ex-Free Officer. Due to internal feuding, the Party has been temporarily disbanded.

Newspaper
al-Ahrar

The National Progressive Unionist Party (NPUP) (al-Tagammu')

History
Along with the NDP and the Liberal Party, the Tagammu' originated as one of the three platforms created by President Sadat before becoming a full-fledged party in 1978. The "leftist" label it held as a platform continues to date with its advocacy of workers' rights; the preservation

and expansion of Nasser's social and economic reform; the expansion of the public sector; social justice and the protection of the rights of the poor. It opposes Islamist movements and, in foreign affairs, is strongly anti-Zionist.

Membership
The Party attracts intellectuals and self-educated workers.

Leadership
Since its establishment, the NDUP has been headed by Khalid Mohyi al-Din, a member of the now defunct Revolutionary Command Council which comprised the group of officers who took power following the 1952 *coup d'état*.

Newspaper
al-Ahali

The Labour Party
(formerly the Socialist Labour Party)

History
The Labour Party was created by President Sadat in 1978 to represent a loyal opposition in his newly established multi-party arena. Until 1984 it officially represented a socialist platform based on government planning, economic development in which the public sector plays leading role, and the promotion of Arab unity. It is strongly anti-Israel. In 1984–7, the Party underwent a dramatic transformation based on Islamic ideology. This move coincided with its electoral alliance with the Muslim Brotherhood in 1987. Its ties with the Muslim Brotherhood continue to date. The Party has also maintained its anti-Israeli position and places more emphasis on the unity of Islamic states than on simple Arab unity. It urges the amendment of the constitution to stress the Islamic identity of Egypt.

Membership

Headed by Ibrahim Shokri, previously Sadat's Minister of Agriculture. In 1936, Shokri, and the late Ahmad Husayn, were among the founders of Misr al-Fatah (Young Egypt), a nationalist political party which until 1984 was considered an important source of inspiration for the Socialist Labour Party. Ironically, it was Ahmad Husayn's brother 'Adel, and son Magdy, both senior Party leaders (and in the case of 'Adel, a renowned Marxist advocate) who played major roles in restructuring the Party along Islamic lines.

Newspaper
al-Sha'b

The Neo-Wafd

History

Originally established as the Wafd Party in 1919 by nationalist-patriot Sa'd Zaghlul, the Party, along with all existing parties, was suppressed following the *coup* of 1952. It regrouped in 1978, but soon dissolved itself in protest against a presidential decree issued by Sadat. It re-emerged under the Mubarak presidency shortly before the 1984 legislative elections. The official platform is derived from its pre-1952 origins. It advocates the following: that the president be directly elected by the people (i.e. the abolition of the affirmative referendum); the genuine encouragement of private enterprise and "true" capitalism; the removal of restrictions on political participation; greater civil liberties and a strict separation of powers in the presidential, legislative and judicial branches of government. It adopts an anti-Nasser stand and, despite its electoral alliance with the Muslim Brotherhood in 1984, it came to hold anti-Islamist views.

Membership

Predominantly comprises upper middle-class professionals.

Leadership
The Chairman (for life) is Fu'ad Serag al-Din, an ageing aristocrat who joined the original party in 1936 and became its Secretary-General in 1942.

Newspaper
al-Wafd

The Arab Democratic Nasserist Party
(the Nasserites)

History
Established in 1991 by a few senior figures from the Nasser era, the Party aspires to carry the Nasser torch. Its official platform rejects Zionism and what it regards as American imperialism. In terms of economic development, the Party advocates self-reliance in which the state plays a central role. Arab unity is also a theme strongly advocated by the Party.

Membership
High-level state officials from the Nasser era who lost favour when President Sadat took power in 1971. Middle-aged people who campaigned for Nasserism as students in the Sadat era also constitute the bulk of party membership. Other members include university students attracted to the Nasser legacy.

Leadership
The Party is headed by its principal founder Dhiya' al-Din Dawud, a cabinet minister and a high-ranking ASU official in the Nasser regime. Dawud spent the entire Sadat era in prison after being sentenced to ten years' imprisonment following Sadat's "corrective revolution" of 1971.

Newspaper
al-'Arabi

The Muslim Brotherhood Organisation

History

Although it does not possess legal party status, the Organisation's participation in the political competition in the Mubarak era warrants its inclusion in this list. Originally founded in 1928 by Hasan al-Banna, the Organisation was banned in 1954 by President Nasser. Its return to the political arena was initially encouraged by Sadat, who hoped it would counteract the perceived threat of leftist ideology. Its platform has changed little since its establishment. It views Islam not simply as a religion, but as a system that deals with all aspects of life. It considers that the source of authority should be derived from the Holy Qur'an and the Sunna (teachings of the Prophet Muhammad). It entered an electoral alliance with the Neo-Wafd in 1984 and in 1987 with Labour and al-Ahrar. It continues to have close relations with the Labour Party.

Membership

It attracts sectors of Egyptian society that comprise largely the educated poor, including schoolteachers, clerical workers and unemployed university graduates.

Leadership

The Organisation's Supreme Guide is Mustafa Mashhur who has occupied the position since the death of Hamid Abu al-Nasr in 1997. The General Guidance Bureau, however, is the executive body responsible for formulating policies and running the activities of the Organisation. The constituents' views are expressed through their own assembly, the Shura Council.

Newspaper

The Organisation has access to the Labour Party's newspaper, *al-Sha'b*. Its own monthly magazine, *al-Da'wa*, was established in 1976 and banned by Sadat in September 1981. It remains banned.

[190]

Splinter Parties:
al-Umma, al-Takaful, Green Party, Unionist Democratic Party, Misr, and the Arab Socialist Party

History
All legalised but none have ever won a seat in electoral competition.

Membership
Made up predominantly of founders with support from friends and associates.

Bibliography

Official Publications

Embassy of Arab Republic of Egypt. n.d. *Mubarak: The Hour Has Brought Forth the Man,* London.

Embassy of the United States of America. 1989, 1993 and 1994. *Human Rights Report for Egypt, Country Report Submitted to Committee on Foreign Affairs,* Cairo.

General Organisation for Government Printing Offices. 1983. *Rules of Procedure of the People's Assembly,* Cairo.

People's Assembly. 1994. *History of Representative Life in Egypt,* Cairo, People's Assembly Press.

—1985, 1988 and 1991. *Asma' al-sada a'dha' al-majlis* (*Directory of members of the People's Assembly*), Cairo, People's Assembly Press.

State Information Service. 1981. *1971 Constitution of the Arab Republic of Egypt,* Cairo.

—1991. *Egypt: A Decade of Peace, Development and Democracy, 1981–1991,* Cairo.

—n.d. *Egypt: The Quest for Peace and Prosperity Continues,* Cairo.

Party and NGO Publications

Amnesty International. 1992. *Egypt: Security Police Detentions Undermine the Rule of Law* (MDE/120192).

—1991. *Egypt: Ten Years of Torture* (MDE/121891).

Centre for Human Rights Legal Aid. 1995. *The First Round of the Legislative Elections,* Cairo.

—1995. *Legislative Elections in Egypt: Rights and Guarantees,* Cairo.

—1995. *Military Courts in Egypt: Courts without Safeguards, Judges without Immunity and Defendants without Rights,* Cairo.

Husayn, 'Adel. 1990. *Al-Islam: din wa hadhara, mashru' lil-mustaqbal* (*Islam: religion and civilisation, a plan for the future*), Cairo, Labour Party.

Husayn, Ahmad. 1991. *Al-Hizb 'ala hady al-Qur'an wa-l-sunna* (*Quranic and Sunni guidelines for the Party*), Cairo, Labour Party.

Independent Commission for Electoral Review. 1995. *Press Release Regarding the Second Round of Elections*, Cairo.

—1995. *Press Release Regarding Election Campaign and the First Round of Voting*, Cairo.

Labour Party. n.d. *Barnamij Hizb al-'Amal* (*Labour Party programme*), Cairo.

Middle East Watch. 1993. *Egypt: Trials of Civilians in Military Courts Violate International Law*, 5:3.

Muslim Brotherhood: Islamic Centre for Studies and Research. 1994. *The Muslim Brotherhood*, Cairo.

Nasserite Party. 1994. *Al-Hizb al-'Arabi al-Dimuqrati al-Nasiri: wathaeq al-mu'tamar al-'am al-thani* (*Nasserite Party's second annual conference report*).

Neo-Wafd Party. 1987. *Barnamij Hizb al-Wafd al-Jadid* (*Neo-Wafd Party programme*), Cairo.

—1986. *Al-Nizam al-dakhili li-l-Hizb al-Wafd al-Jadid* (*Internal Structure of the Neo-Wafd*), Cairo.

Tagammu' Party. 1987. *Al-Barnamij al-intikhabi li-majlis al-sha'b: Hizb al-Tagammu' al-Watani al-Taqaddumi al-Wahdawi* (*Legislative elections party programme: National Progressive Unionist Party*), Cairo.

—1984. *Barnamij li-inqath Misr* (*Programme to save Egypt*), Cairo.

—1984. *Hizb al-Tagammu' al-Watani al-Taqddumi al-Wahdawi: al-barnamij al-siyasi al-'am* (*General party programme for the Tagammu' Party*), Cairo.

Wafd Party. 1993. *Dalil al-Wafd* (*Al-Wafd directory*), Cairo.

Books, Chapters in Books and Dissertations

Albinski, H.S. (ed.). 1987. *Asian Political Processes, Essays and Readings*, Boston, Allyn and Bacon.

Ansari, H. 1986. *Egypt, The Stalled Society*, Albany, State University of New York Press.

Ayubi, N.N. 1994. *Political Islam: Religion and Politics in the Arab World*, London, Routledge Press.

—1991. *The State and Public Policies in Egypt since Sadat*, Reading, Ithaca Press.

Bates, R. 1989. *Beyond the Miracle of the Market: The Political Economy of Agrarian Development in Kenya*, Cambridge, Cambridge University Press.

Bayart, J.F. 1993. *The State in Africa: The Politics of the Belly*, London, Longman Group.

Brown, N.J. 1990. *Peasant Politics in Modern Egypt: The Struggle against the State*, New Haven and London, Yale University Press.

Caciagli, M. and Belloni, F.P. 1981. "The 'New' Clientelism in Southern Italy: The Christian Democratic Party in Catania". In S. Eisenstadt and R. Lemarchand, *Political Clientelism, Patronage and Development*, Beverly Hills and London, SAGE Publications.

Cammack, P. 1994. "Democratization and Citizenship in Latin America". In G. Parry and M. Moran (eds.), *Democracy and Democratization*, London and New York, Routledge Press.

Cardoso, F.H. 1979. "On the Characterization of Authoritarian Regimes in Latin America". In D. Collier (ed.), *New Authoritarianism in Latin America*, Princeton, Princeton University Press.

Chabal, P. 1986. *Political Domination in Africa, Reflections on the Limits of Power*, Cambridge, Cambridge Univerity Press.

Chazan, N. Mortimer, R., Ravehill, J. and Rothchild, D. 1988. *Politics and Society in Contemporary Africa*, Basingstoke and London, MacMillan Education.

Clapham, C. 1990. *Third World Politics: An Introduction*, London, Routledge.

Collier, D. (ed.), *New Authoritarianism in Latin America*, Princeton, Princeton University Press.

Cooper, M.N. 1982. *The Transformation of Egypt*, Baltimore, John Hopkins University Press.

Crecelius, D. 1972. "Non Ideological Responses of the Egyptian Ulama to Modernization". In N. Keddie (ed.), *Scholars, Saints and Sufis: Muslim Religious Institutions in the Middle East since 1500*, Chicago, University of Chicago Press.

Dahl, R. 1971. *Polyarchy, Participation and Opposition*, New Haven, Yale University Press.

Dessouki, Ali E. Hillal. 1983. *Democracy in Egypt: Problems and Prospects*, Cairo, American University Press.

Diamond, L. Linz, J.J. and Lipset, S.M. 1990. *Politics in Developing Countries: Comparing Experiences with Democracy*, Boulder, Colo. and London, Lynne Rienner Publishers.

—1988. *Democracy in Developing Countries: Africa*, Boulder, Colo., Lynne Rienner Publishers.

Eisenstadt, S.N. and Lemarchand, R. 1981. *Political Clientelism, Patronage and Development*, Beverly Hills and London, SAGE Publications.

Eisenstadt, S.N. and Roniger, L. 1984. *Patrons, Clients and Friends*, Cambridge, Cambridge University Press.

El-Gamal, M.Y. "Egypt's Ministerial Elite 1971–1981". Ph.D. thesis, Birkbeck College, University of London, 1992.

Ethier, D. 1990. *Democratic Transition and Consolidation in Southern Europe, Latin America and Southeast Asia*, London, The Macmillan Press.

Gellner, E. and Waterbury, J. 1977. *Patrons and Clients in Mediterranean Societies*, London, G. Duckworth and Co., in association with the American Universities Field Staff.

Giner, S. 1986. "Political Economy, Legitimation and the State". In G.O. O'Donnell, P.C. Schmitter and L. Whitehead, *Transitions from Authoritarian Rule: Southern Europe*, Baltimore and London, The Johns Hopkins University Press.

Goldberg, E. Kasaba, R. and Migdal, J.S. 1993. *Rules and Rights in the Middle East: Democracy, Law and Society*, Seattle and London, University of Washington Press.

Guasti, L. 1977. "Peru: Clientelism and Internal Control". In S.W. Schmidt, J.C. Scott, C. Landé and L. Guasti, *Friends, Followers and Factions: A Reader in Political Clientelism*, Berkeley, Los Angeles and London, University of California Press.

Harb, O.G. 1987. *Al-Ahzab al-siyasiya fi al-'alam al-thalith* (*Political parties in the Third World*), Cairo, 'Alam al-Ma'rifa Press.

Harb, O.G. and Hilal, A.D. (eds.), 1984, 1987 and 1990. *Intikhabat majlis al-sha'b: dirasat wa-tahlil* (*People's Assembly Elections: Studies and Analysis*), Cairo, Al-Ahram Press.

Harik, I. 1974. *The Political Mobilisation of Peasants: A Study of an Egyptian Community*, Bloomington and London, Indiana University Press.

Heikal, M. 1983. *Autumn of Fury: The Assassination of Sadat*, London, Andre Deutsch.

Hermassi, A. 1994. "Socio-economic Change and Political Implications: The Maghreb". In G. Salamé (ed.), *Democracy Without Democrats? The Renewal of Politics in the Muslim World*, London and New York, I.B. Tauris.

Hermet, G. 1978. "State Controlled Elections: A Framework". In G. Hermet, R. Rose, and A. Rouquié (eds.), *Elections Without Choice*, London and Basingstoke, MacMillan Press.

Hinnebusch, R.A. 1990. "The Formation of the Contemporary Egyptian State from Nasser and Sadat to Mubarak". In I.M. Oweiss (ed.), *The Political Economy of Contemporary Egypt*, Washington, DC, Center for Contemporary Arab Studies, Georgetown University.

—1985. *Egyptian Politics under Sadat: The Post-Populist Development of an Authoritarian Modernising State*, Cambridge, Cambridge University Press.

Holt, P.M. 1968. *Political and Social Change in Modern Egypt*, London, Oxford Univeristy Press.

Hudson, M.C. 1977. *Arab Politics: The Search for Legitimacy*, New Haven and London, Yale University Press.

Huntington, S.P. 1991. *The Third Wave: Democratization in the Late Twentieth Century*, Norman, University of Oklahoma Press.

—1968. *Political Order in Changing Societies*, New Haven and London, Yale University Press.

Huntington, S.P. and Moore, C.H. 1970. *Authoritarian Politics in Modern Society: The Dynamics of Established One-Party Systems*, New York, Basic Books.

Jackson, R.H. and Rosenberg, C.G. 1982. *Personal Rule in Black Africa: Prince, Autocrat, Prophet, Tyrant*, Berkeley, Los Angeles and London, University of California Press.

Kaufman, R.R. 1991. "Liberalization and Democratization in South America: Perspectives from the 1970s". In G.O. O'Donnell, P.C. Schmitter, and L. Whitehead (eds.), *Transitions from Authoritarian Rule: Comparative Perspectives*, Baltimore and London, The Johns Hopkins University Press.

Krämer, G. 1994. "The Integration of the Integrists: A Comparative Study of Egypt, Jordan and Tunisia". In G. Salamé (ed.), *Democracy Without Democrats? The Renewal of Politics in the Muslim World*, London and New York, I.B. Tauris.

Lacouture, J. 1970. *The Demigods: Charismatic Leadership in the Third World*, New York, Alfred A. Knopf.

Landé, C.H. 1977a "Networks and Groups in South East Asia: Some Observations on the Group Theory of Politics". In S.W. Schmidt,

J.C. Scott, C. Landé and L. Guasti, *Friends, Followers and Factions: A Reader in Political Clientelism*, Berkeley, Los Angeles and London, University of California Press.

Landé, C.H. 1977b. "The Dyadic Basis of Clientelism". In S.W. Schmidt, J.C. Scott, C. Landé and L. Guasti, *Friends, Followers and Factions: A Reader in Political Clientelism*, Berkeley, Los Angeles and London, University of California Press.

Layne, L. (ed.) 1987. *Elections in the Middle East, Implications of Recent Trends*, Boulder and London, Westview Press.

Lemarchand, R. 1981. "Comparative Political Clientelism: Structure, Process and Optic". In S.N. Eisenstadt and R. Lemarchand, *Political Clientelism, Patronage and Development*, Beverly Hills and London, SAGE publications.

—1977. "Political Clientelism and Ethnicity in Tropical Africa". In S.W. Schmidt, J.C. Scott, C. Landé and L. Guasti, *Friends, Followers and Factions: A Reader in Political Clientelism*, Berkeley, Los Angeles and London, University of California Press.

Lemarchand, R. and Legg, K. 1978. "Political Clientelism and Development: A Preliminary Analysis". In N.W. Provizer (ed.), *Analyzing the Third World*, Cambridge, Mass., Schenkman Publishing Company.

Levy D.C. and Bruhn, K. 1995. "Mexico: Sustained Civilian Rule Without Democracy". In L. Diamond, J.J. Linz and S.M. Lipset (eds.), *Politics in Developing Countries: Comparing Experiences with Democracy*, Boulder and London, Lynne Rienner Publishers.

Linz, J.J. 1978. "Non-Competitive Elections in Europe". In G. Hermet, R. Rose and A. Rouquié, (eds.), *Elections Without Choice*, London and Basingstoke, MacMillan Press.

Lipset, S.M. 1981. *Political Man*, Baltimore, Johns Hopkins University Press.

Martins, L. 1993. "The 'Liberalization' of Authoritarian Rule in Brazil". In G.O. O'Donnell, P.C. Schmitter and L. Whitehead (eds.), *Transitions from Authoritarian Rule: Latin America*, Baltimore and London, The Johns Hopkins University Press.

Mayfield, B. 1971. *Rural Politics in Nasser's Egypt: A Quest for Legitimacy*, Texas, University of Texas Press.

McDermott, A. 1988. *Egypt from Nasser to Mubarak: A Flawed Revolution*, London, Kent, Croom Helm.

Middlebrook, K.J. 1993. "Political Liberalization: Mexico". In G.O. O'Donnell, P.C. Schmitter and L. Whitehead (eds.), *Transitions from Authoritarian Rule: Latin America*, Baltimore and London, The Johns Hopkins University Press.

Migdal, J.S. 1988. *Strong Societies and Weak States: State–Society Relations and State Capabilities in the Third World*, Princeton, New Jersey, Princeton University Press.

Milne, R.S. 1973. "Elections in Developing Countries". In H.G. Kebschull (ed.), *Politics in Transitional Societies*, New York, Appleton-Century-Crofts.

Mitchell, R.P. 1993. *The Society of Muslim Brothers*, Oxford, Oxford University Press.

Moore, C.H. 1970. *Politics in North Africa*, Boston, Little Brown.

O'Donnell, G.A. 1979. *Modernization and Bureacratic-Authoritarianism*, Berkeley, Institute of International Studies, University of California.

Oweiss, I.M. 1990. *The Political Economy of Contemporary Egypt*, Washington, DC, Centre for Contemporary Arab Studies, George-town University.

Owen, R. 1994. "Socio-economic Change and Political Mobilization: The Case of Egypt". In G. Salamé (ed.), *Democracy Without Democrats? The Renewal of Politics in the Muslim World*, London and New York, I.B. Tauris.

—1992. *State Power and Politics in the Making of the Modern Middle East*, London and New York, Routledge.

Palmer, M. 1989. *Dilemmas of Political Development*, Itasca, Illinois, F.E. Peacock Publishers.

Pinker, R. 1993. *Democracy in the Third World*, Buckingham, Open University Press.

Pool, D. 1994. "Staying at Home with the Wife: Democratization and its Limits in the Middle East". In G. Parry and M. Moran (eds.), *Democracy and Democratization*, London and New York, Routledge Press.

Provizer, N.W. 1978. *Analyzing the Third World: Essays from Comparative Politics*, Cambridge, Mass., Schenkman Publishing Company.

Purcell, S.K. 1981. "Mexico: Clientelism, Corporatism and Political Stability". In S.N. Eisenstadt and R. Lemarchand (eds.), *Political Clientelism, Patronage and Development*, Beverly Hills and London, SAGE Publications.

Reeves, E.B. 1990. *The Hidden Government, Ritual, Clientelism and Legitimation in Northern Egypt*, Salt Lake City, University of Utah Press.

Rouquié, A. 1991. "Demilitarization and Institutionalization of Military Dominated Polities in Latin America". In G.O. O'Donnell, P.C. Schmitter and L. Whitehead (eds.), *Transitions from Authoritarian Rule: Comparative Perspectives*, Baltimore and London, The Johns Hopkins University Press.

—1978. "Clientelist Control and Authoritarian Contexts". In G. Hermet, R. Rose and A. Rouquié (eds.), *Elections Without Choice*, London and Basingstoke, MacMillan Press.

Roy, O. 1994. "Patronage and Solidarity Groups: Survival or Reformation?" In G. Salamé (ed.), *Democracy Without Democrats? The Renewal of Politics in the Muslim World*, London and New York, I.B. Tauris.

Sa'id, R. 1990. *Safha min tarikh Jam'iyyat al-Ikhwan al-Muslimun (A page from the history of the Muslim Brotherhood Society)*, Cairo, Ikhwan Morfit Ali Press.

Schmidt, S.W., Scott, J.C., Landé, C. and Guasti, L. 1977. *Friends, Followers and Factions: A Reader in Political Clientelism*, Berkeley, Los Angeles and London, University of California Press.

Schmitter, P.C. 1986. "An Introduction to Southern European Transitions". In G.O. O'Donnell, P.C. Schmitter and L. Whitehead (eds.), *Transitions from Authoritarian Rule: Southern Europe*, Baltimore and London, The Johns Hopkins University Press.

—1978. "The Impact and Meaning of 'Non-competitive, Non-Free and Insignificant' Elections in Authoritarian Portugal, 1933–74". In G. Hermet, R. Rose and A. Rouquié (eds.), *Elections Without Choice*, London and Basingstoke, MacMillan Press.

Scott, J.C. and Kerkvliet, B.J. 1977. "How Traditional Patrons Lose Legitimacy: A Theory with Special Reference to Southeast Asia". In S.W. Schmidt, J.C. Scott, C. Landé and L. Guasti, *Friends, Followers and Factions: A Reader in Political Clientelism*, Berkeley, Los Angeles and London, University of California Press.

Shils, E. 1973. "Opposition in the New States of Africa and Asia". In H.G. Kebschull (ed.), *Politics in Transitional Societies*, New York, Appleton-Century-Crofts.

Springborg, R. 1989. *Mubarak's Egypt: Fragmentation of the Political Order*, Boulder and London, Westview Press.

—1988. "Approaches to the Understanding of Egypt". In P.J. Chelkowski and R.J. Pranger (eds.), *Ideology and Power in the Middle East*, Durham and London, Duke University Press.

—1982. *Family, Power and Politics in Egypt*, Philadelphia, University of Pennsylvania Press.

—1975. "Patterns of Association in the Egyptian Political Elite". In Lenczowski (ed.), *Political Elites in the Middle East*, Washington DC, American Enterprise Institute for Public Policy Research.

Stephens, R. 1971. *Nasser*, New York, Simon and Schuster.

Tripp, C. and Owen, R. 1991. *Egypt under Mubarak*, London, Routledge Press.

Waterbury, J. 1994. "Democracy without Democrats?: The Potential for Political Liberalization in the Middle East". In G. Salamé (ed.), *Democracy Without Democrats? The Renewal of Politics in the Muslim World*, London and New York, I.B. Tauris.

—1993. *Exposed to Innumerable Delusions: Public Enterprise and State Power in Egypt, India, Mexico and Turkey*, Cambridge, Cambridge University Press.

—1983. *The Egypt of Nasser and Sadat: The Political Economy of Two Regimes*, Oxford, Princeton University Press.

—1970. *The Commander of the Faithful*, New York, Columbia University Press.

Weingrod, A. 1977. "Patrons, Patronage and Political Parties". In S.W. Schmidt, J.C. Scott, C. Landé and L. Guasti, *Friends, Followers and Factions: A Reader in Political Clientelism*, Berkeley, Los Angeles and London, University of California Press.

Whitehead, L. 1991. "International Aspects of Democratization". In G.O. O'Donnell, P.C. Schmitter and L. Whitehead (ed.), *Transitions from Authoritarian Rule: Comparative Perspectives*, Baltimore and London, The Johns Hopkins University Press.

Widner, J.A. 1992. *The Rise of a Party-State in Kenya, From "Harambee!" to "Nyayo!"*, Berkeley, University of California Press.

Young C. and Turner, T. 1985. *The Rise and Decline of the Zairean State*, Madison, University of Wisconsin Press.

Zaki, M. 1995. *Civil Society and Democratization in Egypt, 1981–1994*, Cairo, The Ibn Khaldoun Center.

Zartman, I.W. 1990. "Opposition as Support of the State". In G. Luciani (ed.), *The Arab State*, London, Routledge Press.

Articles and Papers

Anderson, L. 1987. "Lawless Government and Illegal Opposition: Reflections on the Middle East". *Journal of International Affairs*, 40.

Bienen H. and Gersovitz, M. 1986. "Consumer Subsidy Cuts, Violence and Political Stability". *Comparative Politics*, 19.

El-Bishri, T. 1983. "The 1952 Revolution and Democracy". In A.H. Dessouki (ed.), "Democracy in Egypt: Problems and Prospects", 2nd edn., Cairo, American University in Cairo Press, Cairo Papers in Social Science, vol. 1, monograph 2.

Cassandra, 1995. "The Impending Crisis in Egypt". *The Middle East Journal*, 49:1.

Cordahi, C. "Strangling the Press". *Middle East International*, 9 June, 1995.

Dunn, M.C. 1993. "Fundamentalism in Egypt". *Middle East Policy*, 2:3.

Fandy, M. 1993. "The Tensions Behind the Violence in Egypt". *Middle East Policy*, 2:1.

Flores, A. 1993. "Secularism, Integralism and Political Islam: The Egyptian Debate". *Middle East Report*, 23:4.

Gauch, S. 1991. "Mubarak's Ten Years" *Africa Report*, 36:6.

El-Ghamry, M. 1995. "A Study of the Constitutional and Legal System of Detention", Cario, The Centre for Human Rights Legal Aid.

Gordon, J. 1990. "Political Opposition in Egypt". *Current History*, 89:544.

Guenena, N. 1986. "The 'Jihad': An 'Islamic Alternative' in Egypt". In Cairo, American University in Cairo Press, Cairo Papers in Social Science, vol. 9, monograph 2.

Harik, I. 1973. "The Single Party as a Subordinate Movement: The Case of Egypt". *World Politics*, XXVI:1.

Hinnebusch, R.A. 1993a. "The Politics of Economic Reform in Egypt". *Third World Quarterly*, 14:1.

—1993b. "Class, State and the Reversal of Egypt's Agrarian Reform". *Middle East Report*, 24:184.

Ibrahim, S.E. 1993. "Crises, Elites and Democratization in the Arab World". *The Middle East Journal*, 47:2.

El-Naggar, S. "Politics and Economic Reform in Egypt", paper presented to the 19th Annual Symposium, Centre for Contemporary Arab Studies, Georgetown University, Washington, DC, 7–8 April 1994.

—1981. "Egypt under Sadat: Elites, Power Structure and Political Change in a Post-Populist State". *Social Problems*, 28:4.

Napoli, J.J. 1993. "Egypt's Third-Term President Facing Daunting Problems". *The Washington Report on Middle East Affairs*, 12:4.

Parfitt, T. 1993. "The Politics of Adjustment in Africa with Special Reference to Egypt". In *The Economics and Politics of Structural Adjustment in Egypt*, Cairo, American University in Cairo Press, Cairo Papers in Social Science, vol. 16, monograph 3.

Radwan, H.H. 1994. "Democratization in Rural Egypt: A Study of the Village Local Popular Council". In Cairo, American University in Cairo Press, Cairo Papers in Social Science, vol. 17, monograph 1.

Rasheed, S. 1995. "The Democratization Process and Popular Participation in Africa: Emerging Realities and the Challenges Ahead". *Development and Change*, 26:2.

Reed, S. 1993. "The Battle for Egypt". *Foreign Affairs*, 69:5.

Al-Sayyid, M.K. 1993. "A Civil Society in Egypt?" *The Middle East Journal*, 47:2.

Singer, H.F. 1993. "The Socialist Labour Party: A Case Study of a Contemporary Egyptian Opposition Party". In Cairo, American University in Cairo Press, Cairo Papers in Social Science, vol. 16, monograph 1.

Index